DISPATCHES
FROM THE EASTERN FRONT

A POLITICAL EDUCATION FROM THE
NIXON YEARS TO THE AGE OF OBAMA

For one of my heroes, Billy Shore, who retains the power to both inspire and instruct.

Gerald Felix Warburg

bancroft press

© Copyright 2014 Gerald Felix Warburg
All rights reserved.

No part of this book may be reproduced in any form or by electronic means, including information storage and retrieval systems, without written permission from the publisher, except by a reviewer, who may quote passages in a review.

Cover design: Ali Abbas
Layout: Tracy Copes
Author photo: Dan Addison/U.Va. Public Affairs

Published by Bancroft Press
"Books that Enlighten"
P.O. Box 65360, Baltimore, MD 21209
410-358-0658 | 410-764-1967 (fax)
www.bancroftpress.com

Library of Congress Control Number: 2012920739
ISBN 978-1-61088-085-5 (cloth)
ISBN 978-1-61088-086-2 (paper)
ISBN 978-1-61088-088-6 (mobi)
ISBN 978-1-61088-087-9 (epub)
Printed in the United States of America

Also by Gerald Felix Warburg:

<u>Books</u>
Conflict and Consensus: The Struggle between Congress and the President over Foreign Policymaking

The Mandarin Club - A Novel

<u>Text Chapters</u>
"Lobbyists: U.S. National Security and Special Interests" and "Congress: Checking Presidential Power" in *The National Security Enterprise: Navigating the Labyrinth*

"Nonproliferation Policy Crossroads: Lessons Learned from the U.S. - India Nuclear Agreement," in *Contemporary Issues in U.S. Foreign Policy*

For three gentlemen, wise and kind:
Dad,
who helped guide us west, and
Andy and Pete,
big brothers who led us forward.

Table of Contents

1. Resignation .... page 1
2. The Nixon Brothers .... page 11
3. The Most Interesting College in the World .... page 21
4. What I Needed to Know at Twenty-One .... page 33
5. Initiation: Working on the Joint Committee .... page 41
6. Playing the Press: Playing with Fire .... page 59
7. Jack Bingham, Giant Slayer .... page 75
8. The Capitol, Through Fresh Eyes .... page 93
9. How Our Laws Are Made .... page 99
10. Roots: Return to Jerusalem .... page 113
11. From the White House to Galvez House .... page 129
12. No Final Victories .... page 141
13. The Catbird Seat: Life on Senate Staff .... page 151
14. Lobbying 101: The View from K Street .... page 173
15. Cold War Days: Inside the Kremlin .... page 191
16. Obama for America .... page 211
17. Renewal .... page 225

Notes .... page 237
Supplementary Sources .... page 245
Index .... page 251
Acknowledgements .... page 269
About the Author .... page 271

"There is nothing you can do except try to write it the way it was. So you must write each day better than you possibly can ... And you must always remember the things you believed because if you know them, they will be there in the writing."

—Ernest Hemingway

"Life can only be understood backwards, but it must be lived forwards."

—Søren Kierkegaard

Chapter One

Resignation

Cody, Wyoming
August 1974

The morning Richard Nixon resigned the presidency and helicoptered away from the White House lawn for the last time, I was busy cleaning the stables at the Dead Indian Ranch, deep in the high country east of Yellowstone Park in Wyoming. My job shoveling horseshit became a conversation starter when, quite improbably, I began looking for a job in Washington, D.C.

I was twenty years old when I watched the last act of Nixon's fall on an old black and white TV, static and snow nearly obscuring the president's face. I hadn't a clue then, but the end of Richard Nixon's three decades in Washington would mark the beginning of mine.

There is an old Chinese saying, variously described as a good wish for a friend or a curse to be hurled at an adversary: "May you live in interesting times." To experience interesting times was a goal of sorts for many of us Baby Boomers who grew up in the comfort of suburban America in the 1950s. There would be no boring Eisenhower-era myopia for us. Adventure lay ahead, if only we would hit the road and find it.

As a restless California teenager, I was uncertain what the future held for me. My dreams were disparate and ill-formed. Turmoil at home offered an excuse to strike out on my own. For reasons I could not articulate, I wanted to flee the bucolic towns north of San Francisco. In Marin County's string of new-money cities, from Sausalito and Belvedere to Kentfield and Ross, it seemed as if everybody's father was in real estate and everybody's mother was unfulfilled.

Our elders were battling something they called a "mid-life crisis," whatever that was. We sensed it must be avoided at all costs. So we determined to live lives without regrets. All around us, the human potential movement was beginning to flower. Californians and returning veterans, shorn of the heavy survival burdens of World War II years, began to question the purpose of their life's work.

In nearby Silicon Valley, new worlds were opening. Steve Jobs, Steve Wozniak, and an eclectic mix of Stanford graduates led an explosion of technology research that would bring about personal computers, the Internet, and the iPad. Even as the Sixties ended and the Vietnam War dragged on, the social climate in the San Francisco Bay Area offered infinite possibilities. On the University of California campus at Berkeley and across the Golden Gate in the Haight-Ashbury district, music was pulsing from local rock groups who had played gigs at high school dances: Steve Miller, Janis Joplin, Carlos Santana, Tower of Power, Boz Scaggs, the Grateful Dead, and the Sons of Champlin. As we listened to their lyrics and considered alternative futures, we determined that no roads would go untaken. We read Emerson and Ferlinghetti, eager to escape.

Beginning at the age of sixteen, I set off on a series of travels that led me far from the California suburbs. They included months of backpacking in Europe, trying to keep up with my mischievous older brothers, Andy and Pete, as we bounced from a Copenhagen youth hostel to a Mediterranean campground. We slept on Greek ferries and in Amsterdam crash pads. We discovered places where the Sixties had never ended.

On the road, tall, bearded young men with no parents in sight could get away with a lot. My brothers, then as now, were not just heroic figures to me, but best friends as well. We talked to strangers. We lied about our age. We inhaled deeply. That, as memoirist

Barack Obama would later confess, was the point, wasn't it?

When I returned to the California suburbs—I still had to finish high school—the privilege and provincialism felt stifling. Soon I headed out to explore once again, this time accompanied by a vague sense of mission.

My destination was simply "Back East." I wanted to make a voyage to what, for me, was a mythical land—Back East, from whence my Harvard and Bryn Mawr-educated parents had come. They had escaped the insular world of childhoods in Manhattan and New Haven, bravely setting out to build a new life in California in 1953, the year before I was born.

By the time I was halfway through Hampshire College in Amherst, Massachusetts, I was still searching for a purpose. The Vietnam War was ending. The great social movements for civil rights and urban renewal were spent. Nothing had risen to replace them as a source of inspiration for the young.

I was a driven but directionless student. By 1974 I had already toyed with a half-dozen possible majors, from theater and history to literature, sociology, and education. I even had dreams one year that a professional baseball career might pan out.

My restlessness was matched only by my growing curiosity. I was trying to figure out what role I might play in the world.

My parents bestowed upon each of their sons a sense of obligation. It was an unspoken but inescapable assumption that public purpose offered a higher calling than the pursuit of private gain. Opportunity was accompanied by responsibility: To whom much was given, much was expected. *Noblesse oblige* meant that growing up to be merely, say, a real estate dealer flipping houses would be a waste of your talents. We were expected to have greater aspirations.

My father, Felix Warburg, had been an early environmental activist. As chairman of the Marin County Planning Commission, he played an important role in the effort to block construction of a commuter city of thirty thousand that developers planned to carve out of the shoreline wilderness. He helped to protect the coastline that would become Point Reyes National Seashore and Golden Gate National Recreation Area.[1] We spent days along the Pacific

Ocean and camped in Mendocino, where he worked with Larry Halprin to design the Sea Ranch, and in Bolinas, where Mom would make us pancakes in the fog on an old Coleman stove.

My mother, Sandol Stoddard, was already an accomplished author and community leader. She had rejected the materialism and prejudice of an Alabama mother and Connecticut Yalie father to become an outspoken supporter of Jack Kennedy and Martin Luther King Jr. Her fierce identification with the underdog and her hunger for justice dominated her work as an activist and writer.

My parents' essential values were made clearer by their broad definition of community. Together with public-spirited neighbors, they repainted the dilapidated Victorian storefronts of Tiburon's Main Street. They volunteered to help build up the local schools. They encouraged us to head out into the world confident we had a capacity to contribute to society and that collective citizen action to engage our government could yield positive results.

Dead Indian Ranch, August 1974.

That summer of 1974, the month I turned twenty, I found myself working as a wrangler at a dude ranch in the Absaroka

Mountains. The nearest town, Cody, Wyoming, was fifty-six miles away on a dirt road, over the eight thousand-foot Dead Indian Pass.

Navajo rugs in turquoise and black hung on the walls, with an old grizzly skull above the fire crackling deep in the stone hearth. Through the television static, a crowd of guests and fellow ranch hands could barely make out the signal bouncing off the hovering mountains. President Richard Nixon was offering his tortured explanation for leaving office in the face of impeachment and a likely conviction.

Sunlight Basin, Wyoming, August 1974.

I saddled horses for wealthy East Coast dudes by day, then played poker down by the creek-side campfire most nights. My only prior interest in politics had been watching nervously as my older brothers maneuvered their way around the Vietnam War draft. Otherwise, Washington seemed a distant land, utterly foreign and unapproachable.

The raw emotion of Nixon's delivery, all jowls and dark gesticulation, fascinated me as we watched. You couldn't make this stuff up—not even a Shakespeare or an Ibsen could. Nixon's anger at his fate was palpable. The stakes of his decision were so profound, the uncertainties for the nation's future so real—no president had ever quit before—that my curiosity about the political arena was piqued.

What was this great drama unfolding in Washington, this contest of good versus evil? A tragedy of mythic proportions, it involved misplaced hopes and hubris, patriotism gone bad, and a struggle to shape the nation's course that had collapsed in spectacular failure. *Who were the men and women who had brought down this all-powerful King Richard, he of the forty-nine-state majority?* I needed to know.

The questions careened about in my head later as I stumbled down the trail to fish out cans of beer from our stash in the creek. *Who were these people who make a life of political contest? How could you get into the arena?* I was just a sophomore heading back to an experimental college in Amherst. I felt as insignificant as any of the thousands of stars that overflowed the black Wyoming sky. Washington seemed so many miles away.

Less than a year later, I was there, inside the U.S. Capitol. In just three years, I would find myself at the White House, standing ramrod straight at the center of power, watching in the Cabinet Room as a different president signed a major nuclear policy bill I'd helped write.

If anyone at the Dead Indian Ranch that night had foretold such developments, I would have thought they were crazy. If anyone had gone on to predict a time when I would work as a Nixon family lobbyist—that I would witness his family's tears and feel just a piece of their horror—then I would have *known* they were hallucinating.

Why do people choose a career in public policy? What makes political contest such an attraction? Why did working in Washington hold my interest for so many years? I could not have answered any of these questions that crisp August night four decades ago. Upon reflection, however, the truth seems clear.

It was the *people* who drew me in. It was the people in pursuit of power who fascinated me—their passions, their oft-compromised principles, and the endless testing of character they experienced. The politicians who populate official Washington, I soon learned, come from country and city, from Ivy League schools and community colleges, from hick towns and boom towns. They are the 4-H Club leaders, and the ambitious class valedictorians, but also the dissenters and rebels, the idealistic critics of the status quo. They share a common sense of mission. All yearn to have some impact on our national affairs. All are eager to leave some mark that can affirm a common existential desire to be present. All hope to leave evidence of their work. Their triumphs, as well as their failures, are reassuringly human.

They are drawn to Washington by the beckoning arena. Some come to do combat over policy. Many want to save the world. Others stay to make money, retailing their expertise to the highest bidder. Some acquire issues and adopt causes only as a means to an end: holding power. "Potomac fever," they call it. It's a disease, like drug addiction. They take just one hit, then cannot escape the craving for more. Their story ends badly, always. The individuals and the institutions they serve suffer as well.

Others seek power only as a means to an end, to advance their chosen cause. Each shares an illusion that Washington is, for a time, the center of the universe. We see the capital as the national movie screen, where we project our greatest hopes for progress. We feel called to Washington to engage, if only in a limited staff role. It is an irresistible call to public service, one fueled in equal parts by altruism and ego.

The following chapters are the stories of the characters I encountered in our nation's capital—characters I came to know along my journey Back East to explore the science of politics. These are stories about the people—from Alan Cranston to Nancy Pelosi, from Jack Bingham to Dianne Feinstein to President Nixon's daughter, Julie Eisenhower—that my work enabled me to know. This is the chronicle of one man's political education amidst such searchers and doers. They were clever, humble, and occasionally profane, the very sort of interesting people whose trials and tribulations give our lives meaning. It is thus, first and foremost, a Washington story.

It is also a story recounting how idealism is tempered by reality. Just as second marriages represent the triumph of hope over experience, political memoirs should offer optimism as an antidote to the cynicism pervading most discussions about Washington. Such narratives need to be enriched by characters one cares about, not just pedestrian villains, of which Washington has plenty.

Memoirs of political life can become exercises in self-justification. Book-of-the-Month Club tomes on "how right I was about the Iraq war" quickly devolve into the settling of old scores. Such an approach is usually rife with cheap shots and self-puffery. Memoirs can slip easily into the realm of fiction.

The stories offered here try to avoid such pitfalls. These stories are true. In many cases, they serve to highlight my own naiveté and flawed judgment. Yet none is retold merely to embarrass or titillate. In thirty-five years in the political trenches, I've encountered plenty of skullduggery. I've known senators and White House aides who abused drink, congressmen who bedded interns, Appropriations Committee chairmen who lived by pay-to-play, and presidential candidates with whom we should never share the car keys.

So what?

Congress is much more like my Redwood High School class of 1972 than the Roman Senate. Any collection of 538 classmates has a few bums. A few years from now, we will not care about idiot congressmen posting lewd photos on their Twitter accounts. Their names are forgotten quickly. Therefore, unless central to narrative or character development, I have omitted most miscellaneous misbehavior as gratuitous. For the record, I screwed up plenty. I had far more than my share of fun, both wholesome and illicit. I plead guilty to zeal, to indiscretion, and to an often sophomoric pleasure in mischief perpetrated just for the thrill of getting away with it. I also cared deeply about the public policy issues I worked on, as well as the business and academic pursuits I followed as a consequence.

The stories that follow share a common point of view, that of a student of political science hoping to shape policy. My career advanced rapidly through a series of lucky encounters. My role was just that of a staffer, one of the thousands of ambitious aides who pass through the Capitol for a year or a decade. I never ran for election, so I wasn't held accountable by voters for controversial positions championed. I shadowed powerful politicians, hovering in the background of camera shots, suggesting avenues of attack, feeding lines and drafting bills. I lived vicariously through risks elected officials took on the Senate floor or in presidential campaigns. I took satisfaction from triumphs shared and worked to weather the stinging defeats that usually followed. Politics humbles even the most righteous and self-confident. I was fortunate to gain admission to the councils of power, then to have a chance to step back and question what draws the moth to the flame.

The book isn't so much about its author, however. Nor is it a personal memoir about the many family members and friends I have loved. It is about a political education in Washington—about how proximity to power tests all who enter the public arena. It describes how it felt to be in the room when the deal was made. It is about the many temptations that threaten to erode principles, only to highlight those convictions that endure. It is an exploration of why people feel called to public service, and a reflection on how the next generation of young men and women can prepare to shape public policy in the real world of our often brutal national politics.

Many of the scenes recounted here were observed as if viewed in a most improbable movie. *A Hampshire College kid applauding in the Cabinet Room less than two years after graduation?* The sensation was surreal, but the experience was genuine. There were weeks when my main source of energy was the adrenaline rush derived from pushing the envelope, from seeing how far I could go as an infiltrator. I would plunge in over my head, stimulated by the pull of the tide. Fear gave me energy and made me a fast talker. The excitement felt like hot coffee in the veins.

The work at hand, however, is neither a Baby Boomer confessional nor a plea for absolution. It is a story of the Washington of our lifetime, of very human characters who populate the drama we call politics. It is a story of patriotic individuals trying, for the most part, to do the right thing. It is a story of the fallible people who come to play a part in the national arena.

In narrative form, it is presented as a compilation of vignettes, betraying the idealism of a once youthful voice fueled by hope and curiosity. These stories are presented here serially, beginning with my first hint of an interest in a Washington policymaking career. They end shortly after the day when, finally, I left. This orderly chronological progress from 1974 to current times is bracketed by even-numbered chapters offering insights that echo parallel themes through the recounting of more recent events. These flash-forwards serve as bookends, looking back at events with wisdom brought by experience.

All are drawn from original notes, preserved from a quaint 1950s habit handed down by my irrepressibly literary mom: Sunday letters sent home. These were letters crafted in the years before e-mail was invented, handwritten in philosophical bursts to be shared with my California family. Letters of self-discovery and overwrought observation. Letters from an earnest and excitable young man reporting on the strange ways of Washington politicians. Letters scrawled feverishly, then bundled and sent off in bulging white envelopes with a haphazard cluster of postage stamps. Snail-mailed dispatches from the Eastern Front.

Chapter Two

The Nixon Brothers

Yorba Linda, California
June 2003

In the searing heat of California's inland desert, we climbed the narrow stairs to the attic of Richard Nixon's childhood home. It was a late spring morning. John Taylor, the avuncular loyalist who served as executive director of the Richard M. Nixon Foundation, was prattling away behind me.

"His mom was a homemaker," John reminded me. "They had a grocery store. His dad worked as a butcher."

I wasn't really listening.

We were in the late president's childhood bedroom. I felt like a voyeur. It was a cramped attic crawl space. He had shared it with three brothers, bunks lining the eaves, as if on a small sailboat. It was not hard to imagine the familiarity he would later find in his close Navy quarters.

"His brother died here," John continued. Then, mercifully, he stopped talking.

I stared at the place. You could sense the anxiety in the household after his kid brother succumbed to flu and fever. A second Nixon brother had died very young as well. Eighty years later—here in the museum setting, amidst the piano with chipped ivory keys where he'd learned to play and his parents' bed, covered with a homespun quilt—the emotions were still present.

We circled the house, which his father Frank had built from a Sears catalogue. Back in 1912, he had ordered it from a book for

$995, and then, weeks later, horses and wagons had dumped the lumber and assembly instructions on his Yorba Linda lot. Today, it remained a tiny cottage with white siding, the president's mother's Quaker touch still apparent.

We walked past President and Mrs. Nixon's graves outside, simple black slabs tastefully offset by a modest garden of wildflowers. We turned and came upon a broad reflecting pool as John recounted the troubled history of their efforts to bring the Nixon Museum and Birthplace into the federally run presidential library system.

I was there to be hired as the new lobbyist for the Nixon family. Some circle had, improbably, been closed. Some profound challenge lay ahead, I believed. Surely, the gods were laughing at this odd turn of events.

I wasn't thinking about the job, however. I wasn't thinking about Washington tactics, about how to get the unionized workers at the Steny Hoyer Research Center that the National Archives and Records Administration (NARA) ran in Silver Spring, Maryland to let go of the Nixon tapes. Thirty years after the fact, some folks still insisted the Nixon tapes had to be held inside the Washington Beltway, supposedly to aid in any possible prosecutions.

I wasn't thinking about earmarked appropriations or riders on an omnibus bill. I wasn't thinking about calling California Representative Nancy Pelosi, or persuading California senators Barbara Boxer and Dianne Feinstein to help.

I was thinking about Richard Nixon, the boy who had been driven so obsessively to succeed. He had felt the snubs, first at Whittier College from the fancy fraternity boys, then later at Duke Law School and on Wall Street from the elitist white-shoe lawyers.

It surprised me to find that I could somehow relate to Nixon's pique. My brothers and I had developed our own contempt for East Coast arrogance, that smug sense of entitlement that accompanied the careers of so many privileged Ivy Leaguers, trust fund fellows who had been to all the right schools and invited into all the exclusive clubs. We, too, had stuck together against the world, though much of our validation came from tight-knit family fabric and from simply bringing home the bacon. We had also left home early, and then urgently recreated our own strong nuclear families.

For Nixon, however, the struggle had never stopped. Life for him had been one endless fight for respect, against enemies both imagined and real. He went from the House to the Senate, where his colleague Jack Kennedy, the handsome war hero, was the life of every party. Nixon endured public put-downs from popular President Eisenhower and the Eastern press, from Georgetown elites and fickle voters.

What was it like, I wondered as we gazed back through the glare at the Nixon birthplace, *to live an entire life with a fifty-pound chip on your shoulder?* Even being twice elected President of the United States had failed to dislodge his burden. He had continued, even at the height of his triumphs, to abuse White House powers; he had continued to make war on his political opponents, blind to the dangers he courted.

Richard Nixon's angst filled the museum grounds, even on a sunny morning. I had read several psychological studies and biographies of the brilliant but tormented president, against whom I had cast my first vote in 1972. None satisfied in solving the many mysteries about him.

The reverence of the tiny coterie of sycophants still on site felt misplaced. They supported him blindly, even now. They had built a Disneyland-style museum, with barely a mention of the Watergate crimes, his vulgar tapes, or his infamous enemies list. It was a fantasy world, where only such historic accomplishments as the opening to China and U.S.-Soviet arms control deals were recounted. With the exception of his daughter Julie and son-in-law David Eisenhower, the hardcore Nixon loyalists seemed still to be in denial. The museum's presentation lent little depth, offering no great insight into an infinitely complicated and accomplished man.

As we went to lunch with aged Nixon Foundation board leaders, I was shocked to realize that here before us were some of the very same men who had supported Nixon's bids for national office. It was as if they'd been released from a time capsule. A few still sported white belts and pastel golf shirts, tan from the good old *Leave it to Beaver* days spent on the type of Orange County golf courses where no women or Catholics were permitted, and no Negroes or Jews were welcome.

Then, as if an apparition, *there was Nixon*. It was Nixon standing in the doorway before me, the familiar silhouette backlit as he shyly said, "Hello."

It was, to my great relief, actually his surviving younger brother. Edward Nixon was the spitting image of the late president. When he smiled, it was eerie: same jowls, same awkward grin, and same pronounced five o'clock shadow. His shoulders were hunched and his eyes deep-set, with brows that arched and pinched as he spoke. He even had the same formal attire his older sibling would have sported. In the desert heat, Ed wore a dark blue suit with pants buckled way too high, a presidential tie clip above the belly.

Ed Nixon, it turned out, was a remarkably unassuming person. Like his brother, he struggled uncomfortably with strangers, yet Ed was noticeably gentle. He introduced himself, then said he was grateful for what we were trying to do; "Probably 'bout time," he observed.

There was poetic justice in the task before me. I had been reared in a home devoted to the Kennedys, where liberal California governor Pat Brown was also revered. Nixon and his Southern California Republican crowd were scorned. I had protested the Vietnam War and Nixon administration policies in high school and college. I had come to Washington as part of the post-Nixon reform fever, the wave of Members and staff swept in by the November 1974 elections. The "Watergate Babies" were a distinctly anti-Nixon crowd. I had worked with California Democrats who had done battle with him and Ronald Reagan, his successor from the right wing, for decades.

Now I was going to work for the Nixon family. It was my job to help do right by history while satisfying my firm's well-paying client. Back in Washington, we needed to draft and lobby for passage of special bills. We'd need to find legislators willing to amend statutes, pass earmarked appropriations, and alter decades of precedent. Our campaign was designed to get all of Nixon's presidential papers together under one roof, not in a loyalists' Potemkin Village-style museum that whitewashed crimes, but in a federally run library in California.

There would be plenty of time to devise a lobbying strategy, and there would be plenty of opposition. Yet, it seemed counterproductive the way Nixon haters still clung to their defining cause. His library *especially* needed to be run from inside the federal system. That was the best way to ensure that professional historians, rather than partisans, controlled access to all Nixon administration documents. My firm was being hired because the legislators most likely to oppose the move, California Democrats, were people with whom I had developed credibility through years of political collaboration.

Once back in Washington, it soon became clear to me that Julie Nixon Eisenhower was the key to the entire project. She understood well that her father would always be set apart from the presidential crowd, and his many accomplishments delegitimized, if his museum was not part of the Archives' historical mainstream. She knew the price of entry: a brutally candid depiction, warts and all, of the criminal activities which also took place in the Nixon White House that culminated in impeachment proceedings. This would inevitably yield exhibits unlike the cheery boosterism evident at all other presidential museums.

Julie proved willing to buck the veteran Nixon loyalists in order to finish the job. She would go around her famously difficult sister and appeal directly to a bunch of liberal Nixon-haters in Washington. It was evident from the outset that Julie was good with people, particularly in a formal setting. Entering the austere Rayburn House Office Building chambers of Republican Congressman Jerry Lewis, she offered a firm handshake to interns and receptionist alike.

"Hi, I'm Julie Eisenhower. How are you?" A confident, pleasant smile, a quick turn to make sure she had not missed anyone, an erect bearing atop practical pumps. Clearly, she was a veteran of many campaigns.

It was only in the privacy of the town car, or in anterooms on Capitol Hill, that I sensed her shyness. This was work for her. It was very hard to be on again, to feel once more all those prying eyes. Watching her, feeling responsible for her well-being and for achieving success in her brave gamble, I felt excruciatingly uncomfortable.

When we visited Congress together for our first round of lobbying calls, I struggled to find safe conversation, asking innocently: "So, uh, when were you last up on the Hill?"

"January 20, 1973," the day of her father's second inauguration.

Of course. I fell silent; I felt like an idiot.

One by one, we made the rounds our lobbying team had prescribed, starting first with California Democratic leaders who might have a home state interest in the project. Next came the Republicans, who were invariably gracious, full of surprising stories about meeting her father early in their careers, and eager to have the Capitol photographer snap a photo of them with the celebrity presidential daughter. Thad Cochran, the silver-haired senator heading the Appropriations Committee, walked us past the grand piano in his private office to show us photos of President Nixon recruiting him when Cochran was still a small-town mayor in Mississippi. Senator Arlen Specter did the same, spiriting Julie off to his private office in the Capitol Building to show her ancient photos of himself, still a young Philadelphia politician, with the grinning president.

David Dreier, chairman of the House Rules Committee, invited us into his Capitol office. It was decorated in soft tones, with an elegant couch covered in Italian fabrics. A roaring fire blazed incongruously while the air conditioning ran: "Just like your dad used to do in his White House hideaway!" Dreier exclaimed too exuberantly, very eager to please her.

We went to see Congressman Tom Davis, a garrulous Republican who had roomed with David Eisenhower, Julie's husband, at Amherst College. Tom told stories of playing all-night board games in the family quarters at the White House. As the wagons were circled late in the Nixon presidency, he and David would lose themselves in the fantasyland of a complex dice game called *APBA Baseball*. It was the very same game my brothers and I had played together for years, through good times and bad.

As we watched, Davis called his Democratic counterpart on a key committee, Henry Waxman. We listened on the speakerphone—Tom was showing off a bit—as he elicited a prompt pledge from Waxman to help get the job done with a bipartisan amendment to a pending bill.[2] We were duly impressed.

Others were more cautious, but nonetheless encouraging. Senator Barbara Boxer, a fellow Marin County liberal, made it clear she would help in any way necessary to get federal funding to move the presidential papers to California. She seemed genuinely moved by Julie's plea. Senator Dianne Feinstein and then-House Minority Leader Nancy Pelosi pledged not to block the effort to get legal clearance for the move, so long as National Archives staff would control access to all Nixon papers.

Julie went with me for a meal in the Senators Dining Room; it would be her first in that elegant setting since the 1950s, when, as a young child, she would visit her dad, then the vice president and the Senate's presiding officer. The high-ceilinged, formal room was warmly done in bright yellows and white, with gold floor-to-ceiling curtains and glass chandeliers. Voices softened within. An old-fashioned gentility reigned as we gazed east through the high windows giving out onto the Capitol Plaza, the Library of Congress, and the Supreme Court. In such ornate surroundings, I felt transported momentarily to a bygone era, a time of bipartisan comity and Old World manners.

One by one, elderly senators from the previous generation came over to say hello to Julie. They *liked* her. Even back in the darkest days of Watergate, they had known she was a steely loyalist. She had stood by her father in the worst of times. She had borne the slings and arrows with a stoicism that must have made him proud. Politicians of all persuasions admired her for this fact. You could see it in their deferential approach and respectful gazes.

After lunch, I led Julie to the darkened interior hallway just off the Senate floor where a white marble bust of her father as vice president rested. I had passed it most working days for more than a decade as I would rush from S-148, the Majority Whip's Office, to the Senate floor. Julie had never seen it, but this was a day for completing unfinished business. She stood before the statue for a long time without speaking. Most passers-by ignored her. A few staffers noticed. They froze in their steps and stared, gawking at the unmistakable likeness between father and daughter: the strong chin, the piercing eyes, and the sloping, ski-jump nose.

"It's not him," she said finally, turning to dismiss the statue. "Too cold. You see, I remember my dad as a warm man, playing the piano for us at home with a big grin on his face."

Our last appointment that day was with the archivist of the United States, in his grand offices looking out on Pennsylvania Avenue. Allen Weinstein was from another world. Academic, Jewish, and a Democrat, he had written a sensational book about Alger Hiss. He concluded, much to most liberals' surprise, that Hiss *had* lied to Congress, as Nixon had insisted, and that Hiss *had* been a fellow traveler with Communists, as Nixon had asserted. Nixon, the slashing opportunist who rode the anti-Communist issue to success in his 1950 Senate campaign, had been right. The controversial Weinstein scholarship delighted hard-liners. Karl Rove couldn't resist making Weinstein one of the token Democrats among senior George W. Bush administration appointees.

As our meeting began, the archivist tried to put Julie at ease, gazing out his windows just as a noisy motorcade headed east up to Capitol Hill. He started reassuring her of his good will, rambling on vaguely about all the water under the bridge.

"Now, Julie"—he paused after a long discourse about the bureaucratic red tape the Nixon Library project still faced—"I know this whole business has been hard on you."

"You have *no* idea, Professor Weinstein," she said sharply.

Julie's eyes grew dark. Something in Weinstein's patronizing tone set her off. Some memory flooded back. Some arrow had pierced her decades-old armor. Her anger astonished us all.

"You have absolutely no idea. There were days when it was all

I could do to just get out of bed. You do not know. You will *never* know."

She silenced him. All of us in the room, including Gregg Hartley, my Republican partner, and Sharon Fawcett, NARA's head of presidential libraries, were looking at our shoes. Julie was right, of course. We did not know how it felt. We could not know.

From that moment on, I saw Julie in a more sympathetic light. I could only imagine her, a young college graduate and newlywed, living in the White House. Her home then was the scene of her family's greatest triumphs, her sister's Rose Garden wedding, gala dinners, and twenty-one-gun salutes. Then it had all turned to horror. She must have felt besieged, and betrayed, lives in flames all around her. Her mother was savaged by the ordeal. The father she revered was nearly destroyed by one thousand cuts, many of them self-inflicted. Julie's bright world of January 1973 had been shattered. It had been left to her, still almost a kid, to be the strong one. She had courageously moved on, emerging from the crucible as a realist.

One sensed she had labored for years to ensure none of her family enemies saw this, the depth of the pain. The vicissitudes of life had thrown her into the center of the public ring. Julie had not volunteered for the role. Yet she had gutted it out and marched ahead, demonstrating both grace and loyalty under intense pressure. She was, I now realized, the ultimate survivor.

Her father would have been proud. That was clear in the archivist's office, as we all averted our eyes sheepishly, waiting for the moment to pass. Richard Nixon would have been proud of his daughter's labors over the next months, as Julie went door to door on the Hill working the problem. I, on the other hand, felt slightly ashamed for the unrelenting vilification my generation had smugly thrown her family's way. I now questioned how we dismissed Nixon's every accomplishment, even those on his relatively progressive domestic agenda—supporting civil rights in the 1950s, establishing the Environmental Protection Agency.

Before we parted that day, I asked her straight up: Why had she been willing to endure the humiliating process to turn the library over to a bunch of historians who would be harsh critics?

"It's something I promised my father I would get done," she said. Her smile was firm, her jaw set just so. "And now it is finally time we finish the job."

CHAPTER THREE

The Most Interesting College in the World

Amherst, Massachusetts
March 1975

Adventurers found Hampshire College through a variety of means. Word of mouth worked best in the early 1970s, in the days before the Internet and text messaging. Free-thinking high school students nationwide began to hear about an academic vision taking form in New England, at a small new college campus being built among the apple orchards below the northern flank of the Holyoke Range. When admittees arrived, this sylvan corner of western Massachusetts seemed the most exciting place on the planet.

For a time, it was our utopia. It offered an alternate universe where all were participants in a grand experiment of creating a fresh approach to campus learning. We were pioneers, launching an educational start-up.

Hampshire College was a new enterprise, one that fostered interdisciplinary studies and reached for an imagined future by rejecting academic traditions. It was to be a community of scholars pledged to lifelong learning; its motto was *non satis scire*: "It is not enough to know." The new college had been sponsored by sons of the Ivy League, spooked by the violent campus protests of the Sixties. These men and women were concerned that their own kids might burn down the Academy, so eager were many to reject Establishment ways. A stepchild of nearby Smith, Amherst, Mount Holyoke, and the University of Massachusetts, Hampshire was given all the resources and support it needed to launch an ambitious experiment.

What ensued was a buffet for hungry minds. We developed our own courses of study. We drew up and executed contracts with advisory committees of professors to conduct our own independent research and complete an individualized series of classes. We wrote our own exams, posing questions we wanted to address. There were no grades, no prerequisites, and few requirements. The College was not just a veritable petri dish for alternative education, but a progressive approach to public policy matters as well.

The day I was admitted to the twelve hundred-member student body was one of the happiest of my life. Demand was intense in those early years, and less than ten percent of applicants got in, an admissions rate lower than any school in the country. Hampshire College, the nation's youngest, was soon to graduate its first four-year class.

My parents in California indulged me. They, too, had charted their own courses as refugees from the East Coast. Dad survived New York's Upper East Side, a Jewish prince destined, like his father and his uncles, for Harvard. Mom had fled a narrow-minded household for the intellectual freedom of Bryn Mawr. They were united by a common determination to take their young family west. They revered the California of the post-World War II years, with its strong public schools and open towns, where young minds were not confined by oppressive traditions and inbred family trees. They sought in California a new ordinary for their children, a public-spirited community with an egalitarian tolerance. From parental passions, my brothers and I took early to the idea that citizen action could combat injustice. Government could actually work.

Mom signs her first book. Dad, and brothers Andy and Pete (to her left), join me in watching. April 1961.

The California of those Wonder Years was full of hopeful families. Because of two war tours as an Army intelligence officer, it had taken Dad more than a decade to get twenty-five hundred miles west from Middlesex prep school to Marin County. He had tried to overcome the social obligations mainstreamed through the DNA of his family of bankers and philanthropists. Unlike his wealthy relatives, he actually worked for a living, as an architect designing homes on the slopes of Mt. Tamalpais. Mom had similarly rebelled against a confining family and its Protestant angst. She published award-winning fiction and nonfiction, and was later to become the leading prophet for the hospice movement in the United States. Together, they tried to shed the burdens they both had known throughout unhappy childhoods.

Our family home on the Belvedere Lagoon looked across the water to the blue-green shoulders of "Mt. Tam," soaring above the small towns on its eastern side. Like so many California communities in those years, it was a place full of possibility. My father had designed our house with floor-to-ceiling plate glass windows and geometric, Frank Lloyd Wright-style lines. My mother had decorated the interior with natural fabrics and *avant garde* art. We had a small sailboat docked in our cool lagoon of a backyard. There was a baseball diamond scratched out in the vacant lot on Peninsula Road where I reverentially followed my older brothers Andy and Pete to play pick-up games.

Pat Brown and Jack Kennedy were household icons, Brown for California's tops-in-the-nation public universities and public works, Kennedy for the intellectual vigor and style he brought to public policy. That both politicians were Richard Nixon's successful opponents was appropriate, for Nixon had harbored a strain of xenophobia we Northern Californians associated with the Southland, from Bakersfield and Whittier all the way to Oklahoma, from which many Angelenos had come.

Sons of an Army veteran, my brothers and I had zero interest in fighting in Vietnam, that lost war to which faraway Washington bureaucrats were sacrificing our young. Andy cleverly exposed himself to the draft December 31, 1971, forseeing a brief window when no call-ups were expected, after which he dropped from number six to number three hundred and seventy-one. Pete exhausted his student deferments, then, when his lottery number came up, presented a medical history just sufficient to avoid being in the last draft pool called up. Both managed to stay west to pursue public-spirited careers and create strong families; only my savvy younger brother Jason ventured east to pursue politics for a time.

As the middle child of five, I had wondered for years about the world my parents had left behind. *What relevance did the mysterious world "Back East" retain for those of us who had fled?* This curiosity, this voyage of return, led me to New England and Hampshire College to figure it out.

This was another world to explore, one quite alien to a Redwood High kid from Larkspur, California. Few in my 1972 graduating class enrolled in colleges east of the Sierra Nevada mountains. I hitchhiked cross-country on the way to college, thumbing from Marin to Reno to Winnemucca to Boise, before dropping south to Boulder. After my final arrival in Amherst, what awaited me was astonishing.

Hampshire College was a place that exalted experimentation. One quiet guy in film class closeted himself to put together a piece on the history of the Brooklyn Bridge. Ken Burns learned his craft well. The school paper was edited by such writers as Tom Kizzia, Chip Brown, and Jon Krakauer, who were just beginning formidable writing careers. I signed up as the photography editor; we published under the juvenile title of *Climax*. Architect Norton Juster taught something called Green Design. My journalism teacher, David Kerr, sharpened our prose by day, then hosted poetry slams and poker games at night.

Hampshire let me take constitutional law my first year: it appeared you did not require a law degree to be a political activist. My English exam contract included a series of articles I wrote about the legal case of an environmental saboteur, a man named Sam Lovejoy. Lovejoy had sought in 1974 to put the entire nuclear industry on trial by committing an act of civil disobedience. He had toppled a weather tower deployed to monitor wind patterns at a proposed nuclear reactor site along the nearby Connecticut River. He then proceeded to transform his court case into an indictment of national nuclear industry practices.

The freedom and intellectual fervor on campus was intoxicating. The women were inquisitive, and altogether liberated. The stimulants were omnipresent; pharmacological research proceeded at a frenetic pace in the dorms. The drinking age was eighteen. It was a time, we all sensed, of enormous possibilities.

We could easily imagine alternative futures, both for each other and for our country. The pain of the Kennedy and King assassinations had begun to recede. Racial strife and generational angst waned. Cultural and sexual revolutions brought greater personal freedom. Our generation was post-Vietnam War, pre-Iran-Contra, after the widespread use of birth control pills, and before the scourge of AIDS. We were living in the sweet spot. We sensed our good fortune, even then.[3]

Hampshire College in 1974 felt like heaven. Directionless, but full of questions and suddenly with the means to find answers, I was as happy as I could imagine being. We called our little corner of the planet, where many strolled barefoot to fall classes, "Camp Hamp, Home of the Happy Feet."

One of the first acquaintances I made was with a real live New Yorker. Lyndsey Gruson filled my every image of a worldly intellectual. He was the first contemporary I'd ever met who read the entire *New York Times* each day. Lyndsey uncorked red wines from a rack in his dorm room, chain-smoked French cigarettes, and worried late into the evening about such obscure issues as the false promise of Euro-Communism. His mother was a foreign correspondent and his father a media executive. He had gone to an exclusive prep school but, like many of our classmates, had talked his parents into letting him attend Hampshire. He was, for me, the epitome of cool, a true sophisticate. I took to reading the *Times* and clipping *New Yorker* cartoons, subtly infiltrating this Eastern salon even while searching to define my own purpose.

Activism was rampant in Amherst. The first issue that engaged me was educational policy. My fascination with the Hampshire experiment led me to contract for a social science exam studying the efficacy of the local Model Cities program. The ghetto of nearby Holyoke, where Puerto Rican millworkers had displaced African Americans at the bottom rung of the socioeconomic ladder, offered a clear vision of public policy challenges. I saw for the first time what happens when national rules are misapplied to local circumstances. The schools failed the kids. Washington offered federal money, but many of its programs were inflexible, ill-suited for local needs. Public education was a crucial element for social progress. Yet throughout Holyoke was evidence of failure and decay. I took to photographing the inner city schools in the harsh winter light and wrote a lengthy research paper on the failures of federal mandates from Nixon's Model Cities program. I began to read eagerly about politics. I began to understand the great power Washington policymakers had over our lives.

West Street, Holyoke, Massachusetts, November 1974.

How could some faraway bureaucrat make sound policy for local taxpayers? My fascination with federal authority began to take root. *Who had the capacity to shape outcomes? Who in Washington contested their power?* I wanted to challenge the status quo, to engage in the debate, somehow, somewhere, to help improve the plight of people ill-served by government. Study of the science of politics loomed.

Meanwhile, we looked hard for stuff to protest. The Hampshire College administration, progressive to a fault, was not obliging. Pioneer Valley activists before us had produced tumultuous anti-

Vietnam war protests, even trying to prevent President Nixon from attending his daughter Julie's Smith College graduation in nearby Northampton. Her family had seethed, but protesters were denied their target when the president cancelled his trip at the last minute.

Hampshire College protest, Amherst Massachusetts, February 1975.

Hampshire College board Chair Franklin Patterson and President Charles Longsworth, February 1975.

In 1975, there was a demonstration at the Hampshire board of Trustees meeting. I marched, but then hung back on the fringe with my camera. I was half in, but uncommitted. I was an observer, not a full participant, abusing my journalistic license to shoot photos for *Climax* without taking sides against administrators I rather admired. Thus did I begin a disturbing pattern of seeking special access without full commitment, a pattern with the potential to haunt me in engagements both professional and personal.

The same *modus operandi* was followed in my reporting on the sensational local trial of Sam Lovejoy. It seems quaint now, but in the 1970s, journalists were expected to demonstrate a reserve. To be a professional meant to maintain an absence of bias. It is a code of conduct that is mostly absent at present, given the partisan commentary that passes for much of contemporary "news" reporting.

As I chronicled Lovejoy's courtroom drama, I struggled to maintain a reserve. The pony-tailed Amherst grad from a local organic farming commune had insisted on serving as his own defense counsel. Yet he managed to put the national nuclear power industry on trial.

"What are you going to do with the radioactive waste?" the cocky Lovejoy would thunder in court. He paced back and forth in a skinny tie and a threadbare suit worn over work boots, his footsteps resounding loudly off the aging floorboards of the county courthouse. He would pause, squinting and pulling at his Ho Chi Minh wisp of a beard. Then he would suddenly erupt with theatrical gestures, flinging his long arms toward the overhead galleries, playing to the last pew as he held the audience in thrall.

Lovejoy admitted toppling the weather tower. He claimed, however, that he was performing a public service. A nuclear power reactor with no permanent waste disposal solution, he maintained, presented a clear and present danger to his neighborhood. "It was self-defense!" he claimed, postitioning himself as a modern-day Paul Revere warning his fellow Massachusetts farmers and merchants.

Shockingly, Lovejoy won. The prosecutor, Lovejoy revealed at the very end of his summation, had zealously filed a faulty indictment. Lovejoy's closing argument was very precise: It was *private* property he had destroyed. The tower owned by the utility company was not, as the charging document stated, *personal* property. The crusty old Yankee judge, more than a little bemused, nodded in agreement. Then he dismissed the case on the technicality.

With this gleeful blow against the legal establishment, Sam Lovejoy became my role model for the day. Here was one man taking on the powers that be—and winning. Not lost on me was the fact that the mercurial Lovejoy did not need a law degree to beat the lawyers. The calculating provocateur had successfully used a small-town courtroom to produce a sweeping inquiry of environmental safety. He had gained national attention and extensive coverage from both *The Boston Globe* and *The New York Times*. In the end, the nuclear plant on the Connecticut River Valley farmland was never built, and Washington regulators of the domestic nuclear industry faced new challenges.

Soon I enrolled in classes in Connecticut River Valley Geology and the Politics of Nuclear Power. My science exam evolved into a study of nuclear reactor siting regulations and focused on such issues as water tables and nuclear waste disposal. A larger lesson seeped in more slowly; many different means could be devised to advance public policy goals. What Lovejoy lacked in terms of a political science doctorate or a law degree, he made up for with imagination and balls.

All around me that spring of 1975 were students who similarly chose to tilt at windmills. They were eager to tear down barriers to fresh inquiry. Even the students' failures were spectacular, if spectacularly wasteful. Bright Exeter-educated kids were lost for months at a time in a thick cloud of cannabis smoke. Talented young poets from Choate and Dana Hall wallowed in existentialist agony, frittering away their parents' tuition dollars in contemplation of navels. Some of the early dissertation topics read like seventh grade science fair projects written under the influence. Then as now, there were striking gaps in the quality of Hampshire academic products, as well as an unforeseen burden that came with liberation from grades. Nobody knew when they had done enough work to advance, a fact that left many lifelong "A" students overwrought.

Here, too, was genius. At Hampshire College, there were mathematicians working with musicians mastering new Moog synthesizers. There were interdisciplinary scholars, classmates like Burns and Krakauer among them, integrating eclectic artistic elements to yield new creative insights. Soon Hampshire was producing a raft of filmmakers, directors, writers, and such actors as Liev Schreiber.

The East Coast elites continued to fascinate me. I would hitchhike north from Amherst on Route 202, then east on Route 2, all the way into Cambridge. I'd stay with cousins from the radical left who lived near Harvard Square. I would pepper my aunt, my father's kindly younger sister, with questions about their screwed-up childhood, conducting my own archaeological exploration of family roots. I went by Greyhound or Amtrak to New York City and took in Manhattan theater with cousins attending Wesleyan and NYU. I admired their maturity, the confidence and adult affectations with which they offered opinions on politics, art, and romance.

Lyndsey Gruson's salon in Hampshire's Dakin Hall continued to mesmerize me. It offered me insight into another world, and a life that might have been if my parents had not, blessedly, taken our family west. There were Bordeaux reds, jazz, chess, and the *Times*, amidst philosophical debate that seemed to never end.

One night in the dorm, well into his cups, Lyndsey saw the future clearly. "We need to go to Washington," he announced.

There was certainty in most every utterance Lyndsey made. His sudden interjection here, however, did make sense. My experiences in Holyoke and at the Lovejoy trial, combined with my family worries about issues as diverse as local parklands or the Vietnam draft, had made clear Washington's power over our lives. So I readily followed his call. The idea was Lyndsey's, but by then I was only too eager to see how things worked in the national capital. Washington was the place of power from which all policy dictates emanated. I needed to find some direction for the nagging sense of public purpose I felt, but one that was struggling to take root in the apple orchards south of Amherst.

When Lyndsey pressed, I didn't protest. Within weeks, we were on an early-morning train out of New York's Penn Station. I wore my only suit, an awkward tan linen number Mom had insisted on buying me before I left home. Using her old hand-me-down Smith-Corona, I'd retyped a résumé so thin that I listed "Wrangler, Dead Indian Ranch" and "Reporter, *Climax* newspaper" near the top, along with a random selection of courses I had completed. There was not a single college class grade to report.

I anxiously reread my Wrangler Résumé in my train seat. Across the aisle, Lyndsey perused his *Times*, sipping a Bloody Mary with Churchillian aplomb. I felt lost. I was out of my league already, and now it seemed as if I was off to the Emerald City.

As towns and bays and freeways flashed by, I struggled to imagine the great capital of Washington. I recalled my fascination with President Nixon's improbable rise and fall, the first stirrings that August night at Dead Indian Ranch. I still felt inconsequential, a presumptuous pretender hoping to infiltrate the strange world ahead. I was afraid—afraid I would be found out and found wanting.

As we neared Washington's Union Station, however, I felt an unmistakable rush. It was the intoxicating surge of adrenaline so similar to that experienced when I'd walk out to the pitching mound, a clean game ball waiting on a pristine field. A reassuring sense of purpose began to take root. I was eager to gain entry to the arena looming before me, to engage in the debates on public policy, to reshape the world.

Before long, my addiction was complete.

Chapter Four

What I Needed to Know When I Was Twenty-One

Charlottesville, Virginia
March 2010

The roads heading west hasten you away from the city of Washington DC, scattering like an ice cube melting on a hot stove. As the tangle of highways spin in spiral webs, you soon enter the South. The land of the old Confederacy begins just beyond the tract homes carved out of the red clay soil of western Fairfax County in Virginia.

After 9/11, the national security apparatus expanded dramatically. Dozens of new buildings sprang up in the Virginia suburbs in the construction boom, as the counterterrorism bureaucracy reached its tentacles past Fairfax and Tyson's Corner. Secret sites with smoked windows and high fences soon sat alongside big-box shopping malls.

Security contractors flush with recession-proof anti-terrorism work helped to make these suburban counties among the richest in the nation. After a few years, the traffic backups on Route 66 stretched all the way beyond Manassas and onto Route 29, headed south. Then, finally, the road would again traverse a land of fruit and corn. Dozens of silver Virginia Historical Society plaques appear, marking Civil War cavalry skirmishes along the creek beds of Gainesville and Bull Run.

One hope-filled early spring morning, I found myself driving south past the split rail fences and fields awaiting shoots of green. The weight of winter's snows, which had exceeded three feet in this, the year of the Great Blizzard, were beginning to lift.

Life surely imitates art, or so I concluded, chuckling to myself in the car. I had once written a novel about a group of eager Stanford graduates who venture Back East to lead complicated Washington careers, only to return, later in life, to the university. On this spring day in 2010, it seemed something similar might be happening to me.

Driving to audition for a professorship and a role helping to build a new program back on campus, I was headed to Charlottesville, not Palo Alto. I was trying to figure out if I was prepared to make the leap.

It began, like most good adventures in life, as a lark. A colleague had shown me a website about a new school of leadership and public policy being established at the University of Virginia (UVa). An acquaintance from Stanford, Harry Harding, had just been named the Batten School's first dean. His challenge was to build a program on the solid foundation of Thomas Jefferson's university. Harding, a brilliant China scholar and a Washington veteran, was hiring professors to help teach graduate students how policy is hammered out in the public arena. The enterprise had all the hallmarks of an entrepreneurial start-up. It offered a fresh opportunity to redefine what students need to know in order to be effective public policymakers. Batten was going to teach leadership skills, strategy, and best practices for policy advocates. Dean Harding hoped to build an incubator for future NGO advocates, civic leaders, and public officials.

The job description seemed tailored for people like me. I had twice left graduate school doctoral programs for Washington challenges, never handing in my Ph.D. thesis, though Harper & Row had published an early draft as a textbook about Congress, the president, and foreign policymaking.[4] I assumed I'd be passed over in any major campus job competition among political scientists—no matter that many of us former Washington types suspected academics knew little about real-world political bargaining. There had been scores of applicants for the UVa job. My hasty submission had somehow yielded a spot in the finals. My curiosity grew.

The next day I was to give a guest lecture to the Search Committee and a group of graduate students. The topic I had chosen was a tutorial on what seemed to have been my life's study: how to prevail in Washington policymaking contests.

I pondered the question as the road curved in a long arc, passing just east of Culpepper, offering a sudden view of the rising Blue Ridge. The low mountains seemed strong and pure, as if shorn of city weight. The thought buoyed me: I felt the same way. With each mile, I was calmed, a fresh perspective taking root.

It was just to the west of here that George Washington, the young surveyor, made his first fortune. It was from here that Virginians, fearing urban crowding 250 years ago, had scrambled through hard mountain gaps to make homes in the vast interior of the American continent, years when Virginia's western boundaries stretched clear to the Mississippi River. The blue-gray of the distant ridgeline beckoned like Mount Tamalpais back in my home California county of Marin. The gentle horizon offered some elusive potential. At that moment, it hinted of an end to the incessant gossip and petty partisan maneuvering that passed for the heart of much life in contemporary Washington, D.C.

I was pulled inextricably towards the university. There on the highway, I began to see it. This was not to be just another speech. It represented a chance for renewal. The audition, I realized, would be a welcome challenge. As adrenaline surged, clarity arrived and themes began to bubble up before me.

What to say? Later that evening, I put the question to my daughter Jenn, who had nearly completed her studies at UVa. Over beer and *Scrabble* at Michael's Bistro in Charlottesville, she offered crucial guidance.

"Tell them how it *really* works, Dad," she instructed as she dropped her tiles on the board—"E-X-A-C-T-L-Y"—on the triple word score. "Tell them the unvarnished truth."

I nodded.

"One hundred ten," Jenn announced matter-of-factly after

toting up her score. "Tell them all the book learning in the world doesn't mean crap if you can't understand your opponent's frame of reference—the personalities involved, what motivates them. When you show up in Congress, you don't just have to know the process. You have to know what they've been arguing about during the ten years before you walked in. You need to know the people and the context if you're going to accomplish anything as a policymaker."

I began scribbling notes frantically on the back of the score pad: "Precedents. Process. Personality." That was it: the three P's. My little alliterative trinity began to take its place. It soon became my catechism for young students: how to use history and analysis to shape public policy outcomes. How to be an effective advocate. How it all really worked.

Later that night, I reflected on the hangover of guilt resulting from the profitable turn my Washington career in public policy-making had quite unexpectedly taken. It seemed that, just like the Hawaiian missionaries, I'd come to town to do good, but stayed and done well. I was committed to public service, eager to help improve lives. I justified the evolution of my work with the notion that I had done my time as a public servant. I still revered the patriots I'd encountered, the nobler sorts in both political parties who put country ahead of party.

I had grown weary, however, of the endless compromises, large and small, one confronted each day—compromises that gnawed away at your sense of purpose. I detested the partisan blather from poseurs who viewed politics primarily as a route to power, not as a means to secure enlightened policy. I was tired of the shallowness of unedited blogs and tweets, the dumbing-down of discourse on television news. Teaching offered an opportunity to help enlighten the next generation of policymakers.

How do you win? I tried to answer the question as I began to speak the next day. The faculty members on the Search Committee had filled up the front row. Their eyes were intent on their clipboards, pens poised in hands as they prepared to score me. They looked like a row of Olympic figure skating judges.

The tableau was intimidating. Yet I felt liberated by the fact that I was such a long shot for the job. It was one I did not need, had not planned to seek, and did not expect to be offered. As a consequence, I was exceptionally frank. I recalled Mom's advice from her theater training: "When in doubt, play to the back row." I determined to look to the students who filled rows in the rear, not the serious faces of the faculty sitting in judgment right in front of me.

I warmed to my subject quickly, weaving into my theme illustrations drawn from years occupying my catbird seat near the center of the floor of the U.S. Senate. I got specific. I named names. I identified winning strategies and tactics. I recalled how to anticipate the quirks of legislators' personalities, the role of process, and the importance of historical precedent. My three P's readily lent structure to the lecture.

"What do you need to know to succeed as a young policymaker in Washington? You need to know there are ghosts in the room. You need to know that every debate you have is haunted by the failures of the recent past. There is blood on the floor and there are loaded metaphors in the air.

"You need to know the precedents: who won and who lost last time, and why. You need to know how to use policy history as an example, and how to prevent 'lessons learned' from being misapplied. You need to understand that behind every member of Congress is the guy they defeated, the guy who strayed too far from the center, who flew too close to the sun.

"Memories are long. The House hates the Senate, for all those tough votes representatives take, only to see their bills stall in the Senate, 'where bills go to die.' The senators hate the House; they look down patronizingly on the 'lower body.' Senators aim to outgrow the provincial partisanship of the more populist House, even as the senators increasingly import bare-knuckle House tactics into their dysfunctional House of Lords.

"Watch out for mischievous roll calls in the weeks before Federal Election Commission fundraising reports are due. Some opponent will misrepresent a vote, if only to shake the money tree for campaign donations via the Internet and direct-mail solicitation.

"Master procedural maneuver. The ill-educated son of a coal miner, former Ku Klux Klan member Bobby Byrd, rose to become one of the most powerful legislators in Senate history by mastering parliamentary tactics. He beat out the celebrated Ted Kennedy for a leadership post.

"Figure out how the deals will be made. Also where and when. Learn the importance of timing. Learn when to compromise, and when to go down in flames, defending a principle absolutely.

"Study the men and women who will decide. Learn the make-up and the quirks of their electoral districts the way kids used to memorize the statistics on the back of baseball cards. Know what motivates decision-makers, their hopes and aspirations.

"Learn the precedents. Study the personalities. Master the process. Be very clear what it is you're trying to accomplish. Learn to distinguish the public interest from special interests. Cultivate and honor loyalty. Know your own heart, and your own principles. Then, and only then, will you be prepared as an effective champion for your cause."

As my words flowed easily from my *Scrabble* discussion notes of the night before, I relished the exercise in synthesis. Removed from the information overload of day-to-day Washington combat, I felt it possible for practitioners to impart decades of experience. I began to isolate the key components, to use them as teachable moments. Enduring truths about public policymaking skills suddenly became apparent. Connections became clear. Work I had performed unthinkingly for years crystallized. The subject *was* teachable. The distance from the Washington Beltway, even just a morning's drive, offered clarity.

Over the course of the day, the team Harry Harding was assembling proved to be remarkably collegial. Each professor I met seemed full of energy, ideas, and optimism. The group included a brilliant political scientist from UC Berkeley, a former JAG and West Point graduate just back from Iraq, and a bright young mother from Duke Law School who offered soup-to-nuts career counseling to the new MPP students. All were committed to the unique Batten School mission, which promised a new direction built on the foundation of one of the nation's best public universities. The University had also just hired its first woman president, Terry Sullivan, a respected scholar and administrator from the renowned state research universities of Texas and Michigan. Joining the team advancing her agenda might offer both new challenges and an opportunity for reflection and growth. Certainly it offered a chance to escape the office politics of both K Street and Capitol Hill for the reflective environment of a community of scholars.

My reaction startled me. The earnest gazes of the students were inspiring. *Maybe you can do this*, I told myself. And then I realized: *You want to do this.* On that day, my Washington work seemed to have run its course. My unusual but interesting career was stalled, a sailing ship stuck in the doldrums. Now this jaunty power boat had come alongside, full of promise and energy, at the perfect moment. *Was I really ready to jump?*

A month passed before the follow-up call came and they offered me the job. To my enduring surprise, I took it.

CHAPTER FIVE

Initiation: Working on the Joint Committee

**United States Senate
April 1975**

It was a balmy spring morning, nine months after Nixon's resignation, when I arrived in Washington for the first time. For the next thirty-five years, I never really left. What held me there?

The accessibility of power is what drew me in, the remarkable openness of the process. I see this now, with the clarity afforded by time. I love the Congress, warts and all, because it is so open. You can walk right in and contest power.

The faults of Congress mirror those of the country. Congress is populist and partisan. Most Members rush to score political points on the daily news. Too many filibuster when the nation is confronted by long-term challenges requiring prompt address. Voters reward flash and sizzle but are slow to honor persistence and moderation. Strident ideology and partisan rhetoric are prerequisites for most primary elections, but then compromise is required to get much of anything done in the Capitol. These failings were apparent from first contact. Yet I grew to appreciate Congress because of the fact that a young man could simply show up and participate in the remarkable world of Jefferson and Madison's design. *That* was the thrill which persisted.

The accessibility amazed me from my first day. As the Amtrak train made its way through Philadelphia, Wilmington, and Baltimore, our car grew increasingly populated by players riding off to some distant drama. They fell into stride as we reached our destination, crossing the cavernous Union Station hall that then separated the tracks from the city, and pouring out through the great brass doors. Tourists with children in tow joined the crowd. Looming above us was the enormous Capitol dome set off against the green oaks and cherry trees, and an impossibly blue sky.

I trailed up the hill behind the crowd. It was a Tuesday, just after 10 a.m., when I entered the Dirksen Senate Office Building for the first time. Down the long marble hallway was Room 106, where the morning *Washington Post* informed me the Appropriations Committee was taking testimony on fiscal year 1976 federal education funding. I peered awkwardly into the doorway, waiting for someone to stop me. Then a retinue of staff brushed by, with Senator Edward Kennedy of Massachusetts in tow.

"Good morning," he muttered as he slid past, grazing my shoulder. His face was splotchy and misshapen, as if from not enough sleep.

You could just walk right in! It was this realization that was most intriguing as I stood in the back of the room, gawking at the ritual presentation unfolding. The senators' dialogue sounded like schoolboy catechism as "distinguished chairmen" were greeted, colleagues "yielded," and legislators seemed to maneuver to outperform each other with flowery rhetorical flourishes from a bygone era. Legislators from different states, different parties, were engaging each other ever so respectfully. Their manner was deferential, yet the issues were so profound. Tens of billions of dollars of federal funding were at stake.

I was spellbound. These were the days before C-SPAN. I had never witnessed any legislative proceeding, not even a city council hearing. I had never met a Member of Congress. Now I was standing in a Senate hearing room, bumping into Ted Kennedy.

Behind the dais, I saw young staffers moving as if in a choreographed dance. They would whisper in senators' ears, slip documents to them. Staff and member would nod gently to acknowledge each other. Several aides weren't much older than I was. Yet clearly the staffers were part of the script and would be helping shape the outcome. The interplay of forces was arresting. I knew immediately that I wanted to find some role to play.

My first appointment was on the sixth floor at 11 a.m. A thrice-retyped cover letter accompanying my lame Wrangler Résumé had somehow produced a response from an aide to one of my California senators. The office manager to Senator John Tunney awaited me. I had no idea if this was just a courtesy informational interview for a home-state constituent, or if I might actually win one of the few legislative internships in my preferred area of education policy.

John Tunney joined here by his senior colleague Alan Cranston, October 1975.

When the time came, I was too naïve to be nervous, but the interviewer who greeted me knocked me off-center. Jeri Thomson was overwhelmingly attractive. Blonde, trim, and sharply dressed, she had a confident businesswoman's command. Her studied gaze through tortoise-shell glasses made me squirm. She was stunning, surely the homecoming queen *and* the charming class president.

Ms. Thomson was no-nonsense as she proceeded, after pleasantries, to zero in on just one line in my résumé. "I see you have studied nuclear energy issues . . ." She paused, testing.

"Uh, yeah." A clumsy silence ensued as I struggled for the best response. I was hoping she did not know about the Sam Lovejoy trial, or some of his over-the-top leftist rhetoric. I was trying to figure out how to get the discussion back to education issues.

Then something clicked in my head. It was a survival instinct, and it saved the moment: *If you can't make the case for yourself, how are you ever going to represent a U.S. senator?* The notion helped prevent me from blowing the opportunity in front of me. I paused just a bit longer, trying to shift gears into a nuclear policy mindset. Then I plunged ahead, drifting perilously toward the realm of fiction.

"Well, uh, yes . . ." I began. "I've been looking into the key questions pertaining to the nuclear fuel cycle. Studying the whole waste-disposal issue. The, uh, implications of the technology and the gap between the unrealized promise of nuclear energy and some of the problems make for a fascinating course of study."

We were interrupted by a phone call, saving me from a pose that had begun to sound as if I'd secured a doctorate in nuclear engineering, instead of taking just one Hampshire College class taught by an anti-nuclear journalism professor.

I am not certain where I got the gift of gab. Mom says it's in my blood; many of her Stoddard, Harris, and Lyons relatives had been distinguished community leaders who could make an eloquent speech about most anything. My kids claim I am a shape-shifter, possessed of an annoying habit: I unconsciously adjust my accent to accommodate foreign guests. As a middle child, I remain eager to fit in, to demonstrate sympathy with my audience. I think out loud too much.

I used to suspect my volubility was a nervous tic, the reflexive calculation of a child of divorce, anxious to fill awkward silences, to move the conversation to common ground. I strained to discern nuance in adult conversation, and to figure out its implications. I gravitated towards the role of peacemaker, quick to move table talk to safe territory. The combination made me a pretty good bullshit artist. And *that* is how I got my first job in Washington.

Ms. Thompson returned with more basic questions. "Honors graduate from Redwood High in Marin County? Ross School valedictorian? Political science major at, uh, *what* college in Amherst?" And then, out of the blue: "When can you start?"

It was that easy. By noon, Lyndsey Gruson and I were headed

for lunch at a nearby restaurant; he insisted we toast my good fortune.

When I returned to Washington to start my internship later that summer, Mom had bought me a second suit. I had a Senate ID and an unpaid job. I was sent to a room in the basement of the Dirksen Senate Office Building to sort constituent mail, but was also assigned as a gofer aide to Bob McNair, one of the senator's legislative assistants, covering his assignment on the Joint Committee on Atomic Energy (JCAE).

The JCAE was one of the most powerful and secretive committees in the history of the United States Congress. It controlled billions of dollars in spending for the nuclear weapons and energy research complex. The JCAE had been the scene of tense, highly classified debates about the future of the hydrogen bomb—lobbying that had accelerated the arms race and cashiered Robert Oppenheimer. Alone among scores of committees in Congress, it was bicameral, reporting bills for action directly to *both* the House and the Senate while retaining exclusive jurisdiction over all things nuclear.

One morning during the second week of my internship, I trailed McNair into the bowels of the Capitol. We scampered through the rabbit's warren of hideaway offices before reaching a grotto later made famous in a ghoulish scene from a Dan Brown mystery novel. It was the crypt directly underneath the dome, the place where the Massachusetts Sixth Regiment guarding the Capitol in April 1861, sleeping on the Senate floor above, had baked their bread.

A bullet-shaped silver elevator tucked away in one corner of the crypt admitted us. Then we rode up to S-407, which the staff in 1975 called "the Room of Secrets." Signing in at the attic security desk, we arrived at a windowless room where, since the beginning of the nuclear age, the Joint Committee had met.

The chamber was a relic of early Cold War days. Before the summer of 1945, few in Congress had known anything about the atom bomb or the Manhattan Project. Even FDR's vice president, Harry Truman, was kept in the dark. Joseph Stalin and his

Los Alamos spies were far better informed about progress in the U.S. nuclear research effort than the man who succeeded Franklin Roosevelt in the Oval Office.

In the aftermath of Hiroshima, congressional powers demanded a greater role guiding sizeable nuclear expenditures. Obsessive secrecy led Hill leaders to agree to a single "joint" House and Senate committee. It would have exclusive powers to regulate and fund the nation's nuclear enterprise. No other committee of Congress could encroach on its legislative jurisdiction. Never did the Committee need to meet in a contentious House-Senate conference.

The Joint Committee's legislative members worked collegially to steer federal spending and jobs to their districts. For decades, the JCAE was the province of an exclusive club, legislators who virtually inherited their states' seats on the panel. Over the years, they included Brien McMahon, author of the Atomic Energy Act that launched the "Atoms for Peace" export program; Lyndon Johnson; Richard Russell; Henry "Scoop" Jackson; Al Gore, Sr.; and Howard Baker.

Many JCAE members hailed from states which received billions of federal dollars in public works for laboratory research and construction—Washington (Hanford), New Mexico (Los Alamos), Kentucky (Paducah), and Tennessee (Oak Ridge). Other members came from states with clusters of new light-water reactors feeding the growing electrical-power grid—Illinois, Florida, and California. Rarely was there a nuclear industry proposal the JCAE did not endorse. Members were ever eager to promote Atoms for Peace exports and to pursue the industry's fantastic dream of "clean" energy that backers promised would be "too cheap to meter."

Never during its initial three decades had an industry critic been a Committee member. I was eager, somehow, to make the unsuspecting John Tunney its first. For my efforts, I should have been fired.

Let me explain.

Tunney, son of a heavyweight boxing champion and supporter

of California agribusiness and aerospace industries, was a prototype of the new, telegenic anti-Vietnam War senator of that era. He had come into a Senate increasingly populated by liberal activists and Nixon critics, champions of environmental and civil rights causes. From the day he arrived in the Senate, a future presidential bid was presumed by reporters covering his meteoric rise.

Nevertheless, Tunney, late in his first Senate term, found himself under political siege. He was being challenged, improbably, from the left, by Tom Hayden, Jane Fonda's husband and an original defendant in the Chicago Seven trial. Tunney was also being challenged, from the right, by an irreverent academic, the plucky S. I. Hayakawa of Marin County, who claimed Tunney was a liberal lightweight. The first test looming was an early Democratic primary to which, with an anti-nuclear power initiative also on the 1976 California ballot, large numbers of Hayden voters were promising to turn out. As Tunney campaigned in the Golden State, senior Senate staffers like Bob McNair were increasingly being pulled back home to California to draft speeches and politic with key constituent groups.

My opening at first was quite slim. The cerebral, trusted McNair was on the road often; he instructed me to sit in the rear of the Joint Committee chamber, keep my mouth shut, and take notes for him on all proceedings. It was there in the back row of the JCAE that I met a new group of role models.

For years, records of many Joint Committee proceedings had been stamped "CLASSIFIED." This routine violation of open-government rules amused members of the club, and kept most would-be critics out of the intimidating hearing room high atop the Capitol building. The tumult of Watergate and the sweeping reforms brought by the Class of the Ninety-Fourth Congress elected in November 1974 nudged the Joint Committee to open more of its hearings.

Young reformers like Chris Dodd of Connecticut, George Miller of California, and Joe Biden of Delaware were assaulting the seniority system in 1975. The good-old-boy network that had Congress ceding too much authority to the "imperial" presidencies of Lyndon Johnson and Richard Nixon was being challenged. With their bell-bottom pants, big hair, and mutton-chopped sideburns worthy of Civil War generals, many of the reform-minded "Watergate babies" set off in search of entrenched powers to challenge. With a 292-143 Democratic edge in the House, and nearly as wide a margin in the Senate, the reformers felt emboldened, if not entitled, to change. Demands for open hearings and recorded votes were only where they started.

Now, sitting in the back row with me, the lowly Tunney intern, was a group of young environmentalists who later became a virtual who's who of the nuclear reform movement. Many would go on to distinguished policymaking careers. In the industry's inner sanctum of S-407 during the fall of 1975, however, they were suspect infiltrators. There was Jim Cubie, a bespectacled and unassuming staffer with Ralph Nader's Critical Mass Energy Project. There was Jacob Scherr, a darkly earnest attorney for the Natural Resources Defense Council. There was NRDC's Tom Cochran, with his Tennessee drawl and walrus moustache; as well as wild-eyed Bob Alvarez from Environmental Action, wearing offbeat ties over ubiquitous blue jeans; and a kindly House staffer named David Rosen, wise behind his Coke-bottle glasses.

Also among us was a group of Senate staffers who served members from other panels. These legislators were reformers. As non-committee members, they were barred from reporting any legislation that might impinge on the Joint Committee's exclusive domain, but they had sent staffers to watch for an opening to challenge the Joint Committee. There was Dick Wegman, chief of staff to Senator Ribicoff, alongside the more cautious Ellen Miller and Connie Evans. Their ringleader was Paul Leventhal, the bow-tied New Yorker who first worked for veteran Senate Republican Jacob Javits of New York. They were lying in wait, united in their determination to change the self-dealing status quo embodied by the JCAE. The Committee remained the epitome of the closed military-industrial complex. Environmental activists, NGOs, and public interest group lawyers were most unwelcome.

Among this group of critics, I stuck out both because of my

youth and lack of fashion sense. Still sporting an Abe Lincoln beard, I stood six-foot-six in my ill-coordinated wardrobe. I often wore my tan suit with a striped Marimekko shirt, the outfit not exactly brought together by a favorite green wool tie I'd bought years before at a street market in Ireland. I was extremely naïve, full of impertinent questions, and still awed by the sense we were being permitted to spy behind the curtains of power in this Oz-like setting.

The Joint Committee interlopers were unfailingly patient. Our gang would whisper in the back row, which someone dubbed the "Group W Bench," from an Arlo Guthrie song about miscreants in trouble with the authorities. In the staff dining room in the Dirksen basement, we'd drink too much black coffee and chain-smoke Marlboro reds as I struggled to figure out how politics and policymaking really worked.

The nuclear policy standoff extant in 1975 was fraught with peril. American and Soviet nuclear arsenals were racing toward the absurd total of sixty thousand warheads. As oil prices soared and more nations purchased reactors and nuclear fuel production facilities, President Kennedy's nightmare vision of a world with fifteen, twenty, or twenty-five nuclear-armed rivals loomed. India had just detonated a nuclear device fabricated in a clandestine military program it had hidden from western suppliers. Staffers to Senators Percy and Glenn had just uncovered evidence Delhi had actually diverted U.S. source materials to help manufacture this nuclear weapon. Atoms for Peace, my staff colleagues argued, could finally be exposed as a fraud.

Facing these dangers, Senate heavyweights Percy, Glenn, Ribicoff, Javits, and Symington saw opportunity. They sought to legislate sanctions against India, and to curb other irresponsible nuclear export practices in the process. This initial effort might also create, for critics, an inroad to challenge the domestic U.S. nuclear industry and its host of unresolved safety and waste disposal challenges. However, they needed a legislative angle to bypass the Joint Committee, and staffers needed a well-placed senator to act as their champion.

That's where I came in. I represented a possible path to reform-minded John Tunney. That's the promise they apparently saw in me, their young trainee at insurgent legislative politics.

The activists pursued their proposed reforms with an enviably clear sense of direction. Their world was a morality play. Their bad guys—from the Indians to European exporters to U.S. nuclear-industry executives—all wore black hats. I had grown up in a household where heroes and villains were similarly identified in absolutist terms; it was part of my Stoddard DNA. Though I had come to Washington as a curious and eager spectator, I was also quite certain of the sharp distinctions between Good and Evil. I had little patience for shades of gray. Nuance was never to be my strong suit.

Here before me, in my first weeks in Washington, was an opportunity to play some small role in national affairs. I just had to figure out how to get Senator Tunney to read my memos.

Tunney, it turned out, was actually a rather awkward private guy; he probably had no business embarking on a public career. The realization that there were shy people in politics gave me hope. Despite his soft hair and rumors of hard partying with his friend and UVa Law School roomate Ted Kennedy, Tunney was quite serious. He was burdened with both a famous name, from his father, the boxer Gene, and the rugged good looks of a square-jawed Hollywood star. Like the Redford character in *The Candidate*, modeled by producers after Tunney in his first Senate race, he appeared uncertain about what exactly his mission was in politics. The handlers and donors and ad men flocked to him; he just looked so senatorial. Everybody had an agenda for John, it seemed, except John.

Tunney had run for the Senate on an anti-Vietnam platform, declaring for the vulnerable GOP-held seat after only two terms in the House. Once sworn in, however, he found the process of negotiating amendments, the nitty-gritty of Senate policymaking, rather boring. Dozens of Tunney staffers scurried about generating work, brainy young lawyers like Mel Levine and Jane Frank (Harman), both of whom later won House seats in their own right.

Handlers pushed Tunney in every direction. He was sent tacking left, then right, his movements so inconsistent that he risked losing his political base. Nixon was gone, replaced by an unelected president, Gerald Ford. There was no more draft to worry about, no Great Society crusade to undertake. For Tunney, this meant no new issue had arisen to galvanize his looming reelection campaign.

Lacking an agenda of his own, Tunney was subject more than most politicians to popular pressures and the manipulations of campaign pollsters. Some people, I learned over subsequent years, came to Washington driven by causes. Liberal or conservative, they are issue activists and political philosophers, men like Newt Gingrich and Barack Obama. They seek power as a means to an end, whether it is deregulation or universal health care.

Their opposites are those who tend to exploit issues as a means to an end—people on the make, like Tom DeLay or Arlen Specter, people who can appear unburdened by any core convictions other than a commitment to their own reelection. They are obsessed by polling data. Their hunger is for power itself, and the accompanying perks, the campaign cash, the TV interviews, the limousines waiting outside every airplane and speaking engagement. They can be for or against almost any issue, depending on what the polls show and the fundraisers want. They are opportunists through and through.

Tunney, it seemed to me from my very first meeting, was neither. As I watched him from the back of a hearing room, or amidst a crowd of California constituents at a Wednesday morning open house coffee, it struck me that Tunney was a thoroughly decent person who was instinctively candid. Tunney had stumbled into politics but was ill-suited to the profession. As a politician, he had to be trained by handlers to dissemble. Seemingly caught in the vortex of forces far bigger than himself, he was driven by people with urgent agendas who failed to inspire. He was an honest guy amidst a gathering of knaves. Presumptuous as it was, I unconsciously began to feel empathy for him.

As the national presidential campaign began to unfold, an

essential passion was lacking in Tunney's politics. The Nixon pardon wasn't enough to make swing voters dislike the amiable Gerald Ford. Appeals to pragmatism began to carry the day. More extreme candidates on the flanks of both parties were faltering even before the presidential primaries began. Ford would ultimately best candidate Ronald Reagan, as Jimmy Carter, the moderate, would defeat liberals like Jerry Brown, Mo Udall, and Fred Harris.

On Capitol Hill each day, I walked my three-block commute to the Dirksen basement, an irrepressible smile on my face. I had a job where my main purpose, other than sorting mail, was to figure out how policymaking power in Congress was wielded. I could learn from the inside, with new friends eager to school me. This seemed a 180-degree reversal from the irrelevance of an undergraduate classroom full of utopian dreamers.

Most days were spent dodging my mailroom duties and coming up with excuses to attend briefings, hearings, or environmental group conferences. Nights were a cornucopia of free food, free liquor, and smart women. My fellow Hampshire interns—six of us were living in a four-bedroom rental on D Street above the grinding construction being completed on the new Washington subway, the Metro—made a sport out of crashing lavish receptions. With our staff IDs, we found we could enter the vast hearing rooms from behind the dais, using the "Senators Only" door, and thereby avoid checking in with the host tables set up at the front entrance. We would eat, drink, and flirt. We'd try to figure out who the event was for on our way out—Russell Long's Louisiana Fish Fry was our favorite—then fill our pockets full of fruit and cookies for the fridge on D Street.

This was bliss for interns. I began trying to scheme how I might be allowed to stay.

A chance invitation opened another door. Clayton and Polly Fritchey, friends of my New York uncle Eddie, were hosting a night at the Kennedy Center to hear the National Symphony, followed by dinner at their Georgetown home. The engraved invitation said "black tie optional."

Out came the tan suit; my zero-income budget made no allowance for tuxedo rentals. I was similarly naïve in not suspecting that amongst the over-sixty crowd at dinner, there would be one single young woman miraculously seated next to me. Warburg was the spare man, it seemed. I lucked out once more.

As it happened, a hurricane skirted the city on the designated evening; Rock Creek overflowed in the downpour. When I arrived late by cab, the pounding rain had transformed my suit into a soggy mess dotted with hundreds of spots. I looked like a bedraggled Dalmatian toweling off in the hallway and trying to make small talk with Tom Braden, the national columnist for the *Los Angeles Times* syndicate. Sliding into my seat, I was grateful that the candlelight hid much of my sartorial shame.

My reward awaited. On my right sat one of the most attractive and intelligent young women I ever met. Slim, with long brown hair cascading over a lacy black cocktail dress, she blushed when she smiled, revealing scores of freckles in the soft light. An English major on leave from Bennington, she was Joannie Braden, Tom's daughter.

My manners lost or forgotten, I neglected to shift with each course and converse, as Emily Post dictated, first left, then right, and then across. I was spellbound, listening intently to Joannie's every word. *What a night!* I thought. *What a city!* The Senate, the salon, the symphony, the reporters, even the various congressmen and senators—everything dazzled me.

Within weeks, Tom and his wife Joan Braden, who was the city's reigning A-list hostess, had made me a regular at the dinners they held at their rambling yellow clapboard house in Chevy Chase. Cocktails at 101 East Melrose were upstairs with many of their eight children, aged thirteen to thirty. We would dress four or five to a room. Random teenagers would bound down back stairs, a cloud of marijuana smoke drifting behind, invariably freaking out the security detail before Secretary of State Henry Kissinger, a regular guest, arrived.

The Bradens would seat me some evenings at the head table with Senator Kennedy, or Senator Percy, or frequent guests David

Brinkley from NBC News and Robert McNamara, president of the World Bank. Tom and Joan adopted me as something of a project—they had decided to try to train the California kid in the ways of Washington.

After the last guest left, the family would linger over a nightcap. Delightful gossip ensued as the course of the evening was dissected. Tom batted around ideas for the national newspaper column he had to file every afternoon at five. Joan shared tidbits from her sidebars with the city's powers. I would listen intently, trying to discern motive, trying to pick up nuance, trying to figure out how things really worked. I was enraptured, engaged in the issues. A worldly young woman shared private observations, escorting me to a salon that offered insights into some of the Capital's secrets. Life could not have been better.

Back at the office, I pressed more intently on my nuclear policy memos. There was no evidence the senator, or even Hadley Roff, his crusty chief of staff, had read them. So I upped the ante.

I proposed in a lengthy memo that Senator Tunney endorse the anti-nuclear initiative on the California ballot. It would be both good politics—taking some wind out of Hayden's sails—and good policy, a shot across the bow for a nuclear industry in denial over waste and proliferation issues.

My buddies on the Group W Bench at the back of the Joint Committee fed me eagerly, suggesting that Tunney also go after the latest industry boondoggle before the JCAE. This was the Nuclear Fuel Assurance Act; it proposed billions in taxpayer-funded loan guarantees to entice U.S. corporations like Bechtel and Chevron to help privatize the costly process of enriching uranium to fuel power reactors. Carefully, I laid out in a memo to the senator both the arguments for attacking this measure, and the tactics that might win the fight on the Senate floor. I labored over my thesis as if it was the most important document I would ever write.

McNair had little time for my scribblings. He glanced at my proposal briefly, then put me off with a patronizing, "We'll see." Down to the basement mailroom I trudged.

The leak came a few days later. I honestly don't believe it was an ego trip, though surely I was looking for a way to join the policymaking game, if only to extend my stay in Washington. *So what? What if circumstances are such that I might help advance the cause of reform while improving my own prospects in the process?* That, it already was clear to me, was how Washington worked.

The opening came over a nightcap.

"Goddamn column," Tom Braden was complaining. "It's like a beast you gotta feed every day or it's gonna eat you."

The lament was not a new one. Then Tom put it to me directly: "Whaddya know? Whaddya hear up there on the Hill? Got anything I can use?"

"The Nuclear Fuel Assurance Act boondoggle!" I blurted out reflexively. Then I proceeded to explain. The nuclear industry was seeking federal loan guarantees and market assurances in order to privatize the business of enriching uranium fuel rods for nuclear power reactors. It was corporate welfare, a taxpayer giveaway to an industry that had not yet addressed critical safety, nonproliferation, and waste disposal issues. As with most of my analysis in those days, the fight was vividly portrayed in black and white—nuclear reformers versus the corrupt Joint Committee powers.

Tom pressed for any documents or committee memos that might be obtained to build a column, asking if a good summary of the issue's stakes existed anywhere. My memo was in my briefcase upstairs, my proposal for John Tunney to lead the nuclear reformers. The memo nobody had read. My Xerox copy was the perfect overview of the issue. I retrieved it, offering it up eagerly to Tom as the best background on the issue.

My thought was that Braden might cite the dispute briefly in his newspaper column as another example of energy industry self-dealing. It never occurred to me he would feature my aspirations for a larger Tunney role.

My analysis made for great copy. Braden's column led *The Washington Post*'s op-ed page the following day.[5]

"Tunney vs. Nuclear Policy" was the headline Tom gave his piece when he dictated his finished column. Or maybe the headline was the night editor's idea. It had not been made clear to

Mr. Braden that the senator had not yet agreed to challenge the nuclear club.

Soon after I arrived in the Dirksen basement office the next morning, October 23, 1975, Tunney's staff was summoned to the senator's sixth-floor suite. We were directed into the senator's personal office, the high-ceilinged inner sanctum that was the only room large enough to hold us all. The walls were covered by the standard "Washington wallpaper" of senator-with-VIP photos. Tunney was slumped glumly below them in a wing chair, his eyes averting mine.

Senator Tunney, I now understand, could have—probably should have—banished me from Capitol Hill. That he didn't end my career before it had even really begun was more than just another piece of good luck for me, in a year when I had had more than my share. It was blind faith on Tunney's part—faith that I would not screw up again, perhaps combined with concern over what such a presumptuous intern might do next with his press connections. Thank you, John Tunney, for your gentle forbearance.

The veteran chief of staff, Hadley Roff, was very tough when he spoke, but he never mentioned my name. A man of many chins, the perpetually rumpled Roff looked like a cross between Jackie Gleason and John Goodman. His trousers strained to contain his bulk and his shirttails, but he was the wise, gray-haired veteran on a staff full of young, ambitious aides. That morning, he was struggling mightily to contain his temper. Every word was slow, hard enough to be its own sentence. Everybody knew who he was talking about as he lectured the staff at some length about never talking to the press without authorization. "We do *not* speculate about the senator's intentions," he reminded us. "We let him speak for himself."

Tunney never said a word. And I was not sent away.

Over time, the folly of my indiscretion became ever clearer to me. It wasn't just that some mailroom intern had tried to shape Senate policy with a leak that ran in California's largest newspaper. It had never occurred to me that the key corporate beneficiaries of the nuclear fuel boondoggle, Bechtel and Chevron, were major California employers and campaign donors.

Tom Braden, an OSS veteran from World War II and an early CIA operative, got a big laugh out of my career crisis.

"So you got his attention!" he snorted as he poured me a Scotch on the rocks later that evening. "Bully for you! Maybe he'll listen to your advice next time."

Of course, there was not to be a next time in the Tunney office. Roff showed great tolerance in not having me frog-marched off the premises; Tunney even grinned a bit mischievously when we sat together the week before my internship ended for an obligatory photo. I served out my last few weeks, however, in the permanent exile of the basement mailroom, SDG-41, warned against venturing out again with the gang from the Group W Bench. (Tunney *would* later decide to take the lead on one high-profile issue important to liberals, but it was limiting U.S. engagement with rebels in Angola, not domestic nuclear policy. Senator Tunney was bloodied by liberals in the June 1976 primary, when Tom Hayden got an astonishing 36 percent of the vote. Then Tunney was finished off in a major November 1976 upset, defeated 50 to 47 percent by Hayakawa, who would become an eminently forgettable one-term senator.)

Tunney and me, December 1975, both sporting a plaid winter suit considered stylish in the disco decade.

Facing the prospect of returning for another year to the far remove of Hampshire College, I nursed my self-inflicted wounds as my last days in Washington approached. The idea that I would soon be talking about politics from afar, instead of acting on my nascent political impulses, made me cringe.

Here before me were divergent paths, a crossroads I would face repeatedly in subsequent decades. A cycle of action, then reflection, appealed to me. I would find it energizing to engage in the arena of public policymaking, then to step back to reflect on first principles. I never had much patience, however, for critics in the press or academia who talked about political change but never tested their notions in Washington's marketplace of ideas. I was hungry for action and skeptical of cautious analysis.

My anxiety heightened in the last weeks of 1975. I so desperately did not want to go backwards. Then my string of good luck was extended once again.

CHAPTER SIX

Playing the Press: Playing with Fire

Washington, D.C.
April 2005

Reporters are omnipotent, or so it seemed to me during my days as a young Capitol Hill aide. In the weeks after my fiasco with the Braden nuclear column, I grew fascinated by journalists' ability to see behind closed doors. Their skills impressed and their efforts seemed heroic.

Bob Woodward and Carl Bernstein were role models for a generation of muckrakers. They had challenged the powerful, emboldened the Congress to act, and taken down a law-breaking president in the process. Schools of journalism saw a spike in applications after Watergate. So-called "public interest" groups sprouted around the country, eager to uncover government wrongdoing. The power of reporters to highlight inconvenient facts and frame issues for action was widely admired. An effective press strategy seemed to me a crucial element of any well-governed community and a key component to any public policymaking strategy.

The reporter's remove also intrigued me. The journalist's ability to observe momentous events, yet hold emotions in check in order to do unbiased reporting, was a cause for envy. I struggled to develop the ability to work an issue without my sentiments clouding my judgment. I took things too personally. Often there was a certainty to my analysis of where virtue lay that made it difficult for me to discern patriotism in the motives of my opponents. I had a tendency to wear my emotions on my sleeve, a righteous sense of justice too transparent. Only at the poker table, where my gift for gab successfully obscured a penchant for outrageous bluffing, did my capacity for misdirection win benefits.

Reporters possess skills I desired as a policymaker. Their license to inquire, their power to shape public affairs and debate, all the while perched above the fight with a 360-degree view, was to be envied. For many lawmakers, actions only mattered if they were reported to a wider audience. Legislators needed the press and hungered for media coverage. Throughout the 1980s, I spent hours as a congressional leadership aide scheming with our press secretary, Murray Flander, and his clever aide, Joy Jacobson, in the office of Democratic whip Senator Alan Cranston. How to get the boss' name and his policy proposals in print was often our challenge of the day.

Hill staffers courted reporters endlessly in Washington, eager to nail a good press "hit" for the boss, or to promote an issue with some page one coverage. We knew that the press play was essential to advance most of the causes we cared about, even if it meant playing with fire.

By the time I'd arrived downtown years later, at the public affairs firm of Cassidy & Associates, I'd developed a more cynical view. As I partnered on several sensitive projects with Jody Powell, formerly President Carter's press secretary, I grew ever more skeptical of journalists. Reporters had great license to challenge authority, to investigate misdeeds, and to help set the national agenda. However, many came to stories with preconceived notions and the baggage of bias that left them in search of anecdotes to confirm their theses. Reporters were also easily manipulated. Worse yet, no matter how friendly the dialogue was, most every conversation between reporter and source was, in the final analysis, transactional.

As a young man, I found that some journalists, like Ellen Hume of *The Los Angeles Times*, were exceptionally good at getting sources to talk. Ellen was fair, honest about both the direction of her reporting and her need for information. She also approached her work with a sense of mission. Yet she had a life beyond the office and kept things in perspective. She would tease herself about the self-importance of the press even as she trolled for tips. She could share a confidence about a piece of a reporting puzzle she was assembling, then trust me to either advance the story or fall silent as my professional obligations dictated. Her reporting was tough and accurate.

Others, like Judy Miller of *The New York Times*, seemed too overtly on the make. Judy was smart and strong, but her ambition was transparent, both for her newspaper and her career. She had an agenda. Even in those days, you could see it, as she coyly twisted her finger in her brown curls and cocked her head just so. It all seemed a bit too much about Judy. To push her stories onto page one, above the fold. To land that spot on the Sunday morning television shows. To get the inside track on White House doings. To beat the *Post*.

One didn't have to be a cynic to know that you were being used. Judy would sound like a sympathetic campus liberal chatting with her Democratic sources, then adopt a hawkish tone with her Republican hard-line contacts. She was always eager to trade, but when she knew something, she always pressed you to give more. Much later, of course, Judy's career with the *Times* imploded. Her use of false leads Bush White House sources had given her about Saddam Hussein's alleged WMD deployments led to a series of *Times* stories in the run-up to the invasion of Iraq so off-base the newspaper later ran a series of lengthy apologetic corrections. Her dealings with Scooter Libby and Karl Rove on the outing of a CIA official named Valerie Plame landed her in jail when she refused to testify in Libby's trial.

Beginning early in my Hill tenure, I planted stories regularly with both Hume and Miller, and with other reporters for California and national publications. The anatomy of a leak was not very complicated. Part of my *modus operandi* after I became an advisor to Senator Alan Cranston working on nuclear nonproliferation was to aggressively advance stories about clandestine nuclear programs in Iraq and Iran, India and Pakistan. If we could feed our information to the right national publications, the impact on policymaking would be significant.

I'd work a tip from an embassy, try to confirm it through a back-and-forth with my CIA sources, and then brief my boss, Senator Cranston, on what I knew and what I suspected. We took care never to get the original information on an explicitly classified basis; he wanted to be free to use it publicly to force the Reagan administration's hand. This method was very much part of the struggle between the legislative and executive branches. Senator Cranston used leaks to the press as a means to limit White House options and to try to force Presidents Reagan and Bush to combat the spread of nuclear weapons.

Cranston wanted voters and policymakers to confront the dangers of proliferation, which he believed was the existential threat of our time. We wanted to do so without committing any felonies for revealing classified data. Once I had gotten some of the details nailed down from my growing number of sources, I'd offer the facts in a face-to-face meeting with Hume or Miller. I was also a regular source for Helen Dewar or Don Oberdorfer at the *Post*, and David Rogers at *The Wall Street Journal*. They'd advance the story further using their own resources, egged on by fears of their journalistic competition, encouraged by non-denials and illicit confirmations from their sources. Then Cranston would lay out all the details we could in a Senate floor speech.

With their additional reporting, reporters tipped off in advance would get their stories onto the front page. As with Hume's "Cranston Sees A-Weapons Danger in Iraq, Pakistan," which ran in *The Los Angeles Times* March 18, 1981.[6] The nonproliferation cause benefitted. The reporters' careers were advanced. So was mine.

With these details in the news, the White House felt pressure to act; Executive Branch officials were unable to deny dangers lurking abroad. Specifically, in the case of Cranston's March 1981 disclosures, the Reagan administration pressured France, Italy, and Germany to curtail their cooperation with rogue nuclear programs or face a cutoff of U.S. supplies. Cranston's disclosures also spurred a reallocation of U.S. intelligence resources to more closely track proliferation in the Middle East and South Asia. This leaking and legislating, riding the pundit reaction and shaping the news cycle, was how the game was played in Washington. It was a win-win for the nonproliferation cause; it was a game I was determined to master.

The reporters collected sources and information for a living. I came to realize that virtually every Washington discussion had an agenda. The best journalists, like my cousin Peter Maass of *The New York Times*, were remarkably skilled at disarming their quarry. Peter is a slight, sallow-faced man, rather nondescript and unassuming in his chinos and unironed Oxford-cloth shirts. His unthreatening demeanor and his calm under fire gave him a remarkable knack for getting dictators to brag about their exploits, on the record. Peter won a national book award chronicling the horror of Yugoslav death camps by sidling up to their administrators. The worst reporters, like hacks at the Sun Myung Moon-owned *Washington Times*, seemed to write their stories in advance. They were lazy. They reverted invariably to caricature, throwing in a few butchered or fabricated quotes to confirm their preconceived notions.

I was biased, too, of course. I used the press for years, and reporters used me even as my success as a policy entrepreneur grew. I respected their power to advance Cranston's agenda, whether it was nuclear nonproliferation, human rights in some Third World nation, or embarrassing Reagan-Bush nominees. We used each other, advancing our careers in the bargain. Yet, I was nervous when reporters shined their spotlight on me. Both *The San Francisco Chronicle* and *The Los Angeles Times* wrote awkward, puffed-up pieces about my work in the Senate.[7] The stories pleased Mom and Dad in California. In D.C., however, my colleagues' eyes rolled, and for good reason. You're supposed to get your boss' name in the paper, not your own. And anybody who gets fawning press in Washington should know that, ultimately, a twisting knife will follow.

A drama that played out publicly during four trying weeks in Spring 2005 captured the horror that could ensue from press stories gone awry. At that time, I was ensconced as a partner at the Cassidy firm, long the city's number one lobbying business.[8] Gerry Cassidy called me into his office to tell me that *The Washington Post* was going to write a series about the history of lobbying. Cassidy's firm was going to be featured in the story, initially titled "The Rise of K Street."

Big trouble could come of this; we all knew it. Publicity might help the firm sign up new clients or retain existing ones. Reporting on the bank-shot maneuvers of lobbyists, however, no matter how ethical their behavior, would read like an exposé of how sausage is made. Journalists weren't going to write about the hospitals Cassidy lobbyists worked for, or about the universities we helped get research grants. They likely had little interest in the personal story of a self-made man like Gerry Cassidy, who built a business that employed hundreds of people, yet started with a five thousand-dollar loan from his father-in-law.

The veteran reporter and editor assigned to the story, Robert Kaiser, proved skillful yet erratic. Cassidy realized that titillation would likely be the way *Post* editors would package the forthcoming articles; they were specifically designed to increase readership and drive traffic to their then relatively new website. Surely that would not be good for the firm's business, nor for our reputation as advocates for nonprofit and corporate clients.

The calculation Jody Powell made was that since the *Post* was committed to doing the series, Cassidy and the firm would do better by cooperating. Kaiser had already talked to dozens of people on the Hill and downtown. So senior lobbyists were asked to give him an interview when he called.

The ensuing stories yielded a twisted caricature of lobbyists, part of a simple theme being developed for a book length treatment. They ran in April 2005 over the course of twenty-six consecutive days—a chapter excerpt per day serialized on the *Post* website, sandwiched between two front-page stories in the Sunday print edition. Not satisfied with details of the firm's internal financials, and predictably fascinated by the firm's apparent coziness with powerful Hill committee chairs, the reporting veered into a thicket of innuendo about private lives. Much reporting was based on anonymous sources and fueled by distorted tales from a handful of former firm employees. It had no place in a serious news story.

Reporting on lawmaking became peripheral as the series stooped to the level of vendetta. Powell and Cassidy decided to punch back. In an unusual but effective counter, they took to running a daily blog assailing errors in the *Post* series. In the Internet age, they decided the new rules were that you had to respond to critics online in the very same news cycle. You had to fight back, if only to deter further assaults.

One of the few admiring stories in the *Post* was, to my horror, a snarky chapter about work done by a team Cassidy and I had managed in Washington for Taiwan's President Lee Teng-Hui.[9] The rest of the series was a savage screed, page after page about evil lobbyists. Subtle it was not.

My relations with the Washington press had long been a mixture of fascination and fear. It had begun with my own excitement as a college kid covering nuclear protestor Sam Lovejoy. It had continued through my rookie mistake with Tom Braden and the nearly fatal Tunney nuclear policy column. Good reporters intrigued me. They shed light into dark corners. Their power was a temptation difficult to resist.

I'd flown too close to the fire earlier in my Senate staff years, and not just with leaks on nuclear proliferation. My Washington career had almost ended again in 1982. Before realizing the risks being run, I had a Senate committee and FBI veterans investigating me. Incredibly, the reason, yet again, was lack of caution in passing around my own memos. It was a stupid mistake from the Braden-Tunney days I'd unwittingly repeated. There was no reason to expect I could escape the consequences twice.

The proximate cause of my screw-up this time was once again zeal. As a pro-Israel staffer, I was horrified when the right-wing government of Prime Minister Menachem Begin crossed the line of decency in its war with the Palestinian Liberation Organization. This was in June 1982, when Israeli forces pursuing PLO terrorists pressed their invasion of Lebanon all the way into the streets of Beirut and the city's refugee camps. My mistake in reacting to developments grew from my hunger for information, my eagerness to trade scraps of detail for more insights into what these actions meant, and my personal torment when I held troubling facts in hand. As a young policymaker, I was slow to master the art of circumspection. It was a challenge that recurred throughout my career in Washington; I found it difficult to remain a quiet witness to bad leadership.

The danger this time came not from my own boss, Senator Cranston. The threat to my job in 1982 was from the chairman of the Senate Foreign Relations Committee, the most civil and friendly Charles Percy, an Illinois Republican.

Percy's committee was full of a who's who of Democratic liberals and GOP partisans, Joe Biden, John Glenn, Claiborne Pell, Dick Lugar, and Jesse Helms among them.

The Senate Foreign Relations Committee, 1983*: (clockwise from top row left side)* . . . **Joe Biden** *(D-DE) was an intense questioner, particularly devastating to such Reagan appointees as arms control czar Kenneth Adelman and failed State Department nominee Ernest Lefever. As he recovered from a family tragedy, Biden was beloved by colleagues—even Jesse Helms—for his humanity. In his thirties still, he regaled staffers with his sharp wit and irrepressible storytelling. He rode home to Delaware every night on Amtrak with his staffer Ted Kaufman, later a senator himself* . . . **John Glenn** *(D-OH) was unflappable, with classic Midwestern common sense. The space and military hero was an effective champion of nuclear nonproliferation. He was a gentle man with a remarkably unswelled head, who went to great lengths to protect his shy wife from media hordes* . . . **Paul Tsongas** *(D-MA) was an earnest post-Watergate reformer and one of seven SFRC members in this portrait to run for president of the United States. His earthy appreciation of irony masked a sharply analytical mind. Tsongas died of cancer in 1997, and his widow Nikki was later elected to his former House seat* . . . **Paul Sarbanes** *(D-MD) was the extremely cerebral but congenitally cautious legislator from Maryland. During the House Judiciary Committee's Nixon impeachment proceedings, his methodical cross-examinations were often the Democrats' most effective* . . . **Rudy Boschwitz** *(R-MN) was a folksy, Jewish Midwestern dairy farmer, who, while wearing a plaid shirt to work, once questioned an appalled Secretary of State, Alexander Haig. A leak critical of a hard-line Israeli government, apparently made by Boschwitz, almost cost me my job* . . . **Richard Lugar** *(R-IN) was such a reliable conservative that he'd once been known as "Richard Nixon's favorite mayor." Assuming a leadership role for Republicans as ballast against the unbridled extremism of the far-right, Lugar became the crucial centrist who helped restore the Committee to a place of prominence in international affairs. Lugar stood up to Reagan administration excesses and was one of the heroes of legislative initiatives to end U.S support for dictatorships, from the Philippines to apartheid-era South Africa* . . . **Howard Baker** *(R-TN) was a popular and highly effective majority leader, vexed by the realization he was smarter than many of the Reagan White House officials with whom he had to deal. He attended SFRC proceedings only when the stakes were high and a GOP party-line position was being put to the test. While on the Joint Committee on Atomic Energy, his handshake closed many a bipartisan deal and his opposition usually spelled defeat for progressive initiatives* . . .

Ed Zorinsky *(D-NE) was a crusty conservative from the Great Plains, reliably pro-Israel, but a hard vote to count for Democratic whip staff . . .* **Larry Pressler** *(R-SD) was a Rhodes scholar, but most certainly not the sharpest tack in the box. Democrats repeatedly took advantage of his good will on procedural maneuvers. His presidential bid was so unlikely as to invite a successful home-state challenge from Tim Johnson . . .* **Jesse Helms** *(R-NC) was a vicious former talk radio partisan. His courtly antebellum manners failed to disguise his scorn for folks with different approaches on matters of race relations, religion, and patriotism. Though unfailingly polite to staff, he struggled to contain his mean streak even as he issued bombastic threats and launched filibusters. An early practitioner of roll call votes designed specifically to script overnight direct-mail fundraising appeals, Helms was pleaded with often by senior Democrats to allow controversial bills to proceed to a vote . . .* **Charles McC. Mathias** *(R-MD) was an elegant liberal and a champion of civil rights and environmental protection. He was an Anglophile who loved French wines and international travel. A proponent of U.S.-Soviet arms control, he was Alan Cranston's preferred traveling company on bipartisan Congressional delegations (CODELs) . . .* **Nancy Landon Kassebaum** *(R-KS) was a cheerful and polite moderate with a willingness to craft bipartisan compromises, especially on issues impacting foreign aid and human rights. She and Senator Baker later surprised all on the Committee when they married . . . SFRC Chairman* **Charles Percy** *(R-IL) was a fabulously successful industry chieftain who had once been the favorite to secure the 1968 GOP Presidential nomination. A liberal internationalist trapped in a conservative political base, he appeared to many observers to be torn again and again between his principles and his political supporters. Savaged unfairly by AIPAC as an anti-Israel "Arabist," Percy lost his gavel and his Senate seat to Representative Paul Simon in November 1984 . . .* **Claiborne Pell** *(D-RI) was a former Foreign Service Officer, born to great wealth and often stuck in a Victorian mindset. Assuming a degree of good will and decency from his adversaries more expected in nineteenth-century croquet than post-Watergate politics, Pell later let Helms run circles around him when they were chairman and ranking member . . .* **Alan Cranston** *(D-CA) was the longest-serving Senate Democrat in California history. A former Stanford sprinter and a newspaperman, once sued by Adolf Hitler for copyright infringement (Cranston published an unabridged version of* Mein Kampf *with commentary intended to warn readers of Hitler's madness), Cranston was the chief* *fundraiser for Senate Democrats. He was the Democratic signal caller for dozens of international issues of the era, from the Panama Canal treaties to nuclear arms control agreements.*

For a generation the Foreign Relations Committee had been the most distinguished of congressional panels. John Kennedy had sought membership on the panel in 1957 to burnish his international credentials—his wealthy father successfully intervened with majority leader Lyndon Johnson to win his son the seat ahead of his rival for the Democratic presidential nomination, Estes Kefauver. Internationalists from Howard Baker to Chuck Percy had joined the committee with an eye toward presidential bids of their own, as would such later SFRC members as John Kerry and Barack Obama.

In June of 1982, Committee members had been briefed in closed session by a senior Reagan administration team. The Israeli Army, ignoring explicit U.S. government warnings, had used their military advantage under General Ariel Sharon to enter the heart of Beirut. Then Sharon stood by, feigning innocence, while Lebanese militia forces under his sponsorship slaughtered Palestinian women and children in the squalid refugee camps. Equipment supplied by the U.S. was used in the Lebanon attacks, in violation of American law.

The Senate Foreign Relations Committee had been informed of these developments in its ornate Capitol Building room, S-116, just below the Vice President's lobby and the east entrance to the Senate floor. Senators were seated around a grand oval table, its aged mahogany covered in green felt. On the walls were fading black-and-white photographs of famous committee chairs, from old Civil War veterans to the recently defeated Frank Church, the smiling Idaho moderate victimized by his courageous vote for the Panama Canal treaties. Overhead, a spectacular chandelier filled the stuffy room with light.

Outside the old swinging doors to the chamber, its thick slatted panels painted a muddy brown, a noisy press gaggle awaited. Inside the room, senators from both parties were furious. Liberal, conservative, Democrat, Republican—they all railed against both the Israelis' unforgivable excess and their stupidity. One of my personal heroes, John Glenn, was especially tough, establishing for the record that Israelis had violated explicit terms under which U.S. weapons had been provided. Cranston had been called to the Senate floor by a leadership caucus, but I remained at the briefing for more than an hour to hear graphic details about the massacre in Beirut, and about Prime Minister Menachem Begin ignoring U.S. calls to stand down.

Horror turned to disgust after the briefing concluded. As I slipped out of S-116 by a side door, I paused to watch the legislators from my revered committee come one by one before the large press stakeout in the Capitol Building hallway. The cameras rolled, with hot klieg lights shining. To a man, however, the senators now sang a different tune. They vaguely lamented the "cycle of violence" and called for peace talks. None had a public word of criticism for our Israeli friends.

After riding the Metro home to Arlington, I stewed, then poured myself a strong vodka and tonic. The next day, after a night of poor sleep, I met with Cranston and handed him an impassioned memo about the state of affairs in Beirut, Jerusalem, and Washington. I imprudently said what was on my mind. Given what I had heard in the briefing, and afterward, I didn't feel I could keep working as his point man on Middle East policy if he did not speak out against the massacre in Beirut. Friends of Israel especially, it seemed to me, needed to rein in the excesses of men like Begin and Sharon.

The senator was taken aback, but it wasn't the first time he'd seen me get worked up into a righteous lather; he promised he would give it serious thought and respond to me soon. To his great credit, Cranston agreed the next day to work with several of us to craft a public letter to Prime Minister Begin. He broke with the Israeli leader and implored him to pull Israeli forces back from Beirut and to act immediately to protect civilian lives. It was such a stunning rebuke by a pro-Israel legislator that *The New York Times* ran the story as a feature and reprinted much of Begin's response verbatim.[10] Angry donors called to complain. Cranston held firm. He put principle ahead of politics, and ahead of his ever-present fundraising interests.

In the interim, however, I compounded my troubles. In the first hours of my crisis of conscience, I was unsure what Cranston would do, so I shared my anguish with a close friend who was writing about Washington's reaction to Israel's out-of-control behavior in Lebanon. Ken Wollack was my best source of wisdom on Middle East issues, a former American Israel Public Affairs Committee lobbyist, but a skeptic of AIPAC's excess, and a trustworthy analyst of Israeli policy matters. He was now a consultant publishing an insider weekly newsletter on Washington/Middle East diplomacy.

By the time we met in a small first-floor dining room on the Senate side of the Capitol, not fifty yards from S-116, Wollack had already heard about the disastrous Senate briefing. I was so angry with the Begin government that I let Ken read excerpts from my memo to Cranston; I thought it was a convenient way to illustrate the challenge facing pro-Israel legislators. I handed him my draft, right there amongst several Senate staffers at nearby tables, and asked what he thought I should do. I wanted personal advice, and guidance, on what I should tell Senator Cranston about my future as a foreign policy advisor. Ken skimmed the memo, told me to hold my fire and to trust Cranston to do the right thing, then casually handed it back.

Twenty-four hours later, *The New York Times* was full of details on the Foreign Relations Committee briefing. It chided senators who offered outrage behind closed doors but fell silent before the cameras. The tagline stunned me: The *Times* credited *The Middle East Policy Survey*, Wollack's newsletter, as a source.

Chairman Percy was furious. How could the Committee do its work, he demanded of colleagues in a blistering memo, if information was routinely leaked from its classified deliberations? Percy's problem was compounded by the fact that in private, he, too, was tough on Israel, while sympathetic in public. Furthermore, he was facing a vigorous, and ultimately successful, election challenge from a Democratic candidate backed by AIPAC supporters, Paul Simon, who made much of Percy's alleged antipathy for Israel.

Senator Percy called in two veteran investigators and ordered every single staffer present for the briefing to submit to interrogation. The prospect of lie-detector tests was pointedly raised. The investigators, we were told, were "on leave" from the FBI.

For a second time, I thought my career shaping public policy was over. I was only twenty-seven. I held what then seemed a huge mortgage on an old Sears and Roebuck house. I had few prospects of a good job if I was fired from Capitol Hill. I had no idea what I could possibly say to the investigators without losing my job.

Years later, I would write a Washington novel about spying. At its heart was the story of the dilemma I faced that week in 1982. In my fiction, longtime friends become reporter and source, lobbyist and leaker. In my imagination, the young Hill aide in *The Mandarin Club* fesses up to the FBI. He resigns and walks out past S-116, down the gold leaf-trimmed corridor of the Capitol one last time. Striding confidently into the spring rain, my mythical hero feels cleansed. The metaphor is decidedly religious.

In reality, my purpose in June 1982 was somewhat less noble. Facing my future, I tried to figure out if there was any way to dodge the awkward facts of my screw-up. I consulted anxiously with Senate staff colleagues Peter Galbraith, Bill Ashworth, and Jim Bond—friends who'd already been questioned by the investigators. I was fishing for details on how the inquiry was proceeding. I was looking for any way to avoid admitting what I feared was my responsibility. I was looking for a way out.

It was my friend Ken Wollack who saved me. To this day, I'm not sure exactly what version of the truth it was that he fed me. I just know it worked, allowing me to retain my job without doing anything illegal.

Like any good reporter, Wollack refused to assist the investigators in disclosing his sources. He asserted his First Amendment rights and promptly ended the effort to interrogate him. What Ken told me in a noisy restaurant the day before I was questioned by the investigators, however, gave me a sliver of hope.

"Don't obsess over it," he said. "I talked to a half dozen people who were in that briefing. I talked to *senators*. It was senators who gave me the best quotes that the *Times* picked up. You think Percy is going to subpoena all of his Republican colleagues? You think Jesse Helms and Rudy Boschwitz and Howard Baker—the majority leader—are going to submit to lie-detector tests? No fucking way."

It then became much easier for me to justify evasion. How could anybody "classify" my impressions of what senators said? Sharing those reflections was indiscreet. It was ungentlemanly. But surely it was not a felony. What the Reagan administration had told us in the Senate that June day wasn't a military secret, I rationalized. It wasn't the formula for some new weapon. And, of course, the Israelis and the Palestinians and the Lebanese knew what had happened in Beirut. So, too, did the families of the victims. It was only the American people who had been kept in the dark. Thus, Chairman Percy's investigation of the leak could be seen as just some political effort to beat up staff for revelations that senators had made themselves. *Why should I walk the plank*, I asked myself, *just to protect the senators who had been Ken's sources?*

Emboldened by these justifications, I faced the two interrogators the next day. We met three blocks south of the Capitol, in overflow office space in the rickety Ford House Office Building. Down by the Southeast-Southwest Freeway, it was a fire trap, full of surplus government furniture and backwater subcommittee staff. Two agents—either on leave from the FBI, or recently retired and hired by the Committee, I was never clear—loomed before me. Just as in the movies, one was talkative, one quiet; one was tall, one was short; one asked most of the questions, one watched from an angle, looking for a tell. Good cop-bad cop was clearly in play.

I gave short, truthful answers but volunteered few details. Calling up all my poker skills, I was determined to act bored. They never asked me the killer question: "Did you show Mr. Wollack any memos?" I would have told the truth.

The longer the session dragged on, the more I had to resist

becoming flip. It was not my place to implicate individual senators. When asked who the source of the leak might be, my reply was factual: It could have been any of the senators appalled by Israeli behavior that led up to the Beirut massacre.

My behavior that month is not a source of pride. I survived, though, and as the years passed, grew more cautious in my dealings with the press. I became more skeptical of the tawdry transactional exchanges. I toned down my willingness to leak, even if it was to advance a preferred policy option. I limited my e-mail ramblings and grew wary of unedited blogs, content unfiltered by discerning minds.

Warning my kids about the lack of privacy on the Internet, I stayed off Facebook. I never opened a Twitter account, insisting that Twitter is for twits. As I matured, I resisted the temptation to spin the press, to play the information trading game, to play with fire.

CHAPTER SEVEN

Jack Bingham, Giant Slayer

U.S. House of Representatives
July 1976

Luck is said to be the happy combination of preparation, chance, and circumstance. Good luck came to me in abundance throughout my first months in Washington. Its repeated appearances drew me deeper into the maze, generating a series of policymaking opportunities that would enrich my experience and make thoughts of any other career paths vanish.

Weeks before the clock expired on my Senate internship and my brief Washington adventure, I was lamenting to a colleague from the Group W Bench the absence of a well-positioned champion amongst the Senate critics of the nuclear industry. My desire not to go backwards was intense. It was a fear of returning to a remote countryside campus, one where leftists talked endlessly about reform, yet few engaged the policymaking establishment.

Going backwards was a source of repeated nightmares. My junior year in high school had been spent abroad, ostensibly as a student at London's Holland Park Comprehensive School. In reality, my major that year was basketball and West End theater, with a minor in pub darts. More often than not, study hall was in the Churchill Arms on Church Street in Notting Hill. Once spring came, any pretense of studying for A Level exams was abandoned, and I set off with my brothers for travel across Europe. For many months, I savored the freedom of the road, only to be required to return to suburban America and to endure a force-feeding of

Redwood High School distribution requirements necessary for a diploma.

For years after that, the same bad dream revisited. I owed some teacher math credits, or science requirements, or another quarter of P.E. I had to go back. It is a nightmare that still floats up on dark nights a few times a year as I approach my sixties, the threat of my own terrifying *Groundhog Day* do-over.

In late 1975, it was just such an undesirable prospect that loomed. I did not want to retreat from the Washington challenge.

"It would be so great to work for somebody who would take these bastards on," I muttered to David Rosen, a sympathetic House staffer over coffee and doughnuts during a break in my last Joint Committee hearing.

David paused, squinting as he pondered my dilemma. "You should take my job." He smiled as he said it, somehow sensing that his novel notion might pan out.

"What?"

"I just told Congressman Bingham this morning that I'm heading to law school next summer," he said. "You should apply to replace me."

Once upon a time, that had also been my plan—to go to law school. Listening to David, my impatience urged me forward. Only a few days after updating my Wrangler Résumé, I secured an interview with Congressman Jonathan B. ("Jack") Bingham's chief of staff.

Gordon Kerr was his name. The son of a foreign service officer, he had grown up in suburban Virginia. After graduating from Yale, he made national press when, as a military officer, he protested the Vietnam War while in uniform. Promptly discharged, he found a job working for Congresswoman Barbara Jordan, a liberal anti-war representative from Texas. Kerr then rose swiftly to a position leading the staff of Jack Bingham, a fellow Yale graduate thirty years his senior.

Gordon would become a lifelong friend. He taught me the rules of golf. He read the New Testament prayer (Ken Wollack the Old) when Joy Jacobson and I married. That late fall day in

1975, however, Kerr intimidated me. He offered a clipped greeting, then launched into a rapid-fire series of questions about my background. His skepticism was apparent as he probed my knowledge of congressional procedure and protocol. He wanted to find out what I knew of Bingham, his House committee assignments, and his policymaking priorities.

Gordon's mind moved so fast, and with such manic energy that I struggled to keep up. It felt like a Ph.D. oral exam, and I was still an undergraduate. He had a dubious wince as he evaluated me, chortling and guffawing at apparent contradictions. I could not tell if he was laughing with me or at me; it was unnerving. It became clear that I did not measure up for a job as a senior House legislative assistant; I was way too raw.

Kerr persisted nevertheless. At first, I was uncertain why. He moved back to my comfort ground—nuclear regulatory issues, especially nuclear export policy. A series of detailed questions ensued. I responded with everything I had learned in months watching the Joint Committee. It felt like a late-inning rally as I poured forth insights gained from David Rosen and my friends from the Group W Bench. Finally, I seemed to be connecting with the energetic Scotsman. Gordon was nodding, cocking his head at an angle with an *entre nous* grin. He was encouraging me instead of pointing out the many glaring holes in my preparation.

Finally, playing his hand, he made his intentions clear. It turned out that the Rosen job *was* beyond my reach, but there was a second job opening up the following spring, that of the office's junior legislative assistant. It would not involve any of the issues covered by Congressman Bingham's assignments on the International Relations or Interior Committees. It was instead the "cats and dogs" portfolio, the miscellaneous leftover issues in Bingham's office, from veteran's benefits to crime control to district correspondence.

My candidacy was alive. This I knew for sure when Kerr moved to close the interview: "Two more questions, Gerry. And these may be deal breakers."

His grin now was unmistakably conspiratorial. "Do you play

poker? And do you play softball? Because the guy you would replace, Greg Zorthian, is a regular at our Thursday night card game, and he's the manager of our Hill league softball team."

Home run.

After a writing test and a rather awkward interview later that week with the congressman, I got the job. I wouldn't start until July 1, 1976, with a beginning salary of eleven thousand dollars a year. It seemed like a million.

I barreled out of the Rayburn Building and hurried down the Hill to D Street. We celebrated heartily that evening; Camp Hamp compatriots made their way to join me at the Watergate Hotel bar, where one of our housemates worked. Drinks were on the house, and we consumed far too many, deep into the evening.

With dawn came the hangover, along with two stark realities. First, I still owed Hampshire College a senior year's-worth of work. Second, I had zero income and faced the prospect of many months more before receiving my first federal paycheck. Even with a ridiculously low rent bill of one hundred dollars per month, no health insurance costs, and no auto expenses, this was a problem.

Some foresight solved the first problem. I had been using my down time in the Tunney operation to draft the equivalent of an honor's thesis to use when I went back to Amherst. I spent long lunches and a few evenings researching the history of school desegregation case law at the Library of Congress, using my Senate intern ID to call up issue briefs prepared by the Congressional Research Service. My plan was to draft the paper in Washington. Then, when I returned to Hampshire College in the spring, I could take whatever classes I wanted, my thesis nearly ready for submission. I thought I was headed to law school, or to a job in education. So my chosen thesis topic seemed to cover both bases: "From *Dred Scott* to *Charlotte-Mecklenburg*: The Supreme Court and School Desegregation."

A series of ponderous U.S. mail exchanges with my examination committee resulted in a decisive gathering on the Hampshire campus the following month. Professors Gloria Joseph and Richard Alpert listened skeptically as I pleaded my case: I had a job waiting for me in Washington. Could I not stay in Washington to pursue this policymaking opportunity?

To my surprise, the committee members agreed: I was simply to mail in the completed product and present myself on campus for a final oral defense of my thesis.

Tom Braden solved my other dilemma. Maybe it was the guilt he felt for the license he had taken with the Tunney memo. Maybe it was his happiness to see the pleasure his daughter Joannie and I were finding those months in each other's presence. Certainly it was the demands of his eclectic work—by then he had a new book out about his chaotic family, and that book, *Eight is Enough*, was being cast as a TV show by ABC. He also had a daily column, and a radio gig about to start, one that ultimately became Braden vs. (Pat) Buchanan on *Crossfire*, first aired on the local all-news radio station, WTOP, then on the first U.S. cable TV news network, CNN.

I was hired to be a leg man for Braden. As a cub reporter, I was tasked with everything from fact-checking and column-editing to phoning in his completed six hundred-word text each night, dictated to a recording machine at the *Los Angeles Times* syndicate. I would attend congressional hearings and press conferences, then after the lunch hour provide Braden with facts and anecdotes from the morning on Capitol Hill. He would bat around a list of possible column subjects with me. Then I would sit opposite him, offering an occasional comment or synonym as he hammered away at his manual typewriter in his attic office, smoking his pipe and swearing like a sailor as he shaped his piece. He paid me four hundred dollars in cash each month, which was enough for me to live on.

I thus earned my first salary in Washington as a reporter, not as a policymaker. I got to ghost a few columns when Braden was too busy or under the weather, including one column that ran nationally under Tom's name, but which he graciously quoted from me in its entirety.[11] With press credentials, I had exactly the kind of access desired by a kid eager to gain entry to rooms full of policymakers. And I got to be a fly on the wall at his dinner table, as he put his guests through their paces while trolling for column ideas.

The months rolled by rapidly. I tailed Braden all over Washington. He took me to lunch in the inner sanctum of the Senators Dining Room with George McGovern. The South Dakota senator and onetime Democratic presidential nominee was philosophical and pedantic. His balding head was set off by bushy eyebrows, which arched when he stressed the irony in points he made about politics. Braden took me to the White House press room, and to dinners at the home of *Post* publisher Katharine Graham. He even sent me out on the road to ride the campaign bus in New Hampshire and Maryland as the 1976 presidential primaries began.

While visiting a new recycling plant in suburban Baltimore, I got to interview "Governor Moonbeam," California's precocious Jerry Brown as he sought the presidency. Brown wore bell-bottomed pants. He was full of irreverent energy so overt that today such behavior would be labeled Attention Deficit Disorder and treated with Ritalin. The rituals of the campaign trail bored Brown, as did press expectations that he respond to their questions with answers; the Jesuit in him led him to fire questions back at his bewildered interrogators, ABC's Sam Donaldson among them.

As 1975 turned to 1976, the mood of the nation was changing. The anger directed at unelected President Ford began to abate as his decency and his humble offer of a return to normalcy began to close the gap between him and any conceivable Democratic challenger. Having relieved us of the prospect of a Nixon trial, Ford became a sympathetic figure as Americans prepared to celebrate the U.S. Bicentennial. Congress continued over these months to chip away at the presidential powers accumulated by LBJ and Nixon, with reform legislation passing on subjects as diverse as the budget process, freedom of information, arms sales, and war powers.

Journalism had an attraction for me not unlike my first internship. It was first and foremost an admission ticket. It offered an inside view of discussions that would impact the whole nation. I could observe the proceedings, unburdened by any commitment. I could watch how the players interacted. I had a seat in the arena.

Even at the beginning of my Washington career, however, I wasn't completely comfortable with the journalist's remove. I lived by my passions, and wasn't sufficiently mature or cautious to contain them.

Reporters weren't supposed to have an overt political agenda in those days. However, I wanted to participate, not merely to watch. I felt a sense of urgency, combined with a sense of obligation. Shaping public policy became my goal.

My eagerness to engage wasn't just a hunger for the adrenaline rush of competition. I wanted to test myself, to test ideas and ideals. Politics, and policymaking, seemed the best place.

Beginning in the summer of 1976, Jack Bingham's office became my second home. It was much more family oriented than the austere Senate setting that confronted interns in the Tunney operation. There was a very clear pecking order in Room 2251 of the Rayburn House Office Building. Several veteran Bingham staffers were quick to put ambitious young upstarts in our place. Yet it was a group of professionals who worked together, then played together via softball and poker. We even won the Capitol Hill softball league championship for Bingham's Bronx Bombers, and Kerr put out a press release, tongue firmly in cheek.[12]

Bingham's pleasant demeanor filled the three-office suite. He was kind and honorable, possessed of a warm smile and a genteel manner. He struck many at first meeting as something of an odd duck, uneasy with small talk. Tall and gangly, with a shock of white hair above his pale forehead, he was utterly patrician in bearing. Bingham was the epitome of the citizen-legislator, from the landowning classes our Founding Fathers had in mind in Philadelphia.

In an era of thick sideburns and loud bell-bottom suits, Bingham favored plaid, and nearly always sported a bow tie. His manners were impeccable, his dissents understated and non-confrontational. Son of Connecticut senator Hiram Bingham—who had discovered the ruins of Peru's Machu Picchu and returned to

Yale with hundreds of Incan antiquities—Jonathan Bingham was decidedly Old School. Formal in most every exchange, he had worked as a policy aide to New York Governor Averell Harriman, first in Albany, then at the United Nations.

Bingham's politics were a web of contradictions. An Ivy League man from Connecticut, he represented an urban New York City district of Democrats that had some of the nation's worst slums, including the South Bronx. His biggest population center was Co-Op City, a crowded high-rise development that housed tens of thousands of elderly, lower-middle-income Jewish families fleeing urban blight in the South Bronx. Bingham's own home was at the district's northernmost fingertip, a gerrymandered piece of Riverdale far removed from Bronx poverty. He won his safe Democratic seat in a primary election upset. He had taken on, then improbably defeated, Charlie Buckley, a formidable House committee chairman. Buckley had failed to take seriously the insurgent reform movement in a district that had adopted Jack Bingham as its candidate.

It became apparent to me that Congressman Bingham, like Tom Braden before him, had taken me on as a project. He intended to train me, to teach me how the world of policymaking actually worked.

It began, for the congressman, with the written word. Bingham would call me into his inner office, close the door, and sit behind his large mahogany desk as I sat opposite him in a straight-backed chair. He would slowly go through some of my draft correspondence with a yellow #2 pencil and correct my grammar. He was teaching me how to write, repeating the editing process two, three, four times for the same letter, before approving each document with a lightly initialed "JBB." For him, good writing meant being clear, formal, and concise. His notes came longhand, cursive, on yellow legal paper, carefully scripted.

There were several weeks of tutorials on VIP correspondence. While I sat alongside, Bingham edited my drafts line by line, toning me down and breaking up long sentences. He'd weed out inflammatory adjectives. He would insert commas, judiciously.

Bingham's teaching, like the reserved legislator offering it, was gentle but firm. There was an ease to our exchanges that felt comfortable. The connection was not made at the time, but upon reflection years later, it is now clear why. This was a form of parental guidance I had relished from a childhood I probably left behind too soon.

My father, the architect, would make baseball score sheets for me with his gold Cross pen and blue tracing paper. I still have his precisely rendered lineups of the 1960 World Series champion Pittsburgh Pirates, with Mazeroski and Clemente. Then Dad would show me how to record the games. Mom, a writer of both poetry and prose, would similarly sit alongside me, editing my compositions from third grade on. Her patience seemed infinite. Her persistence guided me through many an essay, helping me polish words until the piece began to click.

Bingham's ritualistic tutorials thus gave comfort; he became a guide who taught me the inner workings of congressional policymaking. Bingham took me to meetings far beyond my areas of legislative responsibility. He'd offer his predictions of the scene beforehand, then a dry, spot-on commentary after the fact. I learned the House catechism. You distrust the Senate: too full of puffed up egos, too slow to act on legislative proposals, insufferable in its resort to procedural delays.

Bingham's Victorian manner masked his coolly realistic appraisal of power. He taught me to respect the power of chairmen, to strive mightily to gain support from the Speaker's team, to be on the lookout always for potential allies. I learned how to research legislative precedents, how to build coalitions with outside interest groups, and how to reach out for bipartisan partners. Bingham rarely offered a proposal, or even sent a "dear colleague" letter to his House counterparts, without a Republican co-sponsor.

One rainy day, I joined a dozen of Bingham's House colleagues on a walk through the Capitol Building. We headed over to the Senate Banking Committee hearing room in Dirksen for a House-Senate conference committee on a measure shaping international economic powers. At the time, I had no idea how powerful these joint panels were, able to create parts of bills that neither the House nor the Senate had considered, while junking provisions that had been debated and accepted by committees in the respective chambers. There were at least thirty people in the House entourage, including staffers with tabbed binders stuffed with paper, marching along.

Bingham shared his colleagues' fury when they were met by only one senator, who then left it to an imperious staffer, one Stanley Marcus, to icily inform the House delegation of the Senate's terms for conference. Marcus wore a pin-striped banker's suit and examined his manicure as he delivered his ultimatum, unimpressed by the dozen veteran members of the House of Representatives who had come over to hear the Senate's dismissal.

The senior staffers in the congressman's office, including M. J. Rosenberg and Roger Majak, tolerated my tutorials from Bingham with good humor. M. J., especially, had every reason to resent the attention the congressman gave me; that he didn't was a measure of his strong character and friendship. My innocence and ambition amused him. He supplemented the congressman's effort, explaining to me what he did and how he did it. I learned about Middle East issues. I digested a balanced diet of pro-Israel dogma served with a healthy dose of skepticism about the party line dispensed by AIPAC, a lobby that struck me, then as now, as too hard-line and too intolerant of dissent for Israel's own good.

During these first months on the congressional payroll, I developed a rapacious appetite for information. Again, I trace this curiosity to my concern as a kid not just for worldly issues, but also for an assessment of the emotional weather at the family table each day. Most mornings as a junior House staffer, I'd read the *Post*, the *Times*, *The Washington Star*, and even the New York tabloids. I would pore over the bulletins and insider tip sheets circulated by the various reform-minded groups funded by liberal Democrats who gained power after Watergate. These included the Arms Control and Foreign Policy Caucus, the Environmental Study Conference, and the Democratic Study Group. Their summaries chronicled a daily contest of good guys versus bad—a contest peopled by scores of like-minded reformers. Here the issues were laid out, talking points provided, votes recommended, hearing questions advanced. They foretold a dozen scenes of confrontation, lines of attack, and opportunities to shape public policy on many significant national issues. I found them irresistible.

I was also invited to the district office to observe Bingham campaigning. At the appointed hour, I joined him in the backseat of a paneled sound truck. Very slowly, we drove down the Grand Concourse in the middle of the Bronx. Bingham cleared his throat and pressed on the microphone button attached to speakers on the roof.

"Hello. This is Congressman Jack Bingham, Democrat, asking for your support. Please vote Bingham and the Democratic ticket this Election Day . . . Thank you for your support."

Bingham's voice echoed off empty storefronts, a few pedestrians gawking quizzically at our van as they hurried by. We rolled on for almost two hours, through a district savaged by white flight, urban decay, and population loss. Bingham sipped water, grinning sheepishly as he peered out the van windows. Then we quit for the day. (Bingham would go on to win with 100 percent of the vote. He was reelected continually until 1982, when redistricting by Albany powerbrokers obliterated his district.)

Back on Capitol Hill in that fall of 1976, a more serious challenge was brewing. Senate nonproliferation reformers had rallied behind a Ribicoff-Glenn-Percy bill to limit nuclear exports. A narrow House provision authored by Bingham's International Relations Committee colleagues Clem Zablocki (Democrat from Wisconsin) and Paul Findley (Republican from Illinois) was also moving forward. The spark for their initiative remained India's use of Atoms for Peace materials to build a nuclear weapon. An aggressive U.S. response, they argued, was still required.

Despite reformers' success in finally securing a debate on the issue before other panels, the Joint Committee on Atomic Energy easily quashed the measure. India had used U.S. material to make nuclear weapons. Pakistan, Argentina, Brazil, South Korea—even Taiwan—were flirting with developing nuclear fuel cycle capabilities that had military options. At home, U.S. nuclear power production had soared in the previous decade. With sales of new plants suddenly stalled by a recession and a drop in power demand, however, the industry was continuing to make excuses for not resolving waste disposal and safety issues. While resisting more regulatory oversight, it was seeking federal bailouts and loan guarantees to build more uranium enrichment plants and develop plutonium-fueled breeder reactors.

We sought help from the Democratic presidential candidate Jimmy Carter, a nuclear engineer by training. Bingham had me draft a series of memos he edited and sent to Carter on nuclear policy matters.[13] Here was a national security issue where Democrats could take a harder line than the Ford-Kissinger crowd.

The Carter team demurred. On Capitol Hill, even piecemeal nuclear policy reforms seemed impossible. It was all Jack Bingham could do to slow the Nuclear Fuel Assurance Act boondoggle that Tom Braden's column had warned about.

What to do? The solution came from a Nader staffer, of all people. Years later, I came to detest Ralph Nader. His arrogance, I believe, cost Al Gore a victory in Florida in 2000. I even blamed Nader partially for the decade-long Iraq War and occupation because the U.S. never would have started it under a Gore presidency; it was all I could do not to rudely upbraid Nader in public when my kids and I ran into him in Chicago's O'Hare Airport.

In 1976, however, the original idea that turned the tide for the nuclear reformers—and helped my fledgling career take off—came not from Bingham or from me, but from a clever Nader acolyte. It was Nader forces who had first developed the model for the public interest groups then sprouting all over Washington; they had begun as summer intern projects for Ivy League students wanting to take on Nixon's federal bureaucracy. They had grown and multiplied as a new type of non-governmental organization dedicated to challenging executive and legislative officials to advance a reform agenda.

Jim Cubie was the name of the Nader staffer; he worked for CongressWatch and its affiliate, the Critical Mass Energy Project.

Cubie was a pale, bespectacled young man from Vermont who looked like Lara's Trotskyite husband in the film version of *Doctor Zhivago*. We first discussed his notion, I believe, over a beer one evening at a favorite Hill bar, the Hawk 'n' Dove. We were, as usual, lamenting the omnipotence of the Joint Committee, trying to identify some end run to get the Senate reformers' nonproliferation bill a hearing.

"I have an idea I've been batting around with Bob Alvarez and some of the guys," he said, placing his mug squarely on the heavy oak bar, then turning toward me. "Abolish them."

"Right," I said skeptically, not thinking he was serious.

"No, I mean it." He warmed quickly to his subject. "The only way to take them down is head-on."

The idea was so preposterous that, upon further consideration, it was attractive. Abolish them, then legislate fast and furious. Give all the Joint Committee's jurisdiction to subcommittees—many headed by environmentalists—as had been explored by a 1974 committee reform commission headed by Representative Richard Bolling, a widely respected Missouri Democrat.

Joined soon by others from the environmental community, we hatched a plan that actually had a chance. The key to the whole scheme was to exploit the very same set of clubby rules that members of the Joint Committee had used for years to protect themselves and their friends in the nuclear industry.

Wiping out the committee appeared to require a majority vote of both the full House and Senate, if not of the Committee itself. Who would ever willingly cede such power—in this case, absolute power—over all nuclear-related legislation? Stalwart JCAE legislators, including respected national party leader "Scoop" Jackson, would easily block our every attempt.

We did not need to go that route, we soon realized. As we talked and researched precedents, we came to see how exploiting process could profoundly change national policy. Here was a lesson that served me well for decades as a policymaker. Master process first: Policy victories will follow.

All we had to do, parliamentary experts confirmed, was change the standing instructions to the House Speaker on where certain types of legislation were to be referred. Our first move could thus be not in the Senate Rules Committee, or the Joint Committee itself, but in the House Democratic Steering and Policy Committee. Steering and Policy was the Speaker's inner circle. They were the twenty top loyalists to Tip O'Neill, who doled out all Democratic committee assignments and refereed jurisdictional disputes. Jack Bingham was one of the Steering and Policy members. If he could whip the vote in Steering and Policy, then make a few deals with powerful House committee chairmen, who stood to gain significant jurisdiction under his proposal, Bingham just might pull off the coup.

This was the same route followed by the class of the Ninety-Fourth Congress when they moved in January 1975 to impose a series of sweeping post-Watergate reforms. These Watergate babies had dramatically changed the House's power equation. They challenged the power of a seniority system that had for years left control of many committees in the hands of conservative, southern Democrats. The entrenched "old bulls" were legislators who had opposed civil rights and environmental reforms, while supporting Nixon and the Vietnam War. As January 1977 approached, a second wave of would-be reformers was joining the House, eager to strike some similar blows for good government.

To get desirable committee assignments, all of the newly elected members would have to appeal to veterans on Steering and Policy. Bingham and his allies could use the resulting leverage to build support. He then could push for a simple amendment to eviscerate the JCAE, all in the name of House reform. When the House Democratic Caucus proposed rules for the Ninety-Fifth Congress, we told Bingham, there could be a simple amendment offered to the standing rules establishing that no bills would be referred to, or received by the House from, the Joint Committee.

To make all this happen, we explained, Bingham didn't need the support of half of the 538 members of Congress. He didn't need a single supporter in the Senate, as senators would not have any power to block or delay the House action. Bingham needed only one-half-plus-one of the new House Democratic Caucus. That meant we needed only 145 votes, and the incoming class for January 1977 promised to be dominated by progressive voices joining the Watergate reformers swept into the House two years earlier.

The ensuing effort unfolded over a period of weeks at the end of 1976. Most of Washington was distracted by the announcement of Cabinet appointments by President-elect Jimmy Carter. Our nuclear reform issue was, at the time, a decidedly backburner issue, a fact which aided us immeasurably.

When they first got wind of our plan, nuclear industry lobbyists did not take the threat seriously. We used the time (and the neglect) well. Bingham's office became the war room for our band of reformers. Tables were stacked high with documents and vote counts, dated stories about Joint Committee abuses, muckraking stories exposing weaknesses in the domestic industry, and ominous academic studies of the nuclear proliferation threat. Cubie, Speth, Alvarez, Scherr, and Cochran became war room regulars, taking assignments as Bingham and Kerr planned the coup.

We enlisted several government reform groups to produce studies showing how few public hearings the Joint Committee had held on nuclear safety issues. Newspaper editorial boards in key congressional districts were pitched with our talking points about the need for a new congressional watchdog on nuclear exports, nonproliferation, and waste disposal. *The New York Times* editorialized in support. Allies were enlisted to whip the vote, to contact Members one by one and to seek commitments of support in the upcoming test vote in the House Democratic Caucus.

At the center of our little campaign, a seat was opened for me. I became immersed in drafting talking points, calibrating vote-winning tactics, and working with Bingham to shape opportunities. I was a hyperactive twenty-two-year-old guzzling black coffee. The battle concentrated my mind. The overarching strategy resulted in a series of very specific, targeted, tactical moves, enlisting allies on key committees to secure votes from colleagues.

During those weeks in December 1976, I beagn to learn how to run an inside policy campaign. How to frame issues and gain third-party validation. When to ask NGOs to weigh in with issue briefs. How to use media contacts. When to rely on Member to Member lobbying. How to target and count, using Members to whip the vote. What use to make of allies on the president's staff. Consistent with my Hampshire education—the one that let you design your own exams but left lots of holes in your preparation for you to fill—I got to learn by doing.

The key to victory turned out to be the allies Bingham picked up with his proposed redistribution of legislative jurisdiction. He designed a plan to scatter nuclear policy jurisdiction to the four winds in the House, breaking up the iron triangle between the industry, the Joint Committee, and executive branch officials. Domestic, civil nuclear power would be regulated by the Interior Committee, where Bingham was a senior member. His chairman, Mo Udall of Arizona, was a Democratic cloakroom favorite, the liberal runner-up to Jimmy Carter for the Democratic presidential nomination in 1976.[14]

Congressman Bingham (on the right), me, and Chairman Udall's counsel, Dr. Henry Myers (on the left), inspecting the Indian Point, New York nuclear power station, less than forty miles north of Manhattan, on October 28, 1976.

Military programs would fall to the Armed Services Committee, so Bingham had support from his right flank. Nuclear export policy would be handed to International Relations, where—guess who?–Jack Bingham chaired the International Trade and Economic Policy Subcommittee. The regulatory piece, overseeing the newly established Nuclear Regulatory Commission, became a tussle between Udall and House Energy and Commerce Committee power John Dingell (Democrat from Michigan), the latter a champion of the auto industry and no friend of the environmentalists at the time. An eleventh-hour deal was struck whereby Udall and Dingell would share the spoils. Dingell, in turn, used his considerable influence to secure support from his entire committee membership for Bingham's proposal.

By the time debate on our proposal began in the House chamber before the House Democratic Caucus, we knew we had won. Defense of the Joint Committee was led by a Washington state Democrat, Representative Mike McCormack. A nuclear engineer from the Hanford Works, McCormack was an irrepressible champion of virtually every industry request. Short and stocky, with a brain full of facts, he dressed in a plaid suit and wore thick eyeglasses. These only magnified his exasperation as he railed against Bingham's proposal on the House floor.

"Nuclear policy is *different!*" McCormack insisted, his voice rising. He had House pages wheel a library cart full of dusty green-jacketed hearing volumes onto the floor. Waving bound transcripts in the air, McCormack lectured the reformers that they had no idea how much important work the JCAE performed on sensitive nuclear issues. His premise was that, as in Plato's *Republic*, such lofty affairs were best left to a qualified elite.

Lobbyists for Westinghouse and Bechtel and the American Nuclear Energy Council, so accustomed to having their way on the Hill, were now working the hallways, button-holing House Democrats and pleading for support. They reached out to the Oil, Charcoal, and Atomic Workers union and to major nuclear subcontractors, who also worked the Speaker's lobby.

It mattered not. Jack Bingham, the gentleman from Riverdale, had the votes locked up. The final roll call wasn't even close.[15]

On January 4, 1977, the other shoe fell. The first action of the new Congress was a party-line vote adopting the rules package proposed by the House majority. Stripped of its legislative jurisdiction, the Joint Committee no longer had a reason for existing.

The final insult must have been the work of a mischievous night editor whose sense of humor slipped by his boss. The next day's *New York Times* ran reporter Ed Cowan's story on the demise of the JCAE, headlined "Joint Atomic Panel Stripped of Power."[16]

It ran on the obituary page.

Chapter Eight

The Capitol, Through Fresh Eyes

**Georgetown University
June 2009**

A startling perspective was offered by a small window on the seventh floor of Georgetown University's Edmund Walsh School of Foreign Service. Across the expanse of glass and steel to the east, the gleaming white dome of the Capitol rose at the crest of Jenkins Hill. It seemed to beckon students as I observed them on my first day back on campus to lecture.

It was with some surprise that I viewed from afar the familiar home of Congress. The cycles of our lives work in peculiar ways. As the movie rolls on, we catch glimpses of places we've passed by before, under very different circumstances.

Gathered there in the cramped top floors of the Inter-Cultural Center at Georgetown, like survivors from some distant storm, were several of the men and women I had encountered in my previous life as a foreign policy aide. There was George Tenet, who had volunteered to staff Senator Cranston on the Intelligence Committee "for a few weeks" while my security clearance was upgraded, but who rocketed forward into a career at the NSC and CIA. There was Madeleine Albright, who had entertained many of us young Hill staffers in her Georgetown salon as she built a farm system for young Democratic foreign policymakers during the Reagan-Bush years. There was Cas Yost, a key Republican staff colleague of mine and a U.S.-Soviet affairs expert, who was in between stints with the intelligence community. Tony Lake, from the Clinton NSC, was teaching there, as was Chuck Hagel, a Vietnam War hero from Nebraska and long one of my favorite Republican senators. All had arrived at the School of Foreign Service to write and think, fellow refugees from the world of partisan politics.

In this, what became my last summer in Washington, I found myself inside the waiting room of the Senate Hart Building, SH-112. It was my former office, where Joy and I years before worked for Senator Alan Cranston. Our first-born, Jennifer, had visited SH-112 with some frequency in a baby stroller. Now Jenn was the Senate staffer, following her brother Zack, a House page. On this day, she was hosting her visiting father for a sandwich—in the exact same office. Go figure.

Some of my last weeks dealing with Congress had become, like bookends, my kids' first. The entire summer, with its carpool discussions of Senate floor procedures, felt like a farewell tour. Jenn was working for Senator Barbara Boxer, with a recommendation from Senator Dianne Feinstein, two women who had been local activists when we were growing up in the San Francisco Bay Area. Together with Congresswoman Nancy Pelosi, who had often been in Cranston's office working as a Democratic fundraiser, here were three Northern California community leaders in Congress. Improbably, these three had risen to be the most powerful women in California politics. Pelosi was, in fact, the most senior elected woman in American history, second in the succession line to the presidency as the country's first female House Speaker.

As I spoke with my kids each day during our surreal commute, I came to appreciate these three women anew. They were role models for young people who aspired to be change agents in the policy world. Many times when these legislators would come to see Senator Cranston in his ornate Capitol office, they would be stuck waiting, chatting with an ubiquitous floor staffer like me. As with other such California Democrats as George Miller, Leon Panetta, Henry Waxman, Howard Berman, and Mel Levine, they were regular visitors in Cranston's welcoming suite.

Nancy Pelosi had been born to politics. She learned the honor of representing people from her dad, the mayor of Baltimore. While meticulously keeping a "favor file," she fielded calls to the home phone, working with her father to make sure even the poorest family had a holiday turkey. She believed fervently in the power of government to be a positive force in citizens' lives. The fluke of her adult prosperity—her husband Paul made millions from real estate—changed her principles very little. She drove herself each day to pass a progressive agenda, with a damn-the-torpedoes full-speed-ahead attitude about the polls. Like Newt Gingrich, she used her short-lived congressional majority to try to accomplish something meaningful. To her, that was the whole point of attaining political power. You used it. You tried to wield your majority forces to achieve something for the greater good. What people do with the power they accumulate tells you more about their values than most anything else.

From a personal standpoint, Senators Feinstein and Boxer couldn't be more different. One came from old money and one from new. One was a big-business Democrat, one a partisan populist. One was from Stanford and very West Coast Ivy League, one was from a New York community college. One was from Pacific Heights, and one was from the Bronx. Both were aggressive and highly self-confident. Both were impatient and did not suffer fools gladly. Perhaps as a consequence, they were burdened with staffers who consistently distrusted their counterparts. The senators competed for the same financial donors and to champion the same issues. On several ocassions, they cancelled out each other's votes; they were fiercely independent in pursuing their different priorities. Yet they worked together for the good of California, burying the hatchet time and again; they often had to make sure staff got the word when it was time to cease fire.

That summer we all were following hearings on climate change legislation run by Chairwoman Boxer—the same Barbara

Boxer we had known as a community activist in Marin, organizing progressives against the Army Corps of Engineers plan to pave over our local Ross Creek. Boxer had welcomed our family; so had Dianne Feinstein, hosting us in her elegant Washington home to meet a shy, awkward freshman senator from Illinois named Obama.

Nancy Pelosi had worked with Joy on House and Senate campaigns, and the San Francisco Democratic Party Convention. Pelosi, too, has been welcoming, appointing our son Zack to a position as a Congressional page. Zack, the budding liberal, got to shake hands with Speaker Dennis Hastert and Vice President Dick Cheney. He carried Bush veto messages through the long corridor separating the House floor from the Senate, coming to love the drama of raw politics and developing into a *West Wing* junkie. He took his passion for the theater of politics and carried it forward in his studies of nanotechnology and web design.

Observing these legislators anew—and watching the reactions of my students to them—I was curious once more to figure out what launches a public policy career. I questioned the motivations and the lessons learned. And I realized it was a turning of the seasons for me—with the arrival of the young suggesting it was time to usher out the old.

When I was an awestruck intern, I felt the slights when staff higher up the totem pole would dump downwards. I swore I'd never mistreat interns, that I'd try to help the next wave. Now, the time was coming when one should just get out of the way. It felt like that moment on an airplane, after a long cross-country flight, when the urgent pushing forward gently ends. You float, suspended for a time. Then you settle ever so slightly, nose beginning to lower, as gravity reclaims you, the pulling to ground a welcome blessing.

Walking through the courtyard at Georgetown University, I wondered all over again: *How do you teach this stuff? What is the "science" in politics? Do political science professors know much about real-world politics?* When I audited Stanford Business School classes, I remembered thinking: *If they are so smart, why aren't these professors out running Silicon Valley tech companies instead of lecturing on economic theory?*

As a lobbyist, I insisted that my university and hospital clients plan on, even assume, success. "Pretend it is the day after your great victory," I would counsel them, "Ask what exactly did you win? Why? What things did you do that made you able to prevail? Now, go do those things: You have your action plan."

The same approach worked in the classroom: You want to change the world? Pretend you succeeded. Define that success realistically. What is it that you have won? What did you do to accomplish this? How did you uphold your values in the process?

When my Georgetown students talked about change, there was a temptation to focus on the mistakes of the previous generation, and decide to do just the opposite. Arthur Schlesinger wrote a book about the cycles evident in American political history. He chronicled our national tendency to overcorrect for the most recent mistake, like a rookie driver over-steering the wheel of a runaway car, only to spin in circles. History is full of examples: Think of Jack Kennedy coming of age during the isolationist 1930s, then preparing as both senator and president to intervene any place, any time he thought Communists might challenge. Or George W. Bush, the son, belittling his father's caution in Iraq, then using 9/11 as an excuse for a monstrously costly invasion and occupation.

A family friend who had an unhappy childhood says, "Whenever I face a parenting dilemma, I just think of what my parents would have done, then do the opposite." This can be a reactionary, and harmful, philosophy, yet it is one I have sometimes followed myself in making policy. You analyze an initial failure and assume the opposite tack will succeed. In thereby attempting to flee history, you can become, perversely, a prisoner of the past. John F. Kennedy was so haunted by Chamberlain's appeasement at Munich in 1938—and by his father's reluctance to challenge Hitler—that he plunged aggressively into Vietnam, promising to "pay any price" and "bear any burden" in checking totalitarian regimes. LBJ was so haunted by the Democrat-scarring "who lost China?" debate of the 1950s that he could never accept the notion of retreating from his fateful military escalation in Southeast Asia. Veterans of the 1994 Hillary-care debacle—when the White House worked in secret to draft a massive health care reform bill—were determined to use an Obamacare strategy that looked like rope-a-dope. As a result, his White House would leave the messy process of writing and passing a bill too much in the hands of feuding legislative factions on Capitol Hill.

In my Georgetown graduate seminar, we chewed over such historical parallels. Each week, during office hours, the students would line up for advice and counsel. They wanted to work in Congress or the UN. Yet they were not terribly issue-driven. They would not have the common purpose of World War II, or the Cold War, or even Bush's "Global War on Terror." They envied the ease of the good-versus-evil paradigm used by previous generations who battled Hitler, Stalin, Tojo, and Communism.

These students were a veritable Model UN in themselves. They prepped in Azerbaijan and Santa Monica, El Salvador and Warsaw. There were Jewish kids from Milwaukee, Latinas from San Antonio, and a thirty-something mother from rural Pakistan. They were charming young men and women, yet, in their caution, they seemed afraid to be idealistic.

Realpolitik was the hangover legacy we children of the Sixties have given this millennial generation. Its members seemed afraid to take risks, to dream big dreams. With some noble exceptions, many of the young have become flaming moderates.

CHAPTER NINE

How Our Laws Are Made

Washington, D.C.
January 1977-March 1978

Stacked high on the reception desk of most Capitol Hill offices is a delightfully innocent pamphlet titled "How Our Laws Are Made." What the booklet describes is the antithesis of the Rube Goldberg scheme that often awaits those who shape policy. In Congressman Jack Bingham's office, we nevertheless distributed this brochure to unsuspecting constituents who dropped in on their elected representative.

Each decade that hyper-partisan legislative maneuvering accelerates, the booklet fable bears less and less relationship to reality. It portrays a perfect world of "regular order," where proposals are handled entirely on their merits, where predictable procedures are followed, delays are overcome, and consensus reigns. One learns early in Washington policymaking that this is fiction, that unorthodox means to secure legislative ends are the norm, not the exception.

Discerning the patterns of the inside game—a game of three-dimensional chess played for high stakes—was what I was trying to figure out my first years on the staff of Congress. For more than three decades, this systems analysis was the basis of my fascination with all things Washington. Repeatedly, I came back to the same question: How do policymakers produce results?

In most every meeting I had during my first years as a congressional aide, youth and inexperience were serious handicaps. The challenge to overcome as Jack Bingham's junior legislative assistant was this: I did not know what had happened in the years just before I showed up. I did not understand the rivalries, the jurisdictional maneuvers, the stalled proposals that had come before me. I knew little of the mastery of Majority Leader Johnson in shaping the modern Senate, or of the tense and losing battles President Kennedy had with an obstructionist Congress, events which had left indelible marks on the Capitol I entered as a junior staffer.

As historian Ernest May describes it, we have "dead spots" in our history, often made up of the battles that more senior colleagues personally experienced. It is the recent part that cautious high school history books often leave out. So as I set about considering nuclear export policy options, I made it my business to study recent precedents, to learn some of the personalities, and to begin to assess alternatives that had been prescribed in the recent past.

Years later, when I offered courses in policymaking strategy to graduate students, I began to reconsider these key lessons. At Georgetown, they have a practice of assembling all the students in the graduate program, then giving each professor five minutes to pitch their course syllabus. "Why should I take your class?" one student demanded skeptically during my talk, barely looking up from his laptop.

"Because this is the class I needed when I first showed up in town thirty years ago," I responded, somewhat taken aback by the explicit challenge. Then I added: "It will teach you a lot of what you need to know—about precedent, process, and organizational behavior. The stuff they leave out of textbooks." The seminar was fully enrolled within hours.

January 1977 was a heady time to be a young Democrat in the Capitol. The culture wars over Vietnam, civil rights, drugs, sex, and rock and roll seemed to have abated. The era of the Bee Gees, John Travolta, and disco was upon us. Few of us knew quite what to make of Jimmy Carter, the righteous southern Baptist Sunday school teacher from Plains, Georgia. His popularity had plummeted in the months before the election as he lost a thirty percentage point lead in the polls and won the presidency by the narrowest of margins. Yet Democrats still had an overwhelming majority in the House and Senate, and with a bright-faced reformer from Georgia in the White House, all things seemed possible.

For Democrats, and particularly for Jack Bingham, it was a time of great promise. The death blow he had dealt to the Joint Committee on Atomic Energy meant that legislative power over nuclear export policy in the House fell directly to the International Trade Subcommittee he chaired. While I was still responsible for staffing miscellaneous local issues, from citizen anti-crime patrols to swimming pools in the Co-Op City rec center, my legislative work accelerated markedly as I was handed the nuclear portfolio.

Washington was filling up with office-seekers, volunteers from Carter's "Peanut Brigades," frustrated, reform-minded Democrats exiled during the Nixon-Ford years. Washington leaders from environmental groups were getting appointed to White House jobs. Jessica Tuchman Mathews went to the NSC, Gus Speth and Kitty Schirmer to the Council on Environmental Quality and the domestic policy staff.

My apartment at Sixth and A Street in southeast Washington, which I shared with my amiable Bingham office predecessor, Greg Zorthian, was full of Carterites in town for the inauguration. The city was locked in a cold snap of historic magnitude. I took several guests to the Potomac riverbank, laced on ice skates, and raced directly across the river to the Virginia shoreline. The river was frozen solid for the first time in decades. The capital took on the look of a Dutch painting, with couples gliding hand-in-hand and kids playing ice hockey on canals.

On January 20, 1977, screwdrivers for breakfast did little to steel us against the brutal chill. We shivered as we stood on the East Plaza, watching President-elect Carter take his oath. (It was a scene I'd recall thirty-two years later, when we froze for Barack Obama's twenty-degree swearing-in on the other side of the Capitol.) We watched Carter leave the Capitol lunch, then, surprisingly, *walk* to the White House. We celebrated again at Congressman Bingham's office reception before making our way into the night for a blur of vodka-fueled inaugural balls. Soon enough, it would be time for serious work.

Bingham's office once again became the headquarters for those who wanted to rewrite laws governing U.S. nuclear policy. During the waning days of the general election campaign, Bingham had repeatedly encouraged candidate Carter to take a hardline against the spread of nuclear weapons. Now we were, in turn, besieged by suggestions on what a comprehensive export control bill would look like.

The Senate, in typical fashion, moved slowly. Percy, Glenn, and Abraham Ribicoff staffers maneuvered to gain the upper hand and to clarify the new lines of Senate committee jurisdiction. The Senate was also busy approving scores of Carter administration nominees. In the House, however, Bingham's handle on the nuclear nonproliferation issue was unchallenged and his path forward clear.

A steady stream of lobbyists appeared on our doorstep. At the time, I readily caricatured lobbyists as bad guys with special-interest agendas. They could waste your time and try your limited patience. However, I began to see that lobbyists could also perform a service. The best advocates brought concise, distilled messages demonstrating where particular constituencies stood. Equally important, the sharp ones brought good information, sound arguments, and edgy rhetoric. Their talking points framed one specific perspective on an issue. If gathered from a variety of different points of view, these narratives were like reports from a battlefront. Piece them together and a picture begins to emerge that defines the universe of options for victory.

Tom Kuhn sent up his men from the American Nuclear Energy Council (ANEC). They were bankers, investors, and bondholders. They resembled Tom Slaughter, the Kansas man on Wall Street who had controlled the modest college trust fund my grandfather had left me and my brothers. They were Brooks Brothers-suited, buttoned-down guys. Today, they could be extras for an episode of *Mad Men*.

Utilities like Con Ed sent engineers, true believers in the potential of nuclear power. They wore skinny ties and short-sleeve shirts, with pens and pencils in the pocket protectors on their chests.

From the European embassies came nineteenth-century diplomats who liked brandy after a long lunch and cited ancient history in their protestations about extraterritoriality in proposed U.S. nuclear export laws.

The State Department sent a wave of Jesuit-trained lawyers with names like Ronald Bettauer and Louis Nosenzo. They were bland gentlemen, schooled in the art of sighing as they explained why a score of precedents simply would not allow the legislative branch to void existing nuclear fuel supply contracts.

As Congressman Bingham and I listened to their entreaties, I began to develop a mechanistic theory I have subsequently struggled over the decades to refine. It is an altogether optimistic concept, grounded in Madison's *Federalist 10*. It holds that our capital is, by design, a free marketplace of ideas. Factions compete vigorously to define the public interest. Power is wielded not according to some ideal, but in a way that reflects how political power is actually distributed at that moment in time.

It is a flawed system, but the best we have yet designed. Money acts as a megaphone, distorting the relative strength and followership of certain propositions. This is not new. It did not begin with Joe Kennedy's millions or the Nixon shakedown of industry lobbyists, or the Supreme Court's egregious ruling in *Citizens United*. Hamilton and Jefferson used similar tactics, sponsoring poison press assaults on their political adversaries' ideas and character.

What emerges from this Darwinian struggle is, of course, an imperfect product. If you have a cause, you have to make your case, jump into the arena, and join the free-for-all. There is no equity in the distribution of power. The good guys don't always win. The wisest, most forward-looking policies are often rejected. There is no perfect justice, and there are no final victories. Yet, shame on you if you sit back and criticize without ever trying to win in the ring. As Lyndon Johnson liked to say, "A genuinely free society cannot be a spectator society."

Many classmates at Hampshire concluded at a young age that the struggle is fixed. Leftists all, they believed the Establishment would always win. It was a tautology; corporate interests would always have the most money and the most powerful lobbyists. I've found that this analysis misses the mark, however, because the competition is quite open and the corridors of power accessible. From environmental activists to anti-tax crusaders, from Tea Partiers to Nader's Raiders, from Sam Lovejoy to Sarah Palin, and a community organizer named Obama, activists *can* participate. Sometimes they will even win. Popular will can sometimes overwhelm poison PACs and corporate dollars, as in recent years when Wikipedia users shelved the bill impinging on Internet usage.

From my first months in Washington, I found the accessibility of these contests irresistible. It was analogous to Major League Baseball. Sure, the New York Yankees might have, by far, the costliest lineup. On any given day, however, the low-budget Kansas City Royals could beat them. It was an attraction that justifies optimism. When overreach occurred—think of the trusts at the beginning of the twentieth century—democracy facilitated reaction in the form of Teddy Roosevelt, Woodrow Wilson, and a progressive era. Excess begat reform as surely as dawn followed the dark.

This was part of our confidence in pushing for sweeping reform of nuclear policy in 1977. The Joint Committee had functioned so long as the champion of the nuclear industry that a counterreaction was bound to arise; it was one that no amount of lobbying could thwart. It had been necessary for repeated reform efforts to fail before a string of successes could ensue.

An amusing part of being lobbied in those months was to witness the incredulity on some faces when nuclear industry champions came to the House with their appeals. Corporate leaders would appear in Representative Bingham's office to assert the importance of plutonium reprocessing, to argue for more billions in taxpayer funds for the construction of the Clinch River Breeder Reactor, or to explain the inviolable nature of U.S. nuclear fuel supply contracts with Europe and Japan. They would have the highest-priced lobbyists in town. Often they had no choice but to meet with a twenty-two-year-old legislative assistant from Hampshire College. That kids so junior might have sway over major legislation in Washington was taken as an absurd affront by many elders.

The easiest part of my job was assembling the key pieces of a comprehensive reform bill from amongst the many good ideas put forward by my Group W Bench buddies. The hardest part was working with the House lawyers to ensure that the draft effectively represented our intentions. My first draft was titled "The Nuclear Antiproliferation Act of 1977," and was almost a hundred pages long. Broken into five sections, it covered everything from U.S. nuclear export sanctions to what foreign governments could and could not do with U.S.-source materials.

I was a late arrival on the scene, so my work was often highly derivative. Indeed, this is true of most legislation in Washington; you need to build upon the foundation already set, and the bill that fell short in the previous Congress is often the outline for the next initiative. This first draft was a cut-and-paste job. It purposely rescued from the JCAE dustbin the many good proposals put forward by Zablocki, Findley, Percy, Glenn, and Ribicoff. Each proposal had been sidetracked by the formerly omnipotent Joint Committee. Most were revived and brought forward in the package Bingham shared with a handful of nuclear export reform advocates.

The stakes were high. President Carter had cautiously embraced the nonproliferation issue. He brought in respected policymakers to work on multilateral diplomacy and to shape the emerging legislative package, including Joe Nye and Washington lawyer Gerard Smith. The Carter administration began negotiating with European suppliers, whose weak safety standards on nuclear exports were part and parcel of the proliferation dilemma.

The Carter White House could not control events, however, because the president was already embroiled in controversies with Congress, especially over the reaches of executive authority. Carter tried to take on the entrenched powers in Congress by eliminating funds for dozens of water projects he derided as "pork." On this, Tip O'Neill and his lieutenants rolled President Carter repeatedly. In the wake of the imperial presidency of Richard Nixon, Congress was seizing prerogatives anew; it refused to yield on earmarks, one of its powers of the purse. Soon Carter was swimming against the tide, losing ground on almost every issue, from tax cuts to appropriations.

Similar White House efforts to lecture European exporters and Third World nuclear importers of sensitive, weapons-usable technology were brushed off overseas as too much American moralizing. Together, these two factors gave legislative aides a lot of flexibility when it came to pushing Congress to craft a major foreign policy bill changing U.S. nuclear export practices.

Bingham seized the moment. He moved aggressively to occupy the vacuum caused by his elimination of the Joint Committee in January. He introduced his bill, H.R. 4409, on March 3, 1977. It set strict criteria for all U.S. nuclear cooperation agreements and for export licenses, while barring nuclear trade with nations running nuclear research programs not subject to international inspection. He quickly called hearings, rushing the still forming Carter team into reactive mode. They were forced to clear administration-wide statements of White House policy on each element of our controversial proposal.

Soon, Bingham's office was visited by still more State Department lawyers challenging the draft language. The Executive Branch team would insist to us that some provision would be unacceptable to their European counterparts, or would interfere with the Japanese plutonium plant at Tokai-mura. The unilateralism of the Bingham draft was also objectionable to the Carter White House team. They argued that the U.S. could not advance nonproliferation objectives without first securing a broad international consensus. They pleaded for time.

Bingham listened politely to Nye and Smith. They were both old-school gentlemen, the former a brilliant Harvard scholar, the latter a white-shoe lawyer now carrying the rank of ambassador. Smith dripped with disdain for the populist legislature. The Congressman was unfailingly courteous with all the State Department visitors. Then Bingham changed hardly a word of his draft.

In nearly every interaction, industry lobbyists and State Department lawyers seemed somewhat bewildered. For so many years, these people had been dealing with members of their own club—industry captains, investment bankers, nuclear salesmen who wowed the pro-nuclear solons of the Joint Committee. They had been missionaries talking with fellow participants in the nuclear enterprise. They found it hard adjusting to the idea that they had to deal with some reform-minded cabal.

From the start, Bingham's plan was to spirit his measure through the House, banking on goodwill from Speaker O'Neill, who had little invested in the issue. He figured the Senate would be harder, and compromises would be made even before a House-Senate conference committee convened to write the final version. It was in a conference where Bingham predicted the toughest bargaining would be done; the House would have to resist Senate pressures to yield to industry-backed compromises the State Department was sure to push.

Within weeks, Bingham had put together a hearing record he deemed complete. He moved quickly to put his comprehensive bill to a vote, literally a "markup" of the draft measure in his own subcommittee of the House International Relations panel.

Over the course of two long mornings sessions, I was the final witness, joined only by the senior Republican committee staffer, Don Fortier, who had written the Zablocki-Findley amendment. It fell to us to answer any and all questions about the bill from committee members. Sitting at the witness table, looking up at the seats backed by eighty-foot-high curtains and soaring smoked glass windows, we were naturally intimidated.

We had spent days rehearsing explanations for every section of the bill. With Gordon Kerr, Don and I had painstakingly edited the section-by-section analysis of the draft, submitting it to all committee members and staff. We had prepared a committee report to accompany the bill to the House floor. Finally, after a morning testifying before Bingham's subcommittee, and the next day in full committee, we were done talking. A motion was made to report out the bill to the full House.

Then, right before the gavel fell for a final committee vote, a junior congressman named Steve Solarz began to question our rush job, and the fact that we were sprinting past the committee with "such obviously important legislation." A clever young politician, Solarz was calling attention to the fact that the committee was getting steamrolled. His discomfort is still apparent in rereading the decades-old transcript.

"As an act of blind faith in the chairman of the subcommittee who is managing this legislation, and because I do have so much respect for his instincts and for his judgment, plus what I know is the hard work of the subcommittee staff, I won't raise any objections at this time," Solarz intoned as he gazed down skeptically at me and Don, pausing for dramatic effect.[17]

So far, so good.

Once out of committee, the bill sailed through the full House chamber with minimal debate and a favorable vote. Soon enough, though, it was stuck in the Senate, besieged by the lobbying efforts of industry, foreign embassies, and a State Department team determined to water down practically every provision. Chief Senate sponsor John Glenn offered some further improvements, incorporating a new section on international fuel cycle cooperation.

Glenn was soon fighting a defensive action. The politically embattled Foreign Relations Committee chairman, Frank Church of Idaho, home of major nuclear research labs, had joined forces with industry champions, preparing to eviscerate the measure in a House-Senate conference. With amendment after amendment offered on the Senate floor, they "roughed up" the House-passed language. Their maneuvers were not dispositive, but intended to open up each paragraph for conference committee review and rewrite. The plan of bill opponents was to secure a pro-industry majority among Senate-appointed conferees, then hold the conference committee hostage until key provisions were gutted.

John Glenn gamely held the Senate floor for days. For a

national hero who could easily have made a living sitting on corporate boards, he was remarkably diligent in his work, imploring his colleagues to help combat the nuclear danger. He was methodical and honest, and assumed he would win on the merits. His besieged staffer, Len Weiss, sought to neuter, but then accept, amendments designed to open issues for later resolution in a House-Senate conference committee. House staffers watching from the Senate gallery cringed, even as the Carter administration lobbyists worked ever more closely with the nuclear industry in an effort to weaken the key House-passed provisions.

The bill barely escaped the Senate without real damage being done to its core principles. Critics exacted a high price from Glenn for a time agreement to end the stalling and vote for passage on the Senate floor. The bill's opponents won leadership assurances that industry sympathizers on the Senate Energy Committee would be appointed to help shape the upcoming conference committee that would have to reconcile the bill with the House version.

Nearly a year had passed since Bingham had unveiled the strong House measure. Now it appeared as if we were back to square one. In the pending conference committee, House champions faced a battle against a pro-industry Senate majority we couldn't defeat.

Don Fortier and I huddled with senior House aides. The sleight of hand we agreed upon was originally his idea. A conservative Republican who would later serve on Ronald Reagan's National Security Council before dying tragically young of brain cancer, Don was a serious scholar. He had earned his Ph.D. with Albert Wohlstetter as his dissertation committee chair; he had little patience for ideologues. He was also unfailingly kind and inclusive. His proposal was as audacious as any I would hear in all my years on congressional staff.

We were alone in a small chamber behind 2172 Rayburn, the imposing House International Relations Committee hearing room, when he told me.

"We need to duck conference." he said.

"Wouldn't *that* be nice," was all I said. I had no good plan for how to avoid getting rolled by the upcoming industry-White House tag team.

"I'm serious," Don insisted, looking as if he were plotting a coup.

"How?" There was nothing about this option in How Our Laws Are Made.

"We just call up the Senate-passed bill in the dead of night and pass it when nobody is watching. We pass it by U.C. [Unanimous Consent]. Just a quick voice vote."

"What?" I had never heard of such a maneuver. "I mean, they'll object. McCormack will object. Or somebody else will object on behalf of the Carter administration and the nuclear industry. They'll object to the U.C. request."

After Don explained his thinking further, we took his devious plan to Committee Chief of Staff Jack Brady and to Gordon Kerr. Nothing Senator Glenn had been forced to accept on the Senate floor had done any material violence to key House provisions. So we'd wait until cleanup time on the House floor, those five minutes or so before the House of Representatives adjourns for an extended recess. Dozens of minor non-controversial measures are routinely called up and passed by U.C. Only one problem: A bipartisan series of power brokers had to approve this matter getting onto the U.C. list. Jack Brady and Jack Bingham would sign off for the Democrats, Paul Findley and Don Fortier for the Republicans.

Bingham and Brady finessed the issue with committee leadership, selling the move, somewhat disingenuously, as a non-controversial procedure designed to frustrate the common enemy of all members of the House, the United States Senate. The fact that nuclear nonproliferation was such an arcane, technical subject aided Bingham's cause; it didn't hurt that he had both the *chutzpah* and the *cojones* to pull it off.

On a gray February day of snow flurries and northerly winds, minutes before adjourning for the ten-day "President's Birthday Week" congressional recess, the House of Representatives acted by voice vote. The House adopted the Senate-passed version of H.R. 4409 as a substitute. Then it immediately sent the bill for enrollment and on to the White House.

There were less than a half-dozen Members present when the Unanimous Consent motion was made. No objections were heard. Most Members had caught early flights home to avoid the impending storm. If you had blinked, you would have missed it. President Carter could now sign the comprehensive nuclear non-proliferation measure headed to his desk. Or he could veto it.

Don and Gordon let me call the Carter administration team to inform them what we had done. This was in the days before C-SPAN; there was no live broadcast of our parliamentary chicanery. Key State Department nuclear staff, it turned out, were huddled in a meeting room in Undersecretary Joe Nye's suite. Calling from a phone booth just off the second-floor entrance to the House chamber, I asked that Secretary Nye be interrupted.

"We were just going over the bill," he opened cheerfully, "marking out issues for conference. We've all got a lot of work to do on this proposal."

"That won't be necessary," I said, struggling to suppress my wise-ass glee. "We just passed it."

Within weeks, Nye, Weiss, and Fortier stood shoulder to shoulder with Bingham and Glenn in the Cabinet Room of the White House. In the crowded tableau, we smiled awkwardly as President Carter signed the Nuclear Non-Proliferation Act of 1978 into law.[18]

CHAPTER TEN

Roots: Return to Jerusalem

Israel
May 2008

To travel back to where we began and to know the place for the first time—this was what I was hoping for as I flew east once more to Israel. Shifting in my coach seat, I ruminated over T. S. Eliot's definition of wisdom: to arrive where you started and to truly know the place, and know yourself, for the first time.

Accompanying me on this transatlantic flight was my daughter Jennifer. This was the latest of many trips I'd taken over the decades to Israel, beginning thirty years before as an aide to pro-Israel Congressman Jack Bingham, and later as an eager member of delegations from the Senate. This journey to Jerusalem, however, was to be her first.

The trip was my high school graduation gift to Jenn before she began a Washington internship with Ken Wollack at the National Democratic Institute, an organization that promotes pluralism in the Middle East and worldwide. Her great gift to me, the days ahead would reveal, was simply her fresh eyes.

A new perspective was most welcome. My work in Washington had given me leading staff roles on Middle East issues ranging from arms sales and foreign aid, to refugee resettlement and the peace process. I had worked for years with heavy-handed lobbyists from AIPAC, some lifelong friends, some who became adversaries and rivals in Congress for influence over American Middle East policy. In the Senate, I worked closely with individuals bringing information from Israeli intelligence. I flew to Tel Aviv to compare notes on Iraqi and Pakistani nuclear programs, meetings set up in 1987 by a contact of mine at Israel's Washington embassy, Benjamin Netanyahu. Bibi was then a charming raconteur with whom I enjoyed having lunch and brainstorming how to curb the designs of Israel's neighbors to obtain nuclear weapons.

By 2008, however, first principles had grown dated. Old questions needed new answers. I was no longer confident Israeli leaders such as then Prime Minister Netanyahu, or their American supporters, were doing more good than harm. So this trip presented an opportunity. For the first time, I was to be free to roam Israel, shorn of handlers who repeated the foreign ministry catechisms. No embassy briefings, no bus tours, no chattering guides.

After landing in angled evening sunlight, we picked up our rental car and popped in a Doobie Brothers CD. Soon "Jesus is Just Alright" was playing as we traversed the narrow coastal plain near Ben Gurion Airport. For one week, we were determined to drive the country by back roads without any schedule, border to border, rocket fire permitting.

As we left the outskirts of Tel Aviv, that most European of Middle Eastern cities, my daughter looked up from our guidebook. "How can somebody claim an exclusive 'homeland' if there were lots of other civilizations there before, and after, them?" Her question made the Arab-Israeli dispute seem so very recent, considering the broad sweep of time from the Canaanites, Phoenicians, and Ottomans to modern times. *Whose homeland, indeed?*

With a fresh point of view, no query seemed too broad or too basic. As I struggled to respond to Jenn's unrelenting stream of questions, I grew more cognizant of unspoken issues of roots. As a lapsed Episcopalian bearing a well-known Jewish surname, I had suppressed such identity questions for years in Washington.

This journey fulfilled an old pledge. I had promised my parents years before that I would make sure our children, products of two consecutive generations of marriages between Jews and Protestants, would be aware of their ethnic heritage. I was fortunate to have grown up in public schools during California's Wonder

Years. My New York Warburg relatives, starting with our patriarch Felix, my great-grandfather, had been Jewish community leaders. The WASPs on Mom's side had been respected civic leaders going back for centuries to Solomon Stoddard and his grandson Jonathan Edwards. I was aware that one of my parents' greatest gifts in taking us west the day Dad finished his second war-time tour with Army intelligence was that I didn't even know what anti-Semitism was until I was about thirteen, when Nicky Chase's mother made a snarky comment about unwelcome guests at the Lagunitas Club.

That first night in Israel, I drifted off to sleep thinking about myth and history. We concoct our own stories about history, it seemed to me, the same way archaeologists recompose antiquities. We brush away that which obscures. We discard the pieces that clearly do not belong. We try to employ science. Yet, invariably, in reassembling the shards, we create our own truths, our own versions of what really happened. We become deeply invested in the myths we create.

This was true in Washington. We overly revered John Kennedy and Ronald Reagan. We unduly vilified Carter and Nixon without let up. The same applied to the origins of the Arab-Israeli dispute over Palestine. For me, the story had always been a relatively simple one. Mom taught us to root, always, for the underdog. Jewish communities have been persecuted for more than twenty centuries, exiled through the Diaspora, the Inquisition, and the *pogroms* from the Urals to the Black Forest, culminating in the Nazi Holocaust. That survivors realized their dreams of uniting again in the land of Israel was the quintessential story of human triumph. They were brave pioneers who made the desert bloom. Believers in democracy, they overcame hundred-to-one odds to defeat neighboring tribes intent on their liquidation.

This attitude shaped my work for successive pro-Israel legislators in Congress, men who relied heavily on Jewish donors for campaign funds. My Middle East views grew not from Democratic partisanship or ethnic pride, though Dad has long been a fervent AIPAC supporter, but from a sense of fair play. The fact that Arabs and Palestinians saw their lands shrink with each war their generals started (and lost) was the fault of their tragically failed leadership. Actions have consequences. Losing armies forfeit territory. The Mexicans were not given back California. Japan and Germany lost land and temporary governing authority after World War II.

There is one problem with this comfortable construct, though; Jenn and I discussed it each day on Israeli highways and side roads. The Palestinians have suffered such abuse for so long that *they* have now become the underdog. This new reality creates Israel's greatest vulnerability among nations, a danger compounded each year Israel's right-wing government continues its indefensible occupation of the West Bank, squashes Gaza, alienates friends in Turkey, and exacerbates quarrels with Egypt. Few Washington policymakers want to acknowledge this fact: For our kids' generation, the Palestinian farmers on the West Bank are the oppressed, and the Israeli Defense Forces are the oppressors.

The next day we found that one of the great delights of our exploration was the passion with which Israelis themselves debate the issues. We engaged with diplomats and relatives, with cab drivers, Egyptians, West Bank Palestinians, Israeli opposition leaders, and cabinet ministers. All were civil. Yet each had an intensely personal version of history, myths in which they were deeply invested.

Amidst the vigorous debate, one clear truth emerged. It all comes down to real estate. Buying a home was the subject as we rode nervously south from Ramallah, still in the "Greater Jerusalem" part of the West Bank, but such that we were eager to catch the familiar sight of the Old City walls telling us we were back from the political frontier and traveling safer ground. Our driver that day was Youssef, a Palestinian who was explaining some basic truths. Out the car windows, poverty and wealth were juxtaposed block by block. The pricey new condos next to dilapidated hovels offered a stark contrast: It was a crazy mixture of South Africa's Soweto ghetto and California's wealthy Orange County.

"When you buy a place," I asked, "how do you know what country it's in?" My question was tentative, but I was genuinely mystified.

Youssef stopped abruptly at a red light, turned around, and observed matter-of-factly, "Everybody knows what the peace will look like. Everybody knows where the final boundary lines will be drawn. The only question is: How many more will be killed on each side before we get there?"

We set out to consider the pre-Christian era in Caesarea. This ancient port on the Mediterranean, where the apostle Paul had been held before being shipped off to his fate in Rome, was once a glorious harbor. The hippodrome and coliseum next to the palace were perched above an azure sea. We took the scene in amidst relaxed groups of Israelis, who spoke loudly in Hebrew and Russian. Then we continued our journey backwards in time.

We crossed Highway 2 and Highway 4, the modern Israeli roads that run north to south, parallel to the sea. Then we left the coastal plain at Hadera and took Route 99 on a northeasterly track. Soon, fertile farmlands gave way to hills dotted with orchards of olives and plums. Arab villages lined the road that skirted Jenin and the Palestinian towns of the West Bank en route to Afula.

We were in the heart of Arab Israel—lands the UN partition plan of 1947 designated for inclusion in an Arab state, stretching north through Nazareth to the Lebanese border. We paralleled the 1948 disengagement line near Har Megiddo (Armageddon). Yes, *that* Armageddon. We paused to contemplate the crossroads of the lush Jezreel Valley that suddenly bisected the country road as the Band sang on the radio, "I pulled into Nazareth . . ."

There before us was the road from Mesopotamia to the Mediterranean. It was the path the caravans took out of Egypt for the Bosporus. Century after century, this had been a major intersection for marauder and pilgrim alike. It was where the Old Testament prophets foresaw the battle at "the end of all days." At the fateful hour, a current brand of right-wing "born again" Christian preachers earnestly hoped the Jews would control Jerusalem. From our perch, such apocryphal words seemed silly. When we contemplated a seven thousand-year-old crossroads, Jesus just seemed too recent.

Considering the great sweep of the ages, the current Arab-Israeli dispute could seem like a mere blip in time. Great civilizations had fought over these crossroads for eons. Put in context, recent troubles in the neighborhood, as horrific as they had been for soldiers and civilians alike, seemed eminently solvable.

We drove through fruitful fields in a great valley that reached inland from Mt. Carmel to the River Jordan. The swamps were drained by the emigrants in the first great modern *aliyah*, by the Polish and Russian Jews who came even before Herzl and the call to nationhood. There was Mount Gilboa and the ghost of King Saul. There were rectangles of corn and cotton, shooting up in all directions. Brown slopes in the distance were lined with eucalyptus.

The road felt altogether familiar; we could easily have been emerging from the hills of California's Napa Valley. Then we noticed that each irrigation valve was locked, secured behind barbed wire and electric security fences. It was a subtle reminder that here, every inch of land and every gallon of water had been paid for in blood.

We arrived amidst summer-like heat in Beit Sha'an, a sleepy village perched above the River Jordan. We emerged from our car and paid a few shekels for admission to the archaeological digs, but we were wholly unprepared for what we were about to see.

Before us were the ruins of a town five thousand years old. At our feet was Main Street, Roman columns still intact. Just beyond was an enormous amphitheater that once seated crowds of ten thousand. We were standing at the top of a V-shaped valley, with ancient roads reaching down to the Jordan plain, the dusty hills of the Hashemite kingdom beckoning in the distance. Within the sturdy shoulders of the fortress-like setting was a scene right out of Pompeii. This, too, was a place where time felt as if it had stood still. One day in 783, the city was flattened by an earthquake. No one had lived there since. The well preserved mosaics, the storefronts, and the tile work were still being uncovered from beneath generations of accumulated detritus.

Beit Sha'an is several hundred feet below sea level. As we walked along the banked paving stones, we squinted in the searing sunlight. At the foot of the town, we came to the face of a soaring *tel*, ruins of an ancient city built upon layer after layer. Wind and water had sheared the southern face of the mound. As sure as a geologist's cut, the *tel* revealed remnants of civilization, one stacked upon the other, on and on through the ages. All the way up to the summit of a five-hundred-foot hill, we saw the shards of pottery and bone amidst tumbled walls laid down as if by river sediment.

Beit Sha'an, Israel, May 2008.

Here there were Egyptian ruins from the Ramses II period. Here the Canaanites were overrun by the Israelites, who were vanquished by the Philistines, who hung King Saul's body from the Beit Sha'an walls. The Greeks renamed the town "Scythopolis," then were overrun by the Romans, who were fought, in turn, by Arabs, Turks, and Ottoman soldiers. Then, at the turn of the twentieth century, the British took over, finally ceding the turf to Jewish pioneers there on the Jordan frontier.

The Palestinian-Israel dispute? It seemed immature in comparison.

Then we were back in the car, enjoying the open road, channeling Jack Kerouac, laughing at the CD's refrain, "Across the great divide." Route 90 paralleled the bank of the Jordan as we headed north. We were, in fact, a stone's throw from the international border. The road afforded us astonishing views into aging gun mounts lining the opposite bank. Holiday traffic was heading south from the Galilee, flowing back home on the Jerusalem road.

We were driving northwest toward Tiberius in the soft afternoon light. Then suddenly, on a whim, we detoured east, determined not to miss a single corner of the country. We took Route 92 along the U.N.-occupied buffer where Syria once stretched down to the Galilee.

We drove past Kiryat Shemona and then right on 99 East just before the Metulla road. We were at the tip of Israel's northernmost finger that points into the most dangerous parts of the no-man's land south of Beirut and west of Damascus. We passed the Kibbutz Dafna, named for the heroine of Leon Uris' novel *Exodus*. Here we encountered another piece of our concocted historical mosaic, a story we had assumed to be illustrative fiction, but were surprised to find was more reality than myth. There, just above us, were the ruins of the Taggart fort the Haganah stormed, led in the Hollywood film version by a young, shirtless Paul Newman. The incongruously snow-covered peaks of the Golan Heights were shimmering like a mirage in the heat. Just beyond lay Syria, its capital of Damascus less than one hundred miles northeast.

The road narrowed abruptly, then we parked and walked down the cliff along a footpath. The rusted signs posted on barbed wire fences warned of land mines on both sides of the trail. Burned out remains of a machine gun nest stood sentry above the last turn before we wound down into the glade. Then it was before us: the source of the Jordan. The river began in a glorious cascading waterfall that gushered directly from a hillside spring, the lifeblood of farmers and fishermen for scores of miles downstream.

We delighted in the spray, a thoroughly refreshing sensation. After traversing the hills and valleys, to finally stand at this mystical place was a moment of triumph. We were not alone, however, for barreling down the path behind us were dozens of high school kids. Escorted by rifle-toting teachers, they were Israeli-Arab students on a field trip. The girls wore black head scarves and robes that failed to conceal their blue jeans. The guys sported Shaquille O'Neal and Hard Rock Cafe T-shirts, further evidence of a world made flat.

We drove west the next day through Arab hill towns lining the scorched Lebanese border, emerging finally at the coast in Nahariya. Teenage Israeli soldiers with Uzis lounging at the bus stop looked dispirited, apparently headed back to their Army base after leave. We drove south for the balance of the afternoon, all the way through Acre and Haifa until the road down to Tel Aviv opened amid sand dunes alongside the Mediterranean, where kite sailors and windsurfers frolicked. With the sun meeting the sea to the west, I thought of California yet again; the ride so closely resembled Interstate 5 south from Dana Point past Camp Pendleton towards the northern San Diego suburbs.

The next day was Shavuot, the Jewish holiday celebration of ... well, we weren't exactly sure. We tried in vain to nail it down, but we were still ignorant as we made the last turns off the road and up to Carme Yoseff to visit long-lost relatives.

Gabi Unger was the only Warburg I had ever met who lived in Israel. A garrulous agribusiness man, he was also a decorated Israeli Army officer, who helped found Peace Now in the late 1970s as a protest against Israel's prolonged occupation of the Palestinian West Bank.

His welcome was everything we could have hoped for. Teenage kids and twenty-somethings were straggling in to gather for a family holiday meal; it was a familiar drill. Their mother was in the kitchen, welcoming my daughter, involving her in the preparation. Gabi and the dogs were on the porch, savoring the fading light. Below in the valley, Route 1 cut by the ruins of the British fort at Latrun. To the right, the lights of Ramallah in the West Bank twinkled above the Jerusalem hills. To the left, the sun set just beyond the high-rises of Tel Aviv and the old Arab seaport of Jaffa on the Mediterranean Sea.

From here, you could see across the entirety of the country. Here, where the nation was only 10 miles wide, the longing with which so many had ached for this land was palpable. The intense beauty was pierced by our recognition of harrowing vulnerability. The fields before us had seen Crusader slay Muslim, Greek kill Roman, Ottoman and Arab and Jew engage in slaughter after slaughter. From Phoenicians to Philistines, from Canaanites and Israelites, from Caesar's legions to the soldiers of Napoleon and Allenby, one could readily imagine in the fields below the pounding of soldiers' feet. I was transfixed, drawn back to the view again and again.

The vegetarian feast was a delight. We were family; we were at home. The young adults proved to be brilliant. The guys were opinionated, the women clever and sharp. In their informality and passionate debate, they were the embodiment of Israel's future. After we exchanged heartfelt toasts and snapped photos, I found myself captivated listening to Gabi's mother.

Eva Warburg was then ninety-five years old. Yet she retained the spirit of a pioneer and the *sabras* she raised. She had been the last Warburg to make it out of Germany before the Holocaust. It was 1939 when she left Hamburg. For a Jew in Hitler's Germany, 1939 was very late. It was after *Kristallnacht* and after her father Fritz, my great-grandfather Felix's brother, had been sent to a concentration camp. It was after the Warburg family home had become Hamburg's last refuge for the Jewish community, part medical clinic, part departure lounge for suddenly stateless German Jews. Soon thereafter, Eva met a young man named Naftali, who was a leader in Palmach, the group exhorting Jews to make *aliyah*, to immigrate to Israel. Years later, she would marry him during her first days in Israel.

Eva was remarkably clear, despite her advanced years. She shared stories of playing as a child with her American cousin Gerald, my grandfather and namesake. She gossiped with delight about relatives long since dead. Then, before leaving, she presented me with an elegantly wrapped gift.

Later that night, I carefully unwrapped her package. It was a scrapbook. Inside were photographs, many of them sixty, seventy, eighty years old. There were original news clippings, excerpts from memoirs and German news magazines, pictures of groundbreakings and bar mitzvahs—even an infamous family photo of me and my long-haired California brothers from our late 1960s Summer of Love period.

I was incredulous. *How did Eva come to have this collection? Why is she entrusting it to us now?* I read slowly through each page she had collected, sitting alone at 2 a.m. in my hotel room. The papers told of her last days in Germany, of her father being forced by the Nazis to take the name "Israel" Warburg, the only first name Jews were allowed in the Germany of 1939. Her notes recounted how she got her father out of Nazi custody and fled to Sweden. They told of her hopes to make it to Palestine, and later of our cousin Eric Warburg's courageous post-war return to Hamburg.

I read for the first time how the Warburg country house outside Hamburg had been used shortly after VE Day as a recovery home for the handful of Jewish children who survived the Bergen-Belsen concentration camp. I read about how my uncle, a U.S. Army intelligence officer, had interrogated Herman Goering, just as my father had interrogated colleagues of Werner von Braun. I read of Eva's journey to Palestine, of her father's last days on the kibbutz, a nineteenth-century man in a starched shirt marooned amongst pioneers on a hard-scrabble farm.

I saw the notes, some decades old, from her distant American cousins who had long ago left Europe. She reprised the old family story from one day in 1923 when Chaim Weizmann challenged the New York philanthropist Felix Warburg to visit Palestine. Though skeptical of the Zionist experiment, my great-grandpa accepted Weizmann's dare on the spot; Felix set sail from New York within two weeks. He was floored by the efforts of the early Israeli settlers. He agreed to fund several projects, the construction of Hebrew University among them.

Eva's notes were matter-of-fact. Their absence of sentimentality rendered a stark clarity to the stakes involved, the risks and the consequences of decisions made at each crossroad by the Holocaust survivors. As I read her scrapbook, I could not help but think: *What if my family had lingered in Germany? What if I had escaped to Israel? What would be my views of politics and public policy under those* circumstances? Would I have left America and joined the IDF in 1948? What debt do I owe to my Jewish heritage? What impact has it had on my work in U.S. foreign policy?

Eva's testimony to events she lived through was remarkably humbling. Finally I understood her gift to two American travelers. I saw how she wanted us to bear witness to the remarkable—and triumphant—struggle of her years.

We were still grasping for context as we drove the next day up the sinuous path through ancient hills to Jerusalem. Lunch was with a National Democratic Institute country head. James was a self-confessed "democracy junkie." He was a recovering campaign advisor who successively led brave NDI do-gooder efforts to promote democracy in such global hot spots as Ukraine and Gaza, having left the latter post after a hail of gunfire led his wife to force him to choose between job and family.

As we sipped iced tea in ninety-five-degree heat, James explained the challenge of helping build civil society in the Occupied Territories while dealing with roadblocks, terrorists, and Mossad hackers penetrating their hard drives. He acknowledged the burden imposed on him by "political tourists," Washington policymakers who like to drop in during congressional junkets. He dodged the most sensitive questions, explaining with impressive singularity of focus: "I can't afford the luxury of having an opinion about the Israeli-Palestinian dispute. I have to work on building civil society on the West Bank, and just keeping my people from getting shot."

Afterwards, Jenn and I indulged in a madcap treasure hunt. We talked our way past armed guards at the gates of Hebrew University. Then we set off on a spontaneous search to find a statue of an early University donor: Felix Warburg.

At first, nobody could remember seeing his bust. "Maybe he's over in the stacks near Louis Brandeis," one librarian offered brightly.

With our gleeful shouts, we caused a commotion when, at last, we found him in the corner of the oldest building on the Mt. Scopus campus. Felix rested comfortably in marble likeness, grinning through his chiseled bust in a dusty corner of the Law Library.

As I snapped a photo of Jenn with my great-grandfather, a dark-skinned student from Beersheba shook his head in amazement at the family resemblance.[19]

We had another "Eureka" moment in a Jerusalem museum. This time the subject was plate tectonics. It had been a blasphemous running joke with us for days: *How was it that all those crossroads just happened to intersect there? Did Moses, Jesus, and Mohammed take part in some real estate deal?* It could not be a coincidence. Skeptical of divine intervention, we were convinced there was some more rational explanation. Yet none of our Israeli hosts could satisfy our persistent queries.

"Plate Tectonics and the Great African Rift Valley," we read at last. *That* was it. There was a plate rupture that ran from Lake Victoria clear up to the Caucusus. It carved the Gulf of Eilat, the Jordan, and the Galilee as surely as the San Andreas Fault produced California's Big Sur, Point Reyes, and Tomales Bay. You didn't have to be a geologist to discern it; you could see it on any decent map. "Across the great divide," indeed.

We read on. We learned that for eons, birds, animals, and humans alike had migrated the great north-south routes that ran along the fault line. Every few centuries, when the earth shifted, a Tiberius or a Scythopolis tumbled to the ground. Geology explained the crossroads. It explained why the great Mediterranean to Mesopotamia route bisected the same north-south paths that have run for millennia. Control a hill along the route and you become king for a day or a decade. It explained the strategic significance of Beit Sha'an. It explained the fights over the Golan Heights and the Jezreel Valley. It explained Jerusalem, the city on the hill above the crossroads that had stood since the beginning of human history, each successive inhabitant cannibalizing the stones of previous conquerors to renew the fortress.

On our last morning in Israel, we drove down through dusty canyons, through layers of checkpoints manned by heavily armed Israel Defense Forces. Down through desert heat to the Jordan border once more, past the off-limits walls of Jericho, past the haunting cliffs of Qumran where the Dead Sea scrolls were unearthed, we traveled all the way south on Route 90 to Ein Gedi. There we bobbed like corks in the Dead Sea as squealing tourists surrounded us at the lowest spot on the planet.

As we stared up at the sky, the voices from a dozen nations melted together. I reconsidered my Middle East politics. I began to envision Israel as another America, our best and our worst characteristics apparent. Israel in 2008 was a wondrous melting pot—Sephardim, Ashkenazi, Soviet refuseniks. Israelis had a way of consigning their darkest and poorest new immigrants to vulnerable frontier towns like Sderot and Kiryat Shemona where newcomers paid their dues playing the first line of defense against terrorists inhabiting the borders of unstable neighbors.

In Israel we found much greater tolerance of diversity. Conversely, we also found too great a reliance on disproportionate response, the bully boy determination of a Menachem Begin or a Benjamin Netanyahu to settle old scores with a hammer.

Floating in the Dead Sea amidst the cacophony of foreign voices, it struck me: We were so very much alike, Americans and Israelis. We thought highly of ourselves, while scorning our government. Our legislatures were utterly dysfunctional, the Knesset as bad as the Congress. Yet we proclaimed the virtues of democracy, ever eager to export our cure-all institutional nostrums. We were both lands of immigrants, proud of our assimilation, generally tolerant of newcomers.

Both peoples were materialistic, obsessing over cell phones and private cars. We speculated in pricey condos built alongside pockets of abject poverty. We were people of faith, yet majorities distrusted those who wore their religious faith on their sleeves. Moderates in both nations feared the angry fundamentalists and religious zealots amongst us. We did not understand why so many in other nations did not like us.

We caravanned back in anxious silence. A stream of autos accelerated up the long hills past IDF checkpoints to Jerusalem. The cars were homeward bound, travelers eager to get out of the occupied West Bank before nightfall. As we fled in our air-conditioned sedans, our pace quickened.

Once we parked, we hiked up the towers of King David's fort one more time to watch the sunset. A *son et lumière* show was unfolding in the ancient courtyard. As we looked across the Old City, we held in our gaze three of the holiest sites for three of the world's great religions. There was Al-Aqsa, the Temple Mount above the Western Wall, and the Church of the Holy Sepulchre.

We stood a long time without speaking. In the dying light, I was surprised to feel angry. We were staring at the killing grounds before us, where legions had murdered for centuries in the name of Allah, Yahweh, and Jesus. From Canaanites to Crusaders, they killed in some prophet's name, in a vain effort to purge Jerusalem of their predecessors and any memory of their faith. *They killed for what? For a wall? For a rock? For a slab of ground where a preacher died? With all our Tomahawk cruise missiles and Predator drones and nuclear warheads, have we really evolved that far?*

I reflected on my own feeble faith as I brooded. My personal traditions found modest comfort in Saint Francis of Assisi and the Lord's Prayer. I wondered why modern, supposedly civilized people—Muslims, Christians, and Jews—could not finally outgrow and reject religious fanaticism. It seemed obvious that intolerance could not be part of *any* loving god's design.

Tolerance, compromise, hopes for the future: I wanted to find each element there below our perch on the Old City walls. I was eager to believe that the many intelligent moderates among Palestinian and Israeli, Arab and Jew, could unite behind consensus. The peace was right in front of them, waiting to be made. Youssef had it right: They all knew where the borders would end up.

For one week in the middle of May 2008, I was blessed with the chance to see Israel—and consider America—anew. I slept lightly each night, waking to stare at the moon, to ponder old riddles. Dozens of scenes, both imagined and real, replayed themselves in my mind. Allenby and Weizmann traversed my dreams. Ancestors from Eva to Felix smiled down upon me. Lines from Uris and Michener floated in and out of my consciousness as I struggled to sort myth from reality. I thought of the pioneers of 1890, working the malarial swamps of the Jezreel Valley, elated to be free of czarist oppression. I thought of the Palestinian Arab farmers who fled their orchards one night in 1948, never to return. I thought of the future, and still felt that irrational, can-do American emotion: I felt hope.

We flew west the next morning. It was midday for twelve hours, a seemingly endless spring day, as the sun-splashed northern hemisphere passed below us, from Turkey to Germany, Ireland to Iceland, Nova Scotia, to New York and finally Washington.

I was content, fulfilled by the trip. Much as I loved Israel, however, I felt I would never need to visit again. Thanks to the fresh perspective, I had finally *seen* it. After so many visits, I finally knew the place for the first time.

Chapter Eleven

From the White House to Galvez House

Palo Alto
September 1978

"Washington wallpaper" is what cynics call the self-referential tableau that adorns many D.C. offices: scores of photos of their occupants alongside VIPs. The pictures provide a narrative arc for careers spent in public policy, with progressively more powerful figures featured as the office holder matures. Others come from expensive grip-and-grin rope lines at political fundraisers; these hint at a proximity to power, but can be purchased at a high price. Look closely: some of the more candid shots on these omnipresent vanity walls are often inscribed with a trash-talking joke.

It was a frigid morning early in 1978. As we headed to the White House signing ceremony for the Nuclear Non-Proliferation Act, my cousin Peter Bradford from the Nuclear Regulatory Commission (NRC) and I decided to make a game out of getting into a picture we felt we'd earned the hard way. Even then, we sensed a copy of the photograph would probably hang in our offices for decades to come.

There is ritual in such bill signings at 1600 Pennsylvania Avenue. Senior staffers fortunate enough to be invited arrive first, only to be gradually pushed aside. They are marginalized, despite the fact that they were usually the ones who wrote most of the bills being signed into law. Congressmen, including several chairmen who may have done next to nothing to advance the measures being celebrated, but who cannot be excluded based on their power or seniority, arrive closer to the designated hour and crowd the center. Equally busy, but even more self-important senators arrive, just in the nick of time, sliding to a position in front of their infuriated House colleagues. Finally, the door nearest the Oval Office opens. Senior Cabinet members enter to occupy the front row for the signing photo, legislators standing expectantly in what becomes a fawning backdrop for executive authority before the president enters and sits. In spite of themselves, legislators come to resemble courtiers before the almighty royalty; so much for co-equal branches of government.

Peter was an effective advocate of the strongest version of the nuclear nonproliferation bill. He'd warned me of the "crowding out" phenomenon at bill signings. A national environmental leader and a Carter appointee to the newly formed NRC, Peter had helped us for many months to overcome administration fears that a tough bill would irk foreign allies and harm U.S. nuclear exporters. Like me, he was loath to see some office holder who had actually *opposed* the measure press us to the wings at the photo opportunity.

We planned to get to the White House as early as allowed inside. We conspired to stand directly behind the president's chair, resolved to see just how long we could hold our places until some White House functionary shooed us away. We figured we would only last a few minutes, despite the fact that Peter stood six foot eight and weighed over 250 pounds. I came in at six foot six, though skinny as a rail. Among the first escorted into the Cabinet Room that morning, we stood in our selected spot; we weren't easy to move.

We struggled to keep straight faces as the crowd of State Department staffers and Republican legislators, several of whom had actively resisted the bill, grew. They included Idaho Republican Senator Jim McClure, who had worked for months to gut the bill's key provisions. Feet were stepped on. Shoulders were nudged. Proud elected officials jostled for position. Nobody managed to dislodge us. Committee chairmen Clement Zablocki and John Sparkman did slide in alongside. Then the two heroic leaders of the effort, John Glenn and Jack Bingham, arrived moments before the president, barely elbowing into the picture, to the chagrin of Vice President Walter Mondale, his irritation still apparent in the weathered photo.

President Carter signs the Nuclear Non-Proliferation Act on March 10, 1978. Representative Jack Bingham, author of the House measure, was late and had to squeeze in front of a visibly irritated Vice President Walter Mondale. I'm standing in the back row behind President Carter. That is NRC Commissioner Peter Bradford to my right, along with other key staff authors of bill drafts; Don Fortier to the far left of the front row; and Len Weiss with a beard and glasses on the far right, looking over Secretary of Energy James Schlesinger's pipe. The two chairmen between us and President Carter are Senator John Sparkman, an Alabama Democrat, and Clem Zablocki, the Wisconsin Democrat. Five elements were key to the NNPA's successful passage: (1) the Zablocki-Findley and Senate provisions initially blocked by the JCAE; (2) the Bingham initiative to abolish the JCAE; (3) the first House-passed version of the NNPA; (4) the Glenn version of the Senate bill, which included Weiss' improvements, that survived the floor mauling; and (5) the House maneuver to bypass conference, pass the Senate bill, and send the Senate version to the White House for signing.

As the shutters clicked upon President Carter's entry, there we were, Bradford and Warburg, standing frozen in the back row, like presidential bodyguards. Preserved in a now yellowed photograph from the White House Press Office, our faces are pensive, but we were smiling inside. We'd helped pass the bill—and we'd gotten into the center of the photo, striking a blow for staffers everywhere.

Bingham drove me back to Congress in his aging Buick, which he had parked between the Old Executive Office Building and the West Wing. It was a ride to relish. He was as gracious as ever, a boyish grin punctuating his patrician air.

"We did it!" he exclaimed, slapping his knee as we drove slowly through the White House gates and out onto Pennsylvania Avenue. Bingham had accomplished something that seemed impossible just two years earlier. The congressman confessed he did not think we could overcome the Joint Committee, the nuclear industry, the Senate, the State Department, and the White House. He addressed me as he would a contemporary and a colleague. We were both still rather stunned by the success we had improbably wrought. He knew, far better than I, that this would likely be the crowning accomplishment of his forty years of public service.

The impact proved both swift and enduring. Beginning in 1978, the global market for reactor sales was altered profoundly. Atoms for Peace died. For the next thirty-five years, and counting, the U.S. did not sell any power reactors overseas. European suppliers halted their practice of enticing Third World customers with promiscuous offers of uranium enrichment and fuel reprocessing plants capable of producing weapons-grade materiel. No more offers of enrichment plants for Brazil, or plutonium extraction facilities for Pakistan or South Korea. The law worked, mostly because it bought time. Two decades would pass before another nation made a calculated decision to test a nuclear weapon, which did not come until 1998, a much-delayed Pakistani response to India's 1974 nuclear warhead explosion.

Bingham and I could not have foreseen such results when we returned to the Rayburn Building that March day. All I knew for sure was that back at the office, the congressman's chief of staff, Gordon Kerr, awaited. There were stacks of unanswered constituent letters on my desk. There were Department of Justice grant applications to review, letters of recommendation to service academies to pen, "Dear Colleague" letters soliciting cosponsorship of mundane matters such as National Dairy Week to evaluate. The workaday world of a junior House staffer beckoned. It was a return to normalcy, but a norm to which I did not look forward.

2251 Rayburn House Office Building, April 1977.

Gordon called me into his office and closed the door. He was shaking his head.

"Boy, did you screw up!" He was shouting, his tone accusatory, but his exaggerated manner hinted at his purpose.

"You totally screwed up!" he repeated, waving his arms as he worked himself up in mock exasperation. "I mean, what the hell are you going to do for an encore? You could work in this town for the rest of your life, but you have nowhere to go but down!"

He was right, of course. *What next, indeed?* There was no point resisting this arresting truth. So I resolved to prove him wrong, though I really hadn't a clue how.

At a young age, I had developed a slightly anal habit of making lists. Many were simply "to-do lists" of things I needed to get done over the course of the day. Yet as I stumbled back to my desk that March morning, I found it difficult to concentrate on the backlog of routine tasks before me. I stared at the wall of my office cubicle for a long time.

I was thinking, dreaming bigger dreams. Ignoring the stacks of paper on my desk inside our crowded Rayburn Building office, I began to make a list of all the things I hoped to accomplish someday in Washington.

This early bucket list had on it six professional goals. I wanted to travel to both the Soviet Union and China, to see the godless Commies face to face. I wanted to make an official visit to Israel and the Middle East, and begin to sharpen my own views on how the search for peace might progress. I wanted somehow to work with the Senate Foreign Relations Committee, then still the most revered panel in Congress. I wanted to write a novel and have it published. Most ambitiously, I dreamed I'd someday end up back at the university, writing about the process by which legislators tried to get things done in Washington.

Growing up in Marin County, I had never planned any particular career path. Before I graduated from Redwood High, my pitching record let me fantasize briefly about a career in baseball. In my reckless youth, I assumed I wouldn't live past thirty; we took a lot of risks. So as I sat at a desk in Washington jotting down items for my first bucket list, it seemed unlikely many would come to fruition.

I was lost in such daydreaming often that spring. *What was it I was trying to accomplish? How much of infiltrating the Cabinet Room was just an ego trip? What was my enduring purpose in Washington?*

Such cosmic matters weighed on me for weeks after the White House ceremony, as I was beset by some sort of postpartum blues. There were constituent letters to respond to about potholes and traffic lights. There were veterans benefit checks to be tracked down. There were school crossing guards to be congratulated. By providing assistance to an individual Bingham constituent, something tangible had been accomplished that day, but in my self-reflective doldrums, I was a listless and unproductive employee.

Gordon's challenge haunted me. Maybe I *was* just an adrenaline junkie with nowhere to go but down. Maybe working in politics *was* just a hunt for a new rush, an eagerness to gain access to the corridors of power and to make some small mark. As a teenager, I had always wanted to go higher, faster, farther. Some of the mischief I got into was petty, misdemeanors like climbing high fences for a midnight skinny-dip with my high school classmates. I'd sneak out with my kid brother Jason at 2 a.m. to ride bikes through the deserted center of our small hometown. The release of endorphins and the racing of the heart had an effect I wanted to repeat. With young women, I was way too eager to race around first base, then sprint straight for home. I always had an intense curiosity. At poker games, what would happen if I raised again, despite a risky hand? What excitement might another hit bring?

Way over my head in my early days on congressional staff, I feared one thing above all else: the numbing effects of boredom. Having challenged the Joint Committee, and having helped draft and pass the nuclear reform law, I wasn't eager to be consigned to answering the morning mail. Panic set in at the prospect.

There were a few happy interludes. I observed Dianne Stamm, a delightful colleague in Bingham's office, as she labored on a project Bingham and Senate sponsor Charles Mathias had pursued for years. They were trying to get an agreement to place the first statue of a black man in the U.S. Capitol. Senator Barry Goldwater, who thought Martin Luther King, Jr. was a Communist agitator, only relented when Arizona was promised an accompanying Carl Hayden statue. Today, the striking King bust is in the central rotunda alongside those of Washington, Lincoln, and Jefferson.

I also sat in on Bingham's subcommittee hearings, where such patient elders as Roger Majak and Vic Johnson tried to teach me about international economic policy. At my desk each day, however, I felt the quiet terror of tedium.

Gordon was right. I *had* peaked way too soon. I was not going to be content "down on the farm" now that I had seen the big city's excitement. In order to step forward professionally, I concluded, I'd now have to take a step back. The best time to leave a poker table, after all, is when you're on a winning streak.

It was time to fill in the gaping holes left by my funky Hampshire College education. I had no formal training in law or economics. I was thin on history and trade policy. I had studied no foreign countries; I was ignorant of China, Japan, and the Soviet Union, and I knew little about strategic arms control policy.

Three years on Capitol Hill had saved me from one thing, though: law school. I now saw no need for a law degree in order to help save the world. Staffers needed only an idea and a strategy; a quick phone call to Legislative Counsel could produce bill language within hours. Each of my older brothers had found a gratifying niche within the world of the law—I'd looked up to Andy and Pete forever—yet I sensed that a legal education was not essential for the policymaking hopes I harbored.

Off went graduate school applications to London and Cambridge and, almost as an afterthought, to Stanford. I could picture myself at Harvard's Kennedy School of Government or the London School of Economics. I often joked, however, that I'd never had a serious thought about politics inside California state lines.

I was offered admission to all three graduate programs—schools that surely would have rejected my application had it not been accompanied by Congressman Bingham's letter of recommendation and the evidence of my work as a young Capitol Hill aide. As I pondered my good fortune, luck intervened once more.

One night over a few beers, I wrote an article rhapsodizing on the pleasures of working at a young age on policy matters in Washington. It was published in May 1976 as sort of a love letter to D.C. in the Sunday *Washington Star*.[20] Fortuitously, it caught the eye of a former journalist from California named Alan Cranston, who just happened to be the majority whip in the U.S. Senate. Out of the blue, Senator Cranston wrote me a complimentary note and invited me to come say hello sometime in his Capitol office.

My mother did not raise a fool; I called the senator's secretary first thing the next morning for an appointment.

As our conversation about California and nuclear arms control developed—it was clear that Senator Cranston was also an impatient idealist—he invited me to come see him if ever I was ready to make a job change. So when the prospect of graduate school seemed imminent, I returned once more to the Whip's Office in the Capitol for advice.

When I visited one warm day in May of 1978, Cranston congratulated me on my role in helping craft the Nuclear Non-Proliferation Act, and invited me to be his deputy foreign policy advisor. I was flabbergasted, but I was also afraid. If I accepted now, I would be in way over my head once again. My experience with the Nuclear Non-Proliferation Act effectively masked the fact that I had little academic training in foreign affairs, no area or country studies, and no classes in political theory.

I begged off, thanking him profusely.

"What?!" screeched Cranston in reply, a grin splitting his face as he flapped his arms in the air. His seersucker suit jacket flew open like a parachute. "You're turning down a chance to join a senior senator's staff? Do you mind explaining *why*?"

Cranston had a childish sense of mischief, one that put even a young aide at ease. So I laid out my thinking.

"I just have the sense that I need more education, more academic training," I said, rather unconvincingly. He frowned. "I mean, if I don't go back to fill in the holes in my education now, I'll be one of those political junkies forever. You know, a generalist with an opinion about everything, but who doesn't really know what he's talking about. So I'm going to do this two-year Masters of Public Policy program at the Kennedy School. It's likely that I'll be coming back to Washington afterwards."

His face fell deeper, animated into an exaggerated pout. I felt as if I'd insulted him.

He did little to ease my pain, shaking his head incredulously through a long silence as he plotted his next move. His secretary Mary Lou McNeely interrupted us; he was needed on the Senate floor. I rose to leave, thinking our interview was done, my audience in one of the most elegant rooms in the Capitol ending.

"Wait here," he instructed. "I'll be back in a bit."

I sat alone in his office, squirming for nearly half an hour. My discomfort was exquisite. Would I ever have such a great opportunity again? I was sitting in S-148, the office of the Senate majority whip, where LBJ and Bobby Baker used to swing their deals over cigars and whiskey. Out the window, I could see all the way past the Washington Monument to the Potomac River. Tourists aimed their cameras, gazing up at the west front of the Capitol. Taxis and buses bisected the Mall. Planes settled gently into a landing pattern over the deep blue river. *What a view*, I thought. *What an idiot I am for saying no!*

When Senator Cranston returned, he was wearing small reading glasses, eyeing a long tally sheet that had the names of all one hundred senators. He had marked it up in pencil and scrawled a series of symbols next to a dozen names. He was counting, checking votes for the looming Panama Canal Treaty ratification fight. It was, I knew, the whip's daily calling, and Cranston's great forte. Then he took off his glasses and his troublemaker's grin returned.

"*So?* Have you come to your senses?" He clearly wasn't used to being turned down. Nevertheless, I declined again, apologizing for my folly.

He sighed, then added contemptuously, "*Harvard*, huh?"

I nodded.

He paused a few moments more. He was thinking on his feet, devising a proposal. A politician accustomed to spontaneous dealing, he seemed to search, and find, an alternative path to victory. Then he changed my life on the spot.

"Tell ya what," he said, barreling ahead. "You go to Stanford, not Harvard. Take one year for your master's degree, not two. Stay in touch with my office while you're out there. Maybe draft a couple of speeches for me, tag along when I do a road show in the state. Let me suggest some professors I know at Stanford you ought to work with—Lewis on China, George on force and diplomacy, Drell on nuclear—and I'll save the job slot for you 'til you come back. Deal?"

I weighed the offer for about two seconds, then broke into a grin nearly as wide as his. "Yes, *sir.*"

Within months, I was pedaling my blue Schwinn down bike paths amidst the faux Spanish mission courtyards in Palo Alto. I got to spend my days learning the best principles and practices of foreign affairs with some of the leading professors on campus—Alexander George, John Lewis, Sid Drell, Wolfgang Panofsky, Bart Bernstein, and Bob Keohane. The teaching assistants in my courses, several of whom became lifelong friends, were such scholars as Tom Fingar, Chip Blacker, and Roger George. Condoleezza Rice and Harry Harding were also part of their cohort.

They were generous with their time, and were keenly aware of my potential to help support their issues back in Washington. Cranston was a local hero, a Palo Alto native and a Stanford alum. They paired me with the Arms Control Program fellows, the scientists from the Stanford Linear Accelerator, and the China Program scholars, including some of the first post-doctoral exchange students Beijing authorities allowed to study in the West. There were engrossing simulations of U.S.-Soviet strategic arms limitation negotiations. There were private dinners with visiting Japanese trade ministry officials. There was methodical training in how to dissect Beijing's *People's Daily*.

I was in heaven. Weekdays, I was immersed in analysis of the great international issues of our times. Weekends, I was back in Marin County with family, soaking in the smells of laurel and eucalyptus, hiking along the Pacific coastline, or sitting on a deck overlooking San Francisco Bay. I was being schooled by experts whose focus was Washington and the world. My old nightmare of having to go backwards, back to California, back to unworldly Redwood High, was turned on its head. Here was a sabbatical that enriched, a return that renewed and inspired.

I was living in a dream, one I fully appreciated at the time. I would savor it once again, years later, as the memories tumbled forth into a novel I set in Stanford seminar rooms and along the cliffs of Marin's Point Reyes. In my fictional account, *The Mandarin Club*, all the main characters leave California for Washington and intense careers as policymakers, patriots, or spies.[21] Ethical dilemmas confront them mid-life as they must choose between principle and politics, between ideals and self-interested career advancement. In the end, most find their way back to where they first knew great happiness, on university grounds.

In the fall of 1978, life on a sylvan campus surrounded by ambitious dreamers was full of premonition. Even then I was conscious of the eerie foreshadowing. All around me were hints of lives not yet fully lived. As my peaceful present flowed, dreamlike, into my imagined future, I knew that someday, somehow, I too would find my way back.

CHAPTER TWELVE

No Final Victories

San Francisco, California
October 2010

Life imitates art. Art, in turn, imitates life. In my peculiar career, this had become a recurring cycle, even before I turned fifty. I couldn't help but be amused.

When I finally got an unmistakable sense it was time to leave Washington, it was a challenge to channel the energy the decision unleashed. I wanted to once again feel as if I was exploring something new, to find some fresh perspective.

As a young man, I felt an intense desire to take risks, to contribute something meaningful. I first felt the adrenaline rush on the baseball diamond. On the mound, a quirky, unhittable knuckleball gave me a miniscule earned run average and the brief fantasy of shaping events. When I toed the pitching rubber and held the ball, time would stand still. The control freak in me was in charge.

I had the same feeling during my brief tenure as a student actor. Given the lead in the senior class play, Kaufman and Hart's *The Man Who Came to Dinner*, I revealed far too much of my character in the first scene. In no subsequent theater role did I rise above mediocrity. Impatience is a weakness not easily overcome.

Work in Washington offered a daily struggle of good versus evil. It was satisfying, especially to the young; it could reinforce a righteous hunger for justice. Never good at nuance, I supported progressive legislators, and I found great motivation in taking on Ronald Reagan, Oliver North, and similar politicians who insulted my binary sense of right and wrong.

When I left public service and began, to my surprise, to enjoy private enterprise, it wasn't just the salary that gratified. We lobbying partners all had hunter-gatherer roots; we felt validated by the financial harvest. My family lived simply, however. No yachts and no second homes in the country. We saved for college tuition and travel, and cultivated few extravagant tastes. Money was an excellent way of keeping score—accumulating some made you feel you were getting ahead. I liked to win. I liked the contest of ideas, the devising of tactics. Gerry Cassidy explained lobbying to me on one of my first days at his firm.

"We're like a baseball team," he said. "Not everybody needs to hit a homer or throw a shutout. Some guys can just be a LOOGY—you know, a Left-handed One-Out Guy we bring in from the bullpen to retire just one key left-handed batter. You gotta know how to use your team to win."

When I was young, I made many mistakes. My "just do it" approach was not exactly a deep philosophy; we Baby Boomers could be embarrassingly juvenile in our pursuit of excitement.

One of the calming pleasures of later years is to savor the irony. Somehow, as life slows, the gods offer you perspective. The best perspective on life can sometimes be found at thirty-five thousand feet. Flying from Washington, D.C. to California, back and forth across the country over and over again, year after year, I began to gain clarity in my rambling letters home. The scenes I imagined while scribbling notes for a novel threatened to materialize. My notes were part therapy, part recovery.

By late summer 2010, many of the characters from whom I had drawn composites for *The Mandarin Club* were, in reality, returning west. Joy and I were visiting colleges with our youngest son Dylan. At seventeen, he was taken with the West. He seemed to feel a natural affinity for the eclectic minds he encountered from Boulder to Berkeley. He challenged authority, always with a confident commitment to better public policy. He was shaggy-haired, with an Abe Lincoln beard and a hunger for mountain adventures and international travel that reminded me, hauntingly, of my younger self. Dylan was determined, like his brother and sister before him, to head west. A scholarship in environmental engineering at Colorado was one option, California another.

We ended up one October morning rolling up Palm Drive in Palo Alto. As we ambled along the shaded walkways of the Stanford campus, we passed the offices of Chip Blacker, formerly of the NSC during the Clinton administration, and former Secretary of State Condi Rice. Tom Fingar, one of my most respected interlocutors from the intelligence community, had also come home to Palo Alto to write and teach. Jennifer had driven down from her new job in San Francisco—she had moved twenty-five hundred miles west from Charlottesville and was living in my father's house. She was working on urban planning and green cities legislation, yet more evidence that life moves in cycles.

I'd been invited to lecture at Stanford about the politics of nuclear nonproliferation; the forum was with the same program I'd attended thirty years before. Here were the bookends upon which I had based a novel of my imaginings years before.

What to say? We'd been so certain of our convictions back in the day of nuclear nonproliferation purity. In the mid-1970s, we insisted that the United States had to set standards for our nuclear exports, that lowest-common-denominator policies led to promiscuous proliferation, a grave threat to U.S. national security. American policymakers had to buy time; we had to delay the rise of dozens of new nuclear powers President Kennedy had warned about. There would be no final victories in this contest.

Critics had claimed our draconian prescriptions would cripple the U.S. nuclear export business for a generation. They had said India, Pakistan, and North Korea would build nukes anyway.

We were both right.

I said as much in my Stanford reunion speech. The title of my address was a mouthful: "Nonproliferation Policy Crossroads: Lessons Learned from the Strange Case of the US-India Nuclear Cooperation Agreement of 2008."[22] George W. Bush, my least favorite president, had waived key sanctions in the Nuclear Non-Proliferation Act to cozy up to India. Senators Biden, Clinton,

Feinstein, and Obama had voted to approve the deal. My sense of the macabre evolved into a driving curiosity to answer several basic questions: How did a lame duck Republican president get a Democratic Congress to go along? Why did Democratic senators approve?

It took months to research the matter; I was peeling away spare hours from the lobbying business to interview participants in the congressional consideration. It wasn't that hard to figure out, actually. Time passes. The right prescription for 1978 was no longer the best policy thirty years later. I was chagrined to find I agreed with Bush's basic premise.

After answering the last student's question, I slipped away quickly. The Giants were just a couple wins away from a return to the World Series. Friends and family awaited at the Oasis, site of the *Mandarin Club* protagonists' drinking games. It was still the first inning when we arrived, and then I was lost, once more, in a reverie. Amidst the smells of burgers and beer at the Oasis, and shouts from truck drivers and soccer moms wearing Giants hats, I was transported back in time.

One of the most important jobs of parents, it is said, is to be the custodian of their kids' happy memories. When it came to the San Francisco Giants, though, I was never sure who were the adults and who were the kids.

I grew up in a household where, win or lose, love of the Giants was a unifying factor. Dad was a New Yorker, but he and Mom had moved to California late in 1952. I was born north of San Francisco just weeks before the Giants had won their last world championship, which was when they still made their home in New York.

When the Giants joined us in the West in 1958, they were a source of never-ending delight in our home. We collected stacks and stacks of their baseball cards; Willie Kirklands, Johnny Antonellis, Jim Davenports. Some of my earliest memories are of eating peanut butter and jelly sandwiches at Seals Stadium with my cousin Dorothy, or chasing Willie McCovey home runs that would rattle around in the green wooden bleachers of Candlestick Park behind the chain-link fence in right field.

I was sitting with my brothers and Dad at Candlestick on Fan Appreciation Day, Sunday, September 30, 1962. Willie Mays homered in his last batting appearance of the regular season to win the game 2-1. Just after it ended, Russ Hodges was making final announcements to the crowd of forty-two thousand over the public address system. Four hundred and fifteen miles to the south, the last Dodger batter dug in. Suddenly, Hodges shouted: "He pops up to Javier—and we have a playoff!" Mom was so cool that she let us stay home from school to watch the seventh game of the World Series—"World Series-itis," she called it. Conveniently, we all caught the disease.

Our reward was decades of shared pleasure, and decades of heartbreak. For more than half a century, the Giants story was that of Sisyphus and Job, of near misses far more painful than those endured by decades of Chicago Cubs and Red Sox fans, where mediocrity had reigned for years. Like Lucy with Charlie Brown, the baseball gods kept pulling the ball away just when Giants fans were *finally* about to see that satisfying hit. Together, we shared these sorrows. Bobby Richardson snares Willie McCovey's liner, inches from the 1962 World Series win. Giants star Orlando Cepeda gets traded, then wins the MVP and a World Series . . . for the St. Louis Cardinals. Five consecutive divisional second-place finishes, despite the fact that the Giants of the 1960s played with five Hall of Famers.

Years of mediocrity followed. Nevertheless, Andy, Pete, Jason, and I would make annual pilgrimages to Candlestick Park together. We'd share stories from the *Chronicle's Sporting Green* and earnestly believe in Next Year. We moved to different cities to raise our families. Yet we still approached each season filled with hope. We met early one spring at a Giants Fantasy Camp, to which Mom, in a fit of wild extravagance, had paid our way. I even got to pitch to Willie Mays, and he posed with a grin alongside my brothers and Mom.

Still, no World Series title came. As in politics, it seemed, there were no final victories. The curse continued. The 1987 playoff meltdown in St. Louis. The 1989 Earthquake Series, when

Oakland flattened the Giants four games to none with a two-man pitching rotation of Stewart and Welch. The 1993 Giants won 103 games, but ended the last day in second place, one game behind. The Giants' 5-0 lead in the seventh inning of the Series-clinching Game Six against the 2002 Angels? It was horrifically blown, seven outs from victory, amidst a blizzard of rally monkeys that would haunt my dreams for years. So close, so very close—the Champagne was literally set out in the Giants' clubhouse in 2002—but there was no victory to celebrate.

For months each summer, through times of happiness and of trouble, love of the Giants strengthened my bonds with my brothers and our kids. As with Mom and Dad, Giants worship became a special gift I shared with my son Zack. After homework was done, through the miracle of the Internet, we'd log onto MLB.com. There, in his darkened Arlington bedroom, well past the time kids should be asleep, we listened together as the Giants announcers, Mike Krukow and Duane Kuiper, would broadcast the games from the West Coast, chatting with us like two lifelong friends.

I was transported back to foggy nights at Candlestick Park, where the air was heavy with cannabis and catcalls. Zack and I would call the shots, predicting late-inning torture as the Giants' arsonist relievers, Casilla and Wilson, would fan the flames before finally putting out the fires. Zack would indulge me as I shared stories from games of my youth, chasing foul balls and chanting singsong obscenities about the L.A. Dodgers.

It was both therapy for me and a tenderness shared with him. We'd laugh so hard it hurt, as we howled at the one-liners we'd predicted seconds before Kruk and Kuip uttered them. It was companionship and camaraderie at its best, a tie that flowed in the mainstream from father to son. Here were shared memories of joy, of trial and failure, of getting up again and trying once more. Here were lessons from life and politics, ones that readily related to the challenges Zack faced and triumphed over each day of high school.

A Giants World Championship rose to the top of my bucket list. My children teased me about it. *Could we win, just once, in my lifetime?* I eyed the calendar in April 2010 as my brothers and I took Dad, now eighty-six, to a ballgame. I asked my friend, Father Steve Privett of the University of San Francisco, if it was okay to pray for a baseball championship.

"No," he said, smiling gently, "the Lord does not facilitate sports outcomes. But you *could* just pray for the joy of sharing the struggle together."

Later that year, I helped Jenn settle into San Francisco, and we began to sense something magical was afoot, despite the team's remarkable ability (like Democrats) to snatch defeat from the jaws of victory. On my first morning in town, we headed onto the Muni for the Farmer's Market at the Ferry Building.

After days of thick fog, the sun was breaking through on the bay side of town. Riding with us in the old trolley car was a tightly packed late-morning crowd, quintessentially San Franciscan in their diversity. Folks of all ages and all races were dressed almost entirely in orange and black. Little old ladies wore hats festooned with "Croix de Candlestick." Men with canes carried transistor radios. It was clear they were all headed to a Giants game.

"C'mon, Dad," Jenn said firmly, after we shopped at the market. She was pulling at my elbow. "Change of plan."

She steered us south to walk along the waterfront toward the ballpark. By the time we arrived, the stadium was crammed full, another weekday sellout. Chicago was in town. Even though the Giants were in fourth place, the bleachers had a carnival-like mood throughout. Strangers chatted amiably. Cub fans were welcomed by the good-natured S.F. crowd, a spirit of bipartisanship flowering on this, a Ferris Bueller's day off for baseball fans of all persuasions. In the standing room-only section behind an orange line in the concrete, young bankers in suits playing hooky from the office stood next to scruffy junior high school kids on summer break.

The Giants already trailed 3-1 when we squeezed in with two bleacher tickets bought from a scalper. The Giants' Pat Burrell hit the next pitch almost into my lap. We cheered and high-fived, while the foghorn blew in celebration. Three pitches later, Pablo "Panda" Sandoval dunked a home run into San Francisco Bay, setting off fountains and another celebration. Next inning, Burrell came up with the bases loaded, and promptly blasted a grand slam off the foul pole. It was the third Giants homer in less than two innings.

"It's magic, Dad!" Jenn shouted through the delirium. "It's *Giants* magic!"

Some torture ensued—it was the team's trademark that season to leave fans squirming through tense late-inning meltdowns. The Giants blew the 7-3 lead, yet they squeaked out an 8-7 win in the bottom of the ninth. With two outs, a benchwarmer named Aaron Rowand hit a dribbler with a man on third, then dove headlong into first base just as the winning run scored.

As summer turned to fall, the charmed play continued. The team reeled off an impossible run. Zack on the West Coast and I on the East would watch the telecasts; we were virtually together through the power of the Internet. I'd call him on my commute home before a big game: "Beat L.A.!" I'd say. He'd answer confidently, the mantra empowering and reconnecting. From fourth place, seven games behind, the Giants made a dash for glory.

Rookies twirled shutouts. Veterans with torn muscles found new life. Balls bounced crazily on chalk. Misfits from the trash heap—players like Andres Torres and Cody Ross, who had been released by other teams—rediscovered their batting strokes at the party by San Francisco Bay. The Giants buried the Dodgers, the Rockies, the Padres, and then eliminated the Braves.

My brothers began to gather in San Francisco as the playoff run continued. Friends I hadn't heard from in decades found me online, sending notes of shared appreciation for our Giants.

The night before my Stanford lecture, I witnessed a tense playoff game with family. It was a 6-5 walk-off win for the Giants. It broke the backs of the two-time National League champion Phillies, with play after clutch play leading the way. Afterwards, hoarse and exhausted, we walked down King Street as crowds met in the streets, bar denizens racing out to high-five the triumphant fans leaving the park. The whole city was electric.

I couldn't make it back to San Francisco for the World Series. I shared the games in real time, though, on the phone and e-mailing with far-flung family. As the Giants manhandled the Rangers on their way to a 3-1 World Series lead, Dylan and I sat by the fire in Virginia to watch the next game, with Kruk and Kuip on satellite radio to accompany the muted Fox telecast. I texted and called my family out west and my friends from Redwood High. Through cyberspace and the Internet, we counted down the final outs until bearded Brian Wilson blew his cut fastball by the last Texas batter.

That gang of rejects and rookies had done it. There they were, dancing on the mound, shaggy-haired Tim Lincecum riding on the team's shoulders, thrusting his hand in the air.

For the first time in their fifty-two-year history, you could shout it: "The San Francisco Giants are world champions!"

Family and friends who attended the parade two days later confirmed that it was epic. Nearly one million people of all ages celebrated the length of the concrete canyons, the city a cauldron of noise. I watched every minute behind a closed door in my Washington office, speaking with each of my brothers in turn. There I sat in a high-rise building near the White House, a fifty-six-year-old man in a suit and tie, with tears of joy flowing freely.

"You need a new bucket list," Zack said when he called.

The San Francisco Giants had done it, at last. They gave us that one cathartic triumph, that one final victory so elusive in politics and in life. It seemed to blow away all those years of misses, years of losing elections and fumbling playoffs.

Now I really had to believe in the magic. I could believe in the possibility of one completely satisfying victory, be it in politics, life . . . or just baseball.

CHAPTER THIRTEEN

The Catbird Seat: Life in the Senate

Washington, D.C.
July 1979

All statistics freaks are alike, be they Major League Baseball executives or political scientists. Baseball managers and academics both enjoy devising elaborate charts and graphs to determine the odds of success for a hit-and-run play or a cloture vote. Both often fail to factor in the human element, however, the remarkable power of personality to alter the predicted outcome. That is what party whips and ballplayers do for a living.

The power of extraordinary personalities is on display daily in the well of the U.S. Senate, the same Senate which John Kerry, on his last day in office, would note is "a living museum, a lasting memorial to the miracle of the American experiment." Getting to know one hundred different individuals, and trying to predict how each senator would vote, was my job during parts of three decades of my life.

I had a front row seat for each performance in this contest of egos and wills. From the late 1970s into the early '90s, I sat for days on end in a small armless leather chair placed carefully in the first row on the Democratic side of the aisle, wedged between the majority leader's armchair and that of my boss, the party whip, Alan Cranston of California. I was ten feet from the geographic center of the Senate chamber, both witness to and participant in the exercise of legislative power.

I was supposed to be an expert on international matters. My issue portfolio included defense, foreign policy, arms control, trade, and intelligence. My top priority, however, was simple: Count the votes. *Is Bill Bradley with us on the Japanese trade amendment? Will we get Dick Lugar on the South Africa sanctions bill? Can we cut off CIA aid to the Nicaraguan contras if we get John Glenn's vote?* These were the types of questions that drove my agenda each day.

More than the speeches I drafted, more than the articles and amendments I wrote, my job was to figure out the individual personalities. *How many are with us? How many are against us? How do we get to fifty-one?* That's what my boss needed to know. Then, and only then, could we develop good legislative options.

Fifty-one was the magic number then; this was in the decades before the gross abuse of the filibuster required a Senate supermajority of sixty for all but the most meaningless motherhood and apple pie resolutions. This was in the heyday of what one recent author, my former staff colleague Ira Shapiro, has called "The Last Great Senate."[23] These were years when you could still cut bipartisan deals and move intelligent legislation, if you knew how to count and were willing to settle for half a loaf. You could use the Senate's disdain for the House to leverage a position, then exploit the legislators' suspicion of the White House to build a united front. You could get stuff done; Congress was consequential.

We had our own little world there inside the Senate chamber, a windowless room that was surprisingly small. The air was rather stale. During a long debate, you could completely lose track of time. Some evenings, I'd walk out onto the Capitol terrace during a quorum call and, as I squinted toward the setting sun down the Mall in the west, I would be surprised to find an ambient temperature, or witness an approaching storm. I was consumed sometimes for hours, for days on end, by the drama inside. The world of my childhood friends back in Northern California seemed far, far away.

When defense, foreign policy, trade, or intelligence bills were under consideration, I was at Alan Cranston's elbow for the duration. The senator was nearly as tall and skinny as I was. An awkward Scotsman, he had white sideburns, but on top was as bald as a cue ball. Alan would lope up the Senate steps two at a time, grinning mischievously. He always believed the glass of life was more than half full. He thought he could convince even Senator Jesse Helms that welfare moms deserved a break, if only he could get the senator from North Carolina to reason with him for a moment.

Cranston was a reporter by training. He took note of every nuance in his colleagues' remarks. He swapped insights regularly with journalists who covered the Hill. He was an ardent capitalist, from a family with successful real estate holdings in the San Francisco Peninsula. He was also a bit of a utopian, an optimist who believed in the power of reason, who appealed to the self-interest of all, and to the public good. A committed liberal, he'd compromise readily if he could get 51 percent of what he wanted done that day.

As with Senator Hubert Humphrey, politics was a joyous calling for Cranston, an important, if quite serious, game. He had the same attitude with his frequent fundraising. "Dialing for dollars," he'd call it. He was known as "the senator with a pocketful of dimes," so readily would he load the pay phones to solicit funds for his causes, even as he waited for planes at airport departure gates.

Ronald Reagan, Dick Nixon, and the California right wing were his lifelong political enemies. From their opponents, Alan Cranston would raise vast sums of campaign dollars. He'd block out hours during recess afternoons in his campaign office to work with his staff calling rich folks for donations. Many of his colleagues found the task repugnant, beneath the dignity of senators. He'd raise money for his fellow senators and Democratic challengers from all over the country. He'd raise money for the California state party. He'd raise money to register voters in under-represented African American and Hispanic communities. He'd raise money for candidates committed to expanding federal park lands in California and Alaska, to nuclear arms control, and to women's rights.

Cranston made a contest of it. In the early 1980s, he would partner with the most cheerful of his aides, a bright young woman from Southern California by way of U.C. Berkeley named Joy Jacobson. Joy was a marine biology and political science major who had interned in Alan's San Francisco office, then moved east to work for Cranston on California projects. Alan recognized brains and talent; he assembled on his staff a remarkable number of sharp young aides whom he invested with substantial authority—Kam Kuwata, Sergio Bendixen, Demaris Brinton, Dan Perry, Colleen Sechrest, Gina Genton, and Priscilla Burton among them.

California's longest serving Democratic senator, Alan Cranston, with his Washington staff, in December 1983.

Joy was promoted rapidly from a position working on California funding for projects from beach restoration to light rail construction. Soon, she had risen to a deputy position in the press office, and then to a role as the senator's chief fundraiser.

Sometimes, Joy would sit at a small table by the west-facing window in S-148, working with Cranston to develop lists for subsequent calls to potential donors. She'd work from sheets of yellow lined paper, a handwritten call list they would compile from a virtual "who's who" of environmentalists, arms control advocates, Israel supporters, real estate developers, feminists, labor activists, and Hollywood producers—Cranston's core constituencies. Alan would sit behind his large oak desk, which was invariably piled high with stacks of legislative files, newspaper clippings, and staff memos on pending issues. Both would be armed with legal pads with donor profiles and dollar targets. Together they would hunt for political capital.

Joy would tolerate me slipping into the senator's office, where I'd often linger to go over a point of legislative strategy with the senator. She was tough, she had a wicked sense of humor, and she was strikingly attractive. She also had the impeccable taste to be a San Francisco Giants fan. While we would wait as the senator ran up the back staircase of the Capitol to vote, our own conversations developed.

After many years of jousting, we began to date. We kept it secret for months, slipping away together to places like Charlottesville, where we'd walk on the Lawn and picnic in front of Mr. Jefferson's grand Rotunda. It was a doomed office romance, we both suspected, but we were determined to have fun while it lasted. As word leaked out, an office pool of *cognoscenti* made bets on whether we would survive Cranston's improbable 1984 presidential campaign. We beat the odds, married happily, and produced three great kids—but *that* is another story.

In the Cranston office, years in the minority under President Reagan made us all veterans of losing causes. Cranston thought the bloated U.S. and Soviet nuclear arsenals—exceeding sixty thousand nuclear warheads in those years—to be absurd and terribly dangerous. Beginning in 1982, he partnered with Senator Ted Kennedy to push for passage of nuclear freeze legislation requiring a mutual, verifiable halt to the deployment of any more U.S. or Soviet nuclear warheads. Senator Cranston fought battle after battle to curb spiraling U.S. weapons spending. He tried by numerous means to spur U.S.-Soviet negotiations for arms control, talks which had been shelved since the Soviets had invaded

Afghanistan in 1979. He pushed bills, resolutions, amendments, and group letters from senators to the president.

Cranston lost most every vote. He lost in committee when pressing the GOP-led Foreign Relations Committee to adopt the freeze resolution. He lost in opposing the B-2 bomber. He lost in opposing the deployment of more nuclear weapons in the European theater. He lost on neutron bombs and on funding "Star Wars" space weapons. He lost on the Senate floor, trying to cut off funds for new MX missiles—ICBMs which would have carried 10 warheads each and were to be moved about the countryside on rail cars, the better to hide from Soviet warfighters.

Alan was indefatigable, nevertheless, his optimism infectious. By contrast, I was immature. I took most every defeat personally. Senators would offer support for a pending amendment, only to slink away under political pressure, after the White House or home state defense manufacturers turned up the heat. I'd want Cranston to call them out on their breach of faith. He would simply tuck the lesson away for future use, determined to try harder the next time, to count more carefully, and to be more skeptical of someone designated as an "L+" (leaning in favor), on his ever-present Senate roll call tally sheets, who might actually be an "L-" (leaning against).

Democrats were endlessly afraid of looking "weak on defense." The party of FDR, Truman, and JFK shrank under Republican Party attacks, which went far beyond the anti-Communist crusades of Nixon and McCarthy and the "who lost China" insanity of the 1950s. The GOP attacks had grown into the politics of personal destruction, the nonsense that has had war heroes from George McGovern to Max Cleland portrayed by Republican campaign opponents as soft on America's enemies. As Pentagon spending went up year after year, Cranston and arms control activists would lose vote after vote.

Yet, in losing so many battles, Cranston and his allies helped reshape the course of the Cold War. Indeed, very few of those weapons he opposed were ever deployed. American and Soviet nuclear stockpiles finally leveled off, and then began to shrink—now to a fraction of their original size. Arms control negotiations became arms reduction efforts, as Ronald Reagan, under intense pressure from Congress, found an amazingly pliant partner in Mikhail Gorbachev. The last Soviet leader saw the utter folly of a nuclear arms race that had exceeded sixty thousand warheads. While defense budgets soared, the Soviet dictatorship finally collapsed from within. The threat of a nuclear war between Moscow and Washington began to recede.

Reform took time. Efforts to cut nuclear arsenals, like the efforts to desegregate schools or realize voting rights for all Americans, required the ability to weather countless setbacks. In framing the issues throughout the Reagan years, Senate liberals like Alan Cranston, Joe Biden, Chris Dodd, and John Kerry laid the groundwork for future victories.

They lost so many legislative battles. Yet they managed to alter the agenda and advance their issues until a larger prize was won. They could not stop the U.S. intervention in El Salvador's civil war, for example, nor terminate payments to Philippine dictator Ferdinand Marcos. Slowly, the conditions Congress imposed on U.S. foreign aid—land reform, human rights, and democratic elections—*did* take root nevertheless, in more effective U.S. policies from Central America to South Africa, and even toward some of the Arab dictatorships in the Middle East. Soon they had Republican counterparts joining the effort, from Richard Lugar to Charles Mathias and Charles Percy.

In the process, little satisfactions came my way. I got to work closely with my younger brother Jason. He had come east to attend the Georgetown School of Foreign Service and work in the House with an enterprising legislator, Congressman Mel Levine, formerly a staffer with Senator Tunney. We would plot arms control and Central America policy strategy over a weekly lunch in the Capitol, our own family House-Senate mini-conference as we took turns treating each other to a cholesterol feast of cheeseburgers, fries, and hot fudge sundaes. We would edit each other's prose, as Jason crafted pensive fiction enriched by his remarkable emotional intelligence; his work produced many excellent speeches and amendments, and *Believe in Me,* a classic novel about a campaign staffer who goes AWOL with a rock music star.

Senator Cranston and I made it into Malacañan Palace in the Philippines to visit President Corazon Aquino, just weeks after dictator Ferdinand Marcos fled under U.S. pressure. Guards armed with machine guns were ubiquitous. We were told that in the hours after Marcos escaped, scores of blank forms for presidential decrees litered the palace grounds; you could snatch one with a free hand in the courtyard and see the Marcos signature auto-penned on yellow paper, the detritus of a deposed dictator. Mrs. Marcos' infamous fifteen hundred pairs of shoes were still present in the palace closets for us to view.[24]

Cranston and President Corazon Aquino, April 1, 1986, shortly after she was installed in Malacañan Palace.

On trips overseas accompanying Cranston to Beijing and Moscow, we'd pause for an obligatory photo op. I'd pull a San Francisco Giants cap out of my briefcase, then pose for a sophomoric series of *Where's Waldo?* photos in Red Square and Tiananmen Square. It was decidedly puckish stuff. Being childish gave us a smile, however, amidst rather serious times.

Cranston fought for years against CIA interventions in Central America. The clumsy U.S. assistance to Nicaraguan contras was finally banned by Congress through an appropriations bill rider. Nevertheless, senior Reagan-Bush aides lied to our faces in SD-419, the Foreign Relations Committee room in Dirksen, about their schemes to continue illegal aid through the National Security Council. When the Reagan White House, late in its second term, performed an end run, and thereby violated U.S. law, the resulting Iran-Contra scandal might have led to impeachment proceedings. If Reagan had not been a visibly fading lame duck and convincingly clueless about the crimes of his NSC, Congress would have called him to account for the criminal efforts of his senior White House staff.

During the 1982 recession, Cranston felt so strongly that the Reagan presidency was bad for the country that he stunned us all: He announced his own bid for the White House. Alan was a brilliant tactician and a champion of liberal causes, with formidable fundraising skills. Yet he was also a gaunt Senate insider with limited national following. His loyal Senate staff volunteered, and soon we were dispatched to the nation's four corners. Sergio Bendixen cleverly stacked a Wisconsin straw poll in the summer of 1983, garnering national press and a *Newsweek* magazine feature. Joy helped bring in tens of millions from environmentalists, arms control activists, and Hollywood supporters. Dan Perry and John Russonello wrote stirring speeches echoing the campaign slogan of "Peace and Jobs," while the press was handled by Kam Kuwata, who would later become one of the most successful campaign managers in modern California politics.[25]

Cranston never had a chance, of course. For his televised debates, make-up artists put a heavy orange glow on his cheeks, and even on his white fringe of hair. He pummeled Reagan in a tide of TV campaign ads, but Walter Mondale had locked down the support of labor and party centrists, who felt 1984 was the former vice president's "turn." Jesse Jackson was the media darling, eternally entertaining with his rhyming couplets masquerading as policy. Attractive Gary Hart, a close Cranston friend and Russell Senate Office Building neighbor, became the Mondale alternative. Then another liberal stalwart, former senator George McGovern, leapt into the race on the eve of the Iowa caucuses, attacking Cranston, most improbably, from the left.

Through each of these developments, Team Cranston slogged on cheerfully. We drank heavily at night; we knew our cause was hopeless. Somehow my New England schooling landed me in the dead of the New Hampshire winter as a deputy campaign manager charged with organizing towns in that key campaign state. I stayed in a cheap seaside summer hotel which was then providing short-term housing, mostly for Texas steelworkers constructing the nearby Seabrook nuclear power plant: Poetic justice, it seemed.

A foreign policy wonk, I was reduced to dispatching scores of college kids who had to use hand drills to penetrate frozen ground to install lawn signs. The Cranston plan was to finish second to Mondale in Iowa, then storm into New Hampshire with national media in tow. Alan would become the featured alternative to the establishment candidate. Cranston hoped to gain traction as the California senator who had beaten Reagan's reactionary forces in his home state and Washington.

I was instructed to run the day-after-Iowa-Caucuses events. Our goal was to fill a large Portsmouth, New Hampshire auditorium to capacity with a crowd of five hundred enthusiasts, the perfect backdrop for national media coverage of Alan Cranston, the new liberal hope.

The challenge weighed on me for days. I was bereft of ideas on how to get such a crowd to turn out for a faltering candidate. They didn't teach this in political science classrooms at grad school. Then I arrived at my one great insight in presidential politics. Soon the local shipyard and veterans organizations were filled with fliers announcing "Candidate Night with Veterans Committee Chairman Senator Alan Cranston." The trick was in the two essential words I finally figured out to add: "FREE BEER." Thus did we fill the Portsmouth VFW Hall for a truly raucous event. Hart and McGovern had stolen Cranston's thunder in Iowa, however, and the morning after New Hampshire's primary, Alan gracefully withdrew and headed back to the Senate.

After the Reagan landslide of 1984, few victories brought us a sense of closure. Changes in U.S. policy toward South Africa were one notable exception. In those years, progressive legislators took seriously their obligation to challenge executive branch powers on foreign affairs. This suspicion of all-powerful rulers ignoring the will of the people in international affairs was, of course, a central issue in the American Revolution. Even conservative voices, such as that of Indiana's steadfast Republican Richard Lugar, would refuse to give the White House a free hand in the international arena. This was before the so-called global war on terror led Congress to once again grant blank checks to presidents.

The international campaign to bring down South Africa's racist apartheid regime gave birth to an impressive grassroots effort in the United States. The scattered remnants of the great civil rights movement stitched together a new coalition. White churches joined with black activists and Africa specialists in Washington. College students mobilized to push trustees to divest college endowment funds from companies doing business with South Africa. At remote Hampshire College, the efforts were led by activists, and my alma mater became the first campus in the nation to convince trustees to sell stocks in companies profiting in South Africa.

Here was a noble policymaking purpose that seemed to echo some of the great battles of the Sixties, and one that seemed to be simple good versus pure evil. By contrast, the Reagan policy of "constructive engagement" with the apartheid regime moved too slowly, with too few results.

Our coalition met weekly to plot strategy in the dusty Methodist Building across from the Supreme Court. We were joined by young college campus organizers, who sat in folding chairs at old wooden tables. I would sit next to Greg Craig, Senator Kennedy's legislative assistant who was possessed of extraordinary coalition-building talents. We teamed with aging white clerics and young African American activists running the meeting as we developed legislative options.

We pushed a modest package of sanctions through the Foreign Relations Committee. Counting votes one by one in preparation for a floor test, we soon had a majority. We had to convince bill sponsor Ted Kennedy that the better part of wisdom was to get a quick vote to pass the measure in the Senate. Initially, he was crestfallen; Greg Craig had prepared reams of material and a series of progressively tougher amendments for the floor debate.

After hearing us out, Senator Kennedy asked for a few minutes to reflect. Then he bolted out into the public lobby to confidently inform activists of the new strategy he was adopting. The performance was breathtaking, but it *was* his initiative, and it remained important for him as a leader of the Senate's liberal faction to demonstrate his control of the fast-moving issue.[26]

Then we went to conference with an even stronger House bill. The wheeling and dealing was intense. Kennedy stood by, his teenage son Teddy watching over his shoulder, as Cranston tried to shape a deal for the toughest possible bill without losing crucial Republican support. It took a long time for many in the room to see the solution. Because the whole point of the measure was symbolic—we wanted the headline "U.S. Joins Europe to Isolate Apartheid Regime"—it was dumb to argue over such details as how many *krugerrands* private coin collectors could buy.

We convinced House staffers to propose a more moderate package. Representative Steve Solarz then pitched this counterproposal to Senate GOP Chairman Lugar and his chief of staff, Jeff Bergner. Jeff was a good friend and a patriotic conservative with a Princeton doctorate. We readily cut deals because we shared a common commitment to getting stuff done, even if it was only a fifty-fifty compromise. He was blunt, especially in his private evaluations of some of the weaker members on both sides of the aisles. Ultimately, both Bergner and Chairman Lugar embraced our South Africa proposal. At the key moment, late in the evening in the ornate S-116 committee room in the Capitol, a *New York Times* photographer happened by. His photo ran the next day, page one, above the fold; the classic shot captured the moment of decision.[27] The conference report passed.

Then, for reasons that still escape me, President Reagan was convinced to issue one of the few vetoes of his presidency, none of which Congress had been able to override. We were appalled, but responded to the challenge. We worked the well of the Senate chamber and the cloakrooms one vote at a time. Once Kennedy and Cranston got to the magic number of sixty-seven, the dam broke. The Senate overrode a Reagan veto for the first time. The final vote on the Comprehensive Anti-Apartheid Act was 78-21. Three years later, a prostrate South Africa regime released Nelson Mandela from prison. Apartheid died. Like the Congress' challenge to Philippine dictator Marcos, this effort would have failed but for the nimble leadership of Dick Lugar, a conservative Republican.

Another Cranston-led victory of this era, albeit on a domestic fight where I was only a spectator, gave rise to an oft-repeated charge that Cranston and his Senate allies were responsible for launching "the politics of personal destruction." This was the 1987 Supreme Court nomination of Robert Bork. A respected legal scholar, Bork had well-known and widely published conservative views. Washington groups championing minority rights and a woman's right to choose clamored for Bork's defeat. In the process, Bork's record and reputation were savaged. Pro-choice groups had little sympathy for the collateral damage. Cranston was elated by the win, his enthusiasm captured in a nationally run photo of the senator chortling in the press gallery as he held up his trademark roll call tally sheet marking his fifty-eight winning votes.[28]

Today, the jurist's name has lamentably become a verb: Inside the Beltway, to "Bork" someone means to savage them personally, intellectually, and politically with such thoroughness as to prevent their confirmation. Many nonpartisan scholars attribute the terrible mess the modern Senate has made of the confirmation process to the Bork fight.[29]

Having worked in the well of the Senate during those years, I'm quite certain the academics are wrong. From my perspective, the hyper-partisan senatorial challenges to opponents' patriotism was more characteristic of post-World War II times, directly attributable to the McCarthy and Nixon assaults of the 1950s. These Republican senators were the first to question the loyalty of scores of civil servants. McCarthy and his followers ruined many an honest career.

A triumphant Cranston with his trademark Senate roll call tally sheet. October 23, 1987.

The accumulated scars made a generation of Democrats so afraid of being "weak on Communism" that it encouraged them to support engagement in a morass of Asian civil wars. As a presidential candidate, Nixon understandably smarted under the corrupt campaign practices of the Kennedy family; his November 1960 decision not to contest voter fraud in Illinois showed admirable restraint. Candidate Barry Goldwater faced savage LBJ television commercials in 1964, including the infamous "Daisy ad." Nixon's revenge was embodied in the Plumbers unit, which led his presidency directly into the crimes known as Watergate, impeachment proceedings, and resignation.

Vicious Senate confirmation battles took place well before Bork's 1987 imbroglio. After Bork, they just got meaner, beginning with the defeat of John Tower's nomination to head the Pentagon and the unfortunate victory of the most bizarre modern Supreme Court Justice, Clarence Thomas. Yet, prior to Bork and Thomas, Senate opponents of U.S.-Soviet arms control had waged a brutal fight in 1977 against the arms control nomination of Paul Warnke, questioning both his patriotism and character. It was a successful effort to make clear the wounded nominee would face a strong Senate minority capable of blocking any new strategic arms agreement he negotiated.

Years before the Bork fight, members of the Senate opposition regrettably made a practice of assaulting not just the politics of White House nominees, but upon occasion, their character as well. I was a guilty participant, working closely with Foreign Relations Committee Democratic staffers Dave Keaney, Chuck Berk, Gerry Connolly, Peter Galbraith, and Gerry Christianson to collect any information we could possibly use to defeat Reagan nominees. Sometimes these nominees were men and women whose sole crime was being asked to serve an administration with which we disagreed.

Stunned by the Reagan landslide in 1980, which unexpectedly brought a GOP majority to the Senate as well, Senator Cranston used his leadership role to target a handful of administration nominees. These were people he believed were so far out of the political mainstream that they made excellent poster children for Reagan excesses. Our attacks on them, we maintained, were based in policy, legitimately advanced to highlight Reagan administration policies out of step with American values. The public service careers we caricatured and the reputations we sullied were collateral damage to these proxy fights over policy. We were doing to a few Reagan-Bush appointees what hard-line Republicans (and Scoop Jackson Democrats) had done to Warnke. Unlike Joe McCarthy's liquor-fueled conspiratorial rants, our attacks, we believed, were based in fact and did not question opponents' patriotism.

Together with a tough bench of Democratic interrogators on the Senate Foreign Relations Committee, including Biden and Sarbanes, joined later by Kerry and Dodd, Cranston defeated some nominees and bloodied others. Ernest Lefever, a cynical nominee for the top human rights post at State, was rejected on a 13-5 vote when Committee investigators discovered malfeasance in his think tank's use of corporate funds. Ken Adelman, a thoroughly decent scholar miscast as an arms control nominee for an administration skeptical of arms control, survived a humiliating public assault by Senator Biden that revealed his ignorance of nuclear weapons technology.

Other times, we'd go after a nominee we believed had lied to the Committee. These included the unctuous Elliott Abrams, a former Democratic aide, and the respected Donald Gregg. We found clear indication in classified cables that Gregg had briefed Vice President George H. W. Bush about ongoing illegal administration actions to circumvent the ban on aiding Nicaraguan contras.[30]

Given Senator Byrd's isolationist streak and Senator Pell's distaste for personal confrontations, Cranston was invariably the liberals' point man organizing these attacks. For years, senior GOP nominees would come to meet with him early in the process, hoping to get him in their corner. Sometimes, Cranston would emerge as their key defender. He rejected efforts to oppose the nominations of Larry Eagleburger for Secretary of State, William Clark for Deputy Secretary, and John Negroponte for the UN. In the process, the crafty Cranston earned respect from some GOP policymakers and opened a few back channels for dialogue with the Reagan team.

Nevertheless, of all the work I did over three decades in Washington, some of the assaults I helped advance against nominees were the most unsavory. You wanted to take a long shower after one of those nasty confrontations. Watching a nominee's family sobbing in the audience behind them made you feel dirty. It was the kind of hardball politics I grew to disdain and to regret.

Other battles over policy matters domestic and international offered more dissatisfaction. We would debate some bills for weeks in the Foreign Relations Committee, working with legislators to shape a compromise, only to have the measure die in a House-Senate conference committee from the accumulated weight of the junk provisions that had been added. The annual State Department funding authorizations were the worst, consuming weeks of debate yet rarely surviving to enactment. There would be minutes of exhilaration punctuating hours of droning boredom. At such times, the musty Senate chamber was not unlike a foxhole in a stalemated war, and this was before promiscuous abuse of the filibuster sank the Senate's reputation to historic lows.

Sometimes I would plead with Republican staff counterparts to shape a deal; Bergner and Casimir Yost were always ready to listen. Others were less movable. Jesse Helms' staff was hard to read, and harder to pin down.

Bob Dole of Kansas, the longtime Republican leader in the Senate, had an irreverent senior staffer for all international matters named Al Lehn. Al hated the formality of the Senate floor proceedings. He would spend hours holed up in his tiny, windowless office in the back of the Republican leaders' suite in the Capitol, watching game shows on a black-and-white TV and feeding his parrot. I recall negotiating the rabbit's warren of cubicles in Dole's office, then pleading with Lehn to cut a deal on some foreign policy measure being talked to death on the Senate floor. Al's feet were on the desk, and between his squawking bird and Bob Barker on *The Price is Right*, it was difficult to be heard.

For hours on end, I sat in a small staff chair between Cranston and Democratic leader Robert C. Byrd. Byrd was a revered traditionalist and Constitutional scholar, an old-school gentleman who didn't really care for liberals like Cranston. Byrd never hid his disdain for staff; he often expressed his opinion that the Senate chamber should not permit any to be present.

Byrd was a short man, who proudly wore checkered tartan vests many days. He scolded me for standing in his view when I peered anxiously toward the Senate doors for late-arriving Democratic votes. When staff clustered in front of chairs at the back of the chamber or spilled into the well—I was often a guilty party— he would shout: "Mr. President! The Senate is *not* in order! Staff out of the well!" Finally, as president *pro tempore*, he directed that railings be constructed in front of the few staff seats placed at the rear of the chamber; some colleagues blamed me for these walls, which remain to this day.

George Mitchell was a far more engaging leader, who assumed Byrd's post after leading the Senate back to a Democratic majority. Mitchell was brilliant and sharp-elbowed, constantly weighing when to compromise, and when to go down in flames on principle. Unlike the stiff and suspicious Byrd, he engaged Cranston's talents readily. Mitchell relied on him for vote counts on most issues, domestic and foreign. Hour after hour, senators would stroll by Mitchell's desk in the center of the chamber, shopping a deal and inquiring about the timing of the last vote—eager to make it to fundraisers or to family. Byrd moved his desk just behind the leaders; Mitchell and Cranston could sense the West Virginian's steely eyes on their backs as the new leadership team went about its business.

The part of these daily dramas I relished most was seeing these outsized personalities up close, watching them negotiate details of public policy when the stakes were so high.

"Fuck you!" Senator Joe Biden shouted one day at a stunned Senate colleague from Oregon. "Fuck you, Bob Packwood."

We were sitting in the Republican's cluttered Russell Building office, his inner sanctum replete with stereo speakers, wine, and whiskey. (This was before stories came out about Packwood's serial groping of female aides in the same room.) The walls were full of Oregon memorabilia. Heavy mahogany furnishings were covered in green and gold fabrics. A half-dozen pro-Israel senators and a couple of senior staffers were plotting strategy for blocking a Reagan administration package of arms sales to Saudi Arabia.

"Don't you fucking tell me what deals you've cut for us with the White House," Biden growled. "You don't speak for *me*!"

Packwood grew red in the face. He had agreed to a secret deal with Secretary of State George Shultz and Tom Dine, head of AIPAC, the lead pro-Israel lobby group. Biden wasn't buying it.

"I don't care if the Reagan people drop AWACS [command and control aircraft] from the package. I'm *still* gonna fight it. And we'll win, with or without you!" Biden played furious, yet he seemed to be suppressing a smirk. Before unleashing his macho barrage, he had apparently forgotten that staff were present.

Packwood retreated, and the Biden group proceeded to get a strong Senate vote objecting to the Saudi arms sale. I had learned early in Washington that the nastiest fights in the Senate were often to be found among supporters jockeying for position and questioning the bona fides of colleagues. Our pro-Israel friends were among the least tolerant of any dissent.

Other times, I saw young legislators at their best. The Foreign Relations Committee was still considered a great perch in those days, the legacy of its late 1960s stand against LBJ, Nixon, and the Vietnam War not yet having faded. Half its members ended up running for president, including Biden, Kerry, and, later, Barack Obama. As a pre-law student at Georgetown, Bill Clinton interned there; Congressmen Chris Van Hollen and Gerry Connolly had previously been Committee staffers.

One day, an eager-to-please freshman senator from Massachusetts rescued me. I'd worked for hours on a tough line of questioning for Cranston to use on a Reagan State Department witness testifying on arms control. My typescript had elaborate margin notes, with fallbacks and possible follow-up questions highlighted with a yellow marker. Then Senator Cranston got delayed in a Senate cloakroom discussion. All my work preparing elaborate rhetorical traps for him to use would go for naught.

Senator Kerry, the tall young legislator who was then the most junior on the panel, covered me. Kerry had an early reputation—unjust, it turned out—of being a bit of a lightweight, a "JFK wannabe." He discovered my plight, then volunteered to use Cranston's script, going on blind trust in a colleague's staffer.

Kerry picked up my proposed line of questioning without missing a beat; he knocked the stuffing out of the backpedalling witness. It was a most impressive performance. When, eighteen years later, I worked in a drafty Philadelphia warehouse helping run Pennsylvania's Get Out the Vote for Kerry's presidential campaign, I considered it a modest repayment of this earlier debt.

I also saw legislators at their worst. I saw them cynically reversing positions to appease big donors or party leaders. Larry Pressler of South Dakota and Charles Percy of Illinois did it most painfully; you could tell they were voting against measures they wanted to vote for. I saw senators flip-flop on basic policy questions, fingers ever out to test the political winds. Kentucky's Mitch McConnell was the worst in this regard, with tormented John McCain—who was against "immoral," deficit-growing wartime tax cuts before he was for them—close behind.

I saw drunken male senators ogling young women. At one California fundraiser hosted by Senator Mitchell, I was assigned to protect female staff from an especially randy Democratic senator who shall remain nameless. I saw legislators who were quite creepy; the first time I was asked, at the age of twenty-two, to give an after-hours policy briefing to a Member in his private House office, it took me a few minutes to realize the legislator in question had no interest whatsoever in nuclear nonproliferation. He was merely trolling for a male date, feigning interest before asking me out to dinner. My hasty exit was extremely awkward.

I saw legislators high on drugs—even on the Senate floor, as with a first-term Republican. The senator was apparently battling multiple inner demons during the go-go Eighties, leaving a wild party late one evening where a mutual friend confessed she'd witnessed him snorting cocaine before racing, disoriented, into the Senate chamber for a vote.

Over time, however, my righteous judgments lost their edge.

I loved the Congress. It was so open, so accessible. Yet it was so arcane in its ways. The congressmen and congresswomen? They represented a tautology, a perfect reflection of how imperfectly power is distributed in America. Any time you confine 538 men and women, originating from across the fifty states and several territories, in one small space, you'll get a representative cross-section. It truly is a lot like high school, where you have your quota of straight-A students, a few natural-born leaders among them. You also have your jocks, your Romeos, your drama queens, your boozers, and your bums.

As one Nebraska legislator named Roman Hruska famously observed, "Even the mediocre deserve to be represented."

When you think about it, Senator Hruska had a point.

CHAPTER FOURTEEN

Lobbying 101: The View from K Street

Washington, D.C.
April 2007

A Horatio Alger figure, Gerry Cassidy was reared in hardscrabble Red Hook, the tough docklands of Brooklyn, New York. He came to Washington after working to get legal aid for migrant farm workers in Florida. Then he ran a hunger study for a bipartisan congressional committee headed by the unlikely team of George McGovern and Bob Dole.

Cassidy borrowed five thousand dollars from his father-in-law. Then, through extraordinary business savvy, he parlayed it into a multi-million dollar corporation. Cassidy bought and sold the firm more than once. Then he repeatedly emerged to lead it in its next incarnation. His company, Cassidy & Associates, was the most successful lobbying firm in Washington for decades.

Cassidy's was the classic rags-to-riches story retold, a Sixties political activist who first came to Washington as an idealist, and parlayed his interest into a highly successful business. For years, his firm ranked first in annual revenues, yet he rarely sought publicity. His offices were between the White House and Capitol Hill, not on K Street, lobbying's traditional center in Washington. The firm's button-down, Brooks Brothers formality felt more like an old-school Boston investment firm than a D.C. lobby shop. Then Cassidy was encouraged to cooperate with a reporter working on a series of articles, ostensibly about the growth of the lobbying profession. The subsequent pieces, however, turned out to be a lengthy caricature of lobbyists.

When I was first introduced to Cassidy, friends said simply: "He's a guy who always keeps his commitments." It was a compliment that resonated. At the time, I was in one of my periodic career transitions—leaving a secure job once again, this time departing the Senate for academe. Bored with the glacial pace of progress in the Senate, I decided to pursue my longtime goal of finishing my Ph.D. I had interrupted my studies at Stanford years before; this time I was leaving congressional staff to teach and write at Georgetown.

At that time, an era of divided government, Cassidy's business was thriving. As an international policy wonk wary of congressional appropriators, however, I knew little of his niche. The firm's specialty was helping schools and hospitals secure some of the federal funding controlled by the peer review buddy system. In places like the Bay Area, Cassidy explained, Cal and Stanford received five hundred million dollars annually from the federal government. The nearby University of San Francisco, however, which trained first generation college kids who went right to work in the city, got zero. The firm's nonprofit clients were counseled on how to secure federal funds by creating programs capable of winning earmarks in Congress and ongoing executive branch support.

The firm was expanding once again, this time into more international, corporate, and state government work. The enterprise already supported nearly one hundred employees; its leadership understood far better than I did how I might help grow the business.

In my job interview, I was rather clueless. A lifelong public servant, I had no idea how to make money or create jobs in the private sector. I was headed to a college campus, with an interest in doing some research and consulting on the side. Cassidy promised to show me how the business worked. He was determined to build the legitimacy of lobbying until the profession was on par with that of lawyers and doctors. He hired smart people who knew how to navigate our dysfunctional Washington government. He provided a service of substantial value to corporate and non-profit clients alike. The firm was demanding, and its professional services contracts with clients all required long-term retainers.

I was just looking for a one-day-a-week consulting job to supplement the teaching salary Georgetown had offered. Within sixty days, however, I was hooked. I withdrew from the Georgetown Ph.D. program and accepted a full-time position at Cassidy & Associates. I'd publish my draft thesis about inter-branch struggles over foreign policymaking as a Harper & Row book, the title a bit of a mouthful: *Conflict and Consensus: The Struggle between Congress and the President Over Foreign Policymaking.*

The draw was irresistible. Decades spent in Congress opposing Ford and Reagan and Bush usually meant being *against* things. Work in the Senate felt many times like running in place; you rarely made it to your destination. The Senate could truly be the "cave of winds." As I listened week after week to Jesse Helms drone on in yet another filibuster, the yellow-walled chamber truly became the place where bills went to die.

With the departure of many veteran legislators, the Congress seemed less and less relevant. Many of the newer legislators were shallow, blow-dried hacks. Some juvenile members—Rick Santorum and Anthony Wiener spring to mind—were grating partisans. They were forever posturing for fundraising, looking for cheap sound bites to land themselves on shouting TV talk shows. They were not exactly the larger-than-life figures I'd first encountered on the Senate Foreign Relations Committee. Fulbright and Javits, Church and Jackson, McGovern and Goldwater were gone. Irritating lightweights had replaced them.

Capitalism was an adrenaline rush of another order. Days began with 8 a.m. strategy sessions and hurried rides to the Hill. Crisply run appointments at congressional leadership offices, advanced with military precision, followed. In the afternoon, we would recalibrate our strategy with our clients, evaluating angles, preparing bank shots. Then came evenings full of conversation at banquets, fueled often by liquor, gossip, and campaign donations.

Ambition was palpable, the dollars coming and going became an easy way to keep score, and the work was results-oriented.

What surprised me most was how interesting the individual clients were. Steve Privett, the president of USF, was a Jesuit priest and human rights champion, a man who'd nearly been murdered by right-wing militias in El Salvador. Yet Father Steve took joy in counseling me about issues as diverse as liturgy and the San Francisco political scene. Bud Selig was a proud former used-car salesman who became the commissioner of Major League Baseball and a long-time client of the Cassidy firm. Chris Connor began his career with Sherwin-Williams during high school weekends in San Leandro; he was now the CEO.

"What was your first job?" I asked Connor one day as we waited to see the HUD secretary.

"Sellin' paint, man. Sellin' paint. Over the counter for Sherwin-Williams."

Here in the marketplace were businessmen and women who took enormous risks with jobs, careers, and capital. Many were brilliant conversationalists, Fortune 100 CEOs, mayors, and university presidents. They all came to Cassidy & Associates with either a problem or an opportunity. They had a vision for their school, their town, their medical center, or their company. They just needed Uncle Sam to offer up a grant, to commit to the first contract, or just to get out of the way and let them pursue their business initiatives freely.

As a lobbyist, I would find myself in the most improbable of situations. Part of a Cassidy team advising Major League Baseball, I was standing in an anteroom behind the dais of the Senate Commerce Committee one day in 2003. One of a half-dozen handlers prepping Commissioner Selig for steroids testimony before Chairman John McCain's panel, I saw out of the corner of my eye a quiet older man standing alone in the back of the room.

I walked over and introduced myself. It was Henry Aaron, "Hammerin' Hank," holder of the untainted all-time home run record. Aaron seemed completely out of his element. On my turf, he looked shy and a bit lost. We spent fifteen minutes talking about wrists and curve balls; he seemed grateful for the company as we waited for a parade of senators to return from a roll call. I asked if he'd sign a note for my kids. His hands were enormous, the long, thick, leathery digits of a bass player. His smile was gentle and projected the profound dignity of a Nelson Mandela.

Other conversations with clients had greater international consequences. For years, we would communicate with the president of Taiwan, Lee Teng-Hui, through long memos sent via an informal channel. Our messages were conveyed by an economics professor Lee had befriended decades before whilst working on his Ph.D. in international development at Cornell. Dr. Lien Fu-Huang was a serious scholar, but his face would erupt in a nervous smile when Cassidy was able to help President Lee. Yet, I never met the president, the man at the other end of the communications chain. Several of our frank memos on Communist China's maneuverings in Washington were leaked by intelligence services and made for sensational press stories on both sides of the Taiwan Strait.

Another consulting challenge put me in the backseat of a town car riding through darkened Cleveland streets. Leon Panetta was sitting next to me, after helping me lead a corporate board discussion on seismic safety. We were bored, and not looking forward to turning in at the local Hilton at 8:30 p.m. Then we pulled by the outfield bleachers of the new baseball stadium, Jacobs Field. We looked at each other, smiled, and said, almost in unison: "Let's go!"

Not many months before, Panetta had been chief of staff to the president of the United States. Now he watched in amusement as I tried to talk our way into a stadium that was sold out. We started at the box office, then we strolled the sidewalks looking for straggling scalpers. It was more than an hour after the first pitch and nothing was to be found. I pleaded with the security guard, who recognized Panetta, but still we failed to get in. We ended up standing in our coats and ties at a fence beyond the bleachers, trying to peer through the bars like two kids. We would strain to follow the game via the roar of the crowd when a ball hit high into the lights cleared the fence.

The clients' problems were surprisingly interesting. Our job was to design strategies for them, to provide solutions to complicated challenges. Backed by a broad and deep roster of Cassidy & Associates lobbyists—we bragged we were one friendly phone call away from any of the 538 members of Congress—we felt at times almost omnipotent, like policymakers on steroids.

First and foremost, our clients needed something in Washington. They needed ideas on how to overcome the challenges. Then they needed a guide who could demystify the arcane processes of their own government. To navigate the labyrinth, they needed very specific battle plans that could offer multiple routes to success in the legislative game. It felt as if we were clever doctors. People came to us with ailments; the Cassidy firm could offer both diagnosis and cure.

Reforms made in the 1970s, fueled by reactions to Vietnam and Watergate, resulted in the wide dispersal of power in Congress. Reformers ensured that authority was spread to dozens of subcommittees. Many of the obscure panels, in turn, became small power centers. Relative backwaters, chaired by inexperienced freshmen, became optional venues for those searching for champions. Lobbyists now had dozens of routes to choose from to achieve legislative success. The Cassidy stable included a number of veteran minds, such as former Marine Corps general P. X. Kelley and former White House press secretary Jody Powell; so we often knew where and when key decisions were made.

The work was enjoyable. I had not come to Washington to make money, but now shaping policy and producing measurable results for clients yielded big returns.

The first two clients I signed were the University of San Francisco, thanks to my brother Jason's introduction, and a coalition of U.S. companies formed by a Stanford friend, Frank Hawke, which led the effort to end the U.S. trade embargo on Vietnam.

The following year, the Cassidy staff took out a complicated loan to buy 49 percent of the company's ESOP stock. After the deal went through, Cassidy appeared in each of our doorways the last Friday afternoon before the Christmas holiday. He smiled like Santa Claus as he handed out large bonus checks. The job was profitable.

Cassidy collaborated with fellow team members on our most visible and challenging accounts, including the controversial Taiwan project. President Lee had created an international incident in Hawaii when low-level State Department protocol officers refused to let him disembark from his plane, for fear of offending Communists in Beijing. Lee then used a think tank funded by Taipei supporters to hire Cassidy & Associates to overturn the U.S. policy of shunning Taiwan in favor of Beijing. Our challenge was to get the Taiwan president an American audience on U.S. soil. Secretary of State Warren Christopher assured the Chinese foreign minister it would never happen. Lee gave Cassidy & Associates twelve months to reverse this diktat.

We schemed with Hill allies, reporting dutifully to President Lee, even as we suspected the State Department and the People's Republic of China were reading our messages. Jody Powell helped us reframe the issue: Why should Americans let Communist Party bureaucrats decide with whom we could meet on American soil? Our lobbying team went door to door on Capitol Hill, exploiting anti-China sentiment. Then we influenced editorials in dozens of national and local newspapers, while ghostwriting a number of opinion columns. Finally, we got to a group of key senators meeting with President Clinton. Each pressed for a change in Taiwan policy. The White House soon undercut Secretary Christopher and admitted Lee.[31]

Taiwan's president made the cover of *Newsweek*. Taipei was delighted. We were asked to help draft remarks for Lee's U.S. speech, and I was called by senior State Department officials with pleas, bordering on demands, that we soften Lee's rhetoric. President Lee's ensuing speech was anything but subtle: "Communism," he declared, "is dead." Lee's pronouncements provoked a major international incident: The PRC responded with a military escalation—live-fire missile drills that bracketed Taiwan. We were accused of nearly starting World War III. Yet it was China that had overreacted. The Cassidy firm was rewarded with years of lucrative fees and challenging Taiwan projects.

Gerry Cassidy remained a clever talent scout. His business grew, in part, because of the license he gave a dozen go-getters like Marty Russo, Jim Fabiani, Vince Versage, Kai Anderson, Gregg Hartley, Barbara Sutton, Terry Paul, Dan McNamara, Mary Shields, and Arthur Mason to bring in and service the grinding lobbying business. Cassidy usually stayed one step ahead of the market; his small boutique firm grew from his tiny personal investment to a company with more than thirty million dollars a year in revenue. He added public relations, grassroots services, and polling well before competitors did. In the summer of 1994, sensing President Clinton's early first-term troubles, Cassidy bought a respected Republicans-only firm. It became a key weapon in the firm's quiver with the astonishing arrival of the Gingrich Revolution.

Lobbying had all the rhythm of a baseball season. There was a new game each day, a new challenge to stir the adrenal glands, and the unmistakable results most legislating lacked. If we did a good job, the firm got paid and our contract was renewed. If we didn't, the firm got fired. The clarity, in marked contrast to Senate filibustering, was refreshing.

I loved the action. You accomplished tangible results for ambitious clients. You took risks to try to shape policy, always framing your request as consonant with local and national interests. It was more akin to high-stakes blackjack in the noisy haze of lights and free liquor than to any academic seminar in political theory. The riverboat gambler in me enjoyed it all, even the marketing part.

My brothers wondered why I was any good at it, yet it was precisely because I was a product of a large family. From a young age, I was anxious to pick up the slightest cues, using equal parts emotional intelligence and survival skills. Adult conversations had substantial consequences; I had been calculating domestic strategy from my earliest days.

Every day, it seemed, we were presented with some terribly complicated problem. In order to get paid, we had to devise a good plan to solve it. When we were hired to help get the Nixon Library into the National Archives (NARA) system, most of Nixon's supporters were dead. Years of denial had earned his surviving sympathizers the contempt of most historians. The whitewashed version of history on display at the privately financed Nixon Library did not inspire public investment. It was not an easy job Julie Nixon Eisenhower asked us to do. Thirty years after Watergate, we succeeded in winning the library millions in earmarks and a detailed agreement to join NARA. Today, the library is federally run; it is open and accessible, and it tells a version of history far more in tune with historical reality.[32]

Cassidy was hired by a small hospital near Monterey devastated by California's Loma Prieta earthquake and desperate for FEMA funds to rebuild. Our team had to develop a strategy for inspiring the California delegation in Congress to require, through legislation, that FEMA make the hospital whole financially. Otherwise, the primary health care facility for thousands of farm workers, and the jobs of hundreds of medical professionals, would vanish. Ultimately, the Watsonville Community Hospital received $52 million in federal funds. Then we helped St. John's Hospital in Los Angeles get $140 million to rebuild after the Northridge quake. We helped secure transition and clean-up dollars for the bankrupt city of Vallejo after the Navy left Mare Island—and 150 years' worth of toxic waste on the site for the city to clean up.

Former junk bond dealer Mike Milken's CapCure Foundation hired us to secure a billion dollars for prostate cancer research funding. During our first year of work, we helped them get forty-five million dollars earmarked in the Department of Defense budget. We patted ourselves on the back, but then Milken fired us.

"I said a billion and I meant it," Milken growled. I still had much to learn about rough-and-tumble capitalism.

Most successful engagements led to another. I offered to help my brother Pete get one million dollars to continue the youth drug intervention program he and colleagues had spent years developing in Lane County, Oregon. Several members of our firm worked for free to help him restore funding after it had been cut. Soon, the Board of Supervisors, who had been promised federal funding when environmentalists curbed local logging, asked us to help them and eighty-seven other counties collect the $3.7 billion in transition support they had been promised. It took two years and five different attempts, but a team of Cassidy partners, led by Kai Anderson, managed finally to get it passed by both the full House and the Senate.[33] Helping rural schools and cops get billions of dollars they were due was far more gratifying than watching paint peel on the Senate walls during yet another filibuster.

Our Major League Baseball work gave us entrée to an eclectic gathering of lobbyists: the Sports Coalition. Seated around a large law firm conference table each month were representatives from all the major sports leagues, the NCAA, and the U.S. Olympic Committee. Most of their issues had to do with telecommunications, labor laws, and drug testing. Yet the conversations were always sprinkled with political intelligence and statistical trivia, the business of sports. Counsel came from all parts of the political spectrum, many longtime Hill adversaries cooperating on behalf of the sports leagues to advance the common interest of maximizing the profits of generally unpleasant owners.

Some potential clients were sleazeballs, but Cassidy didn't push us to work an account we couldn't believe in. Cassidy was ardently pro-life, and refused to work for Planned Parenthood. I balked at working the Saudi Arabia account because their mistreatment of women and democracy advocates was so far beyond the pale. There were projects I became involved in, however, that gave me second thoughts. I helped an Israeli company cozy up to Central Asian autocrats, even as they passed along blunt American diplomatic messages imploring the dictatorship to clean up its act or face U.S. sanctions. Colleagues at the firm tried to play a similar role helping U.S. diplomats engage Equitorial Guinea, an oil-rich, pro-American dictatorship in Africa. These were tough, bare-knuckle assignments, and not for the faint of heart, but we had a payroll to meet. During business downturns, when layoffs loomed, senior rainmakers would walk the Cassidy hallways and feel anxious eyes upon us. These belonged to support staff, coworkers whose faces were virtually pleading: "Save my job."

Plotting policymaking strategy was a compelling team exercise. Sometimes we'd collaborate in the office with veteran strategists we had opposed in our previous lives as Hill staffers. We'd share intelligence and insights, spending hours planning tactics and challenging each other's strategies. Would Feinstein talk to Harman about this? Could we convince Cantor to reach out to Boehner in support of our client's position? How could we get Dicks to talk to Murray? Would Cantwell call the White House and ask for more funding from DOE? There was always somebody at the firm who seemed to know which arguments would be received best, and by whom.

There was political science involved, but psychology, too. Statistics were also crucial. You had to know Members' districts and figure out which way the polls were moving, then decide how to present an issue. The key was framing: You had to be able to legitimately present every request for support as being consistent with the national interest, while advancing the prospective champion's often parochial objectives. Lobbyists would deliver amendments and talking points to legislators, complete with suggested committee tactics and fallback strategies. We'd commission polls, plant newspaper opinion pieces, and stir up grassroots support. We'd draft speeches, amendments, and bills. Then we'd watch with delight as the play unfolded as we had designed it. We'd script clients' Capitol Hill visits right down to the last talking point, then appear prescient when staffers played the roles we had predicted.

Sometimes doors would get slammed in our faces. A grumpy legislator or an ill-conceived request could result in embarrassing setbacks in front of clients. As the city's best-known lobbying firm, we Cassidy professionals also had targets on our backs every single day, even before a former law professor from Illinois named Obama rode to the White House railing against "special interests" and promising to bar lobbyists from using the revolving door.

For even the most ethical lobbyists, the landmines were everywhere. There were overly aggressive business development officers, Foreign Corrupt Practices Act amendments, and some slimy international business folks you wanted to avoid. There were lying reporters who impersonated potential clients as they secretly taped your pitch for their business. There were too many free sports tickets and expense-account dinners. There were complex lobbying disclosure forms to fill out. There were FBI scams, efforts to entrap legislators, schemes with legal consequences far more serious than the work of journalists who had written their good-versus-evil stories before conducting their first interview.

The most dangerous characters I met in my time in the lobbying business, however, were not renegade peddlers of influence, or out-of-control clients. The greatest peril to our reputation was usually the members of Congress themselves. The addiction of both Democrats and Republicans to campaign cash from lobbyists threatened the integrity of the entire lawmaking process. It created at least the appearance of malfeasance daily.

Most elected officials hate raising money. All are upset by the hours the task consumes day after day. It is an obscene misallocation of our elected leaders' time, and surely one that would have made our Founding Fathers' skin crawl. Virtually every office we visited to make a case, with Members' constituents in tow, kept a list of folks who had sought help. That list wasn't itself a problem.

The problem came from the appearances taken on by the Washington dance. Fundraisers were often scheduled for the busy legislative season: April, May, June, and September. Invariably, these fundraising events were held on the days before key votes, where provisions lobbyists cared about, and which might mean millions of dollars to clients, were decided.

It didn't require a paranoid journalist to produce sensational charges purporting to link campaign contributions with official actions. The fact is that House rules require Members to avoid even the *appearance* of impropriety. This rule continues to be violated routinely in Washington, and will in the future, until Members have the guts to bar people doing business with the federal government from giving them money. Few do.

Cause and effect was never crystal clear. The vast majority of lobbyists' campaign donations went to support incumbents whose positions were well known and irreversible. To the outside viewer, however, skepticism was understandable. The lines were crossed when Capitol Hill people whom you had visited, and who had helped your client, began to call. They would call serially, and they would call aggressively. You'd pick up your private line, and there would be a Member, dialing for dollars from some campaign office. Some didn't even have an opponent. They did, however, have a title: "Chairman of the Ways and Means Committee" or "Chairman of the Defense Appropriations Subcommittee." It was very hard to say no.

So where did those contributions go? Look at the staff directory of many Members' campaigns. Sometimes it seemed as if every living relative of the incumbent was listed there, pocketing the campaign support as just another part of doing business in Washington. Or look at a man of modest personal means like Jesse Jackson, Jr., or an admired party leader such as John Boehner. Boehner was from a blue collar family. He owned a small home in Ohio and an apartment in D.C., where he had a full-time job leading House Republicans. Yet he played over 130 rounds of golf in one year, many at fancy resorts with lobbyists picking up the tab. As Seth Myers would say on *Saturday Night Live*'s "Weekend Update," "*Really?!?*"

Sometimes you could dodge a fundraising invitation. Other times, you had to show up, mostly as a return favor to a firm partner who had helped you under similar circumstances. You wrote the check, and mentally wrote it off as a tax, a tithe for the lucrative work. In the end, however, most involved in the process, including the elected officials and the donors, felt cheapened.

Periodically, Congress makes lame attempts to clean up the campaign fundraising mess. The only way you can reform the process is to make it so the Members cannot ask, not for tickets to the big game, not for their spouse's favorite charity, not for a corporate jet ride. Ban federal campaign contributions from any and all registered lobbyists doing business in Washington. End the fiction that millionaire lobbyists like Newt Gingrich and Dick Gephardt, who take lobbying fees as "history consultants" or "strategic counselors," are not influencing policy. (One competitor, Tommy Boggs, had scores of his firm's lobbyists "de-register" after Obama took office, effortlessly dodging new White House restrictions on meeting with lobbyists.) Then make all lobbyists try to sink or swim on the merits of the case alone. Firms like Cassidy would thrive.

As my work at the firm continued, I was struck repeatedly by the less than six degrees of separation that marked the inbred world in Washington. A good example was work on issues related to Pakistan. Back in the 1980s, when Senator Cranston was harshly critical of both New Delhi's and Islamabad's clandestine nuclear weapons programs, my mischievous Foreign Relations Committee colleague Peter Galbraith invited his college classmate, Benazir Bhutto, to dinner at our home. She was charming, joining us in our renovated Sears & Roebuck house for a sober evening of conversation and debate. Peter teased me about my public alarms over the prospect of a "Moslem bomb," pointing to books in our living room condemning the Pakistani weapons program Benazir's father had launched.

Benazir was witty, attired in beautiful silk robes and heavily made up with black eyeliner and alluring lipstick. Even with her escort (a virtuous woman must not dine alone with men in a private home), Benazir spoke freely, with a delightful British accent that elegantly framed her fervent nationalism. She was unwavering in her belief that her country needed a nuclear deterrent to counter the Indian threat, dismissing concerns that nuclear weapons did little to advance her impoverished nation.

Two decades later, the Musharraf dictatorship was in power and Benazir was once again in foreign exile. Pakistan was facing intense Washington pressure, this time for greater cooperation and transparency in fighting al-Qaeda and the Taliban. Throughout the summer of 2007, a massive U.S. aid package was being debated on Capitol Hill. The "Kerry-Lugar-Berman" bill would place stringent conditions on further U.S. assistance to Islamabad.

Pakistan's Washington ambassador was under pressure from ardent nationalists to rebuff these policy riders, considered by

Islamabad as a terrible affront to its national sovereignty. To plead his case that the Musharraf government was making great strides towards restoring civilian rule and soon would allow Benazir Bhutto back in the country to take part in national elections, Pakistan's Washington embassy needed help. Cassidy & Associates was hired for a very large retainer.

My partners and I would meet frequently at the Pakistan embassy in September and October of 2007, on a heavily guarded cul-de-sac in Washington, near the Israeli embassy compound. As we bantered freely with the ambassador and his staff, passing memos and notes back and forth, we were conscious of at least five intelligence services likely capturing parts of our exchanges, including the CIA. In fact, when appropriate, we shared our own views with senior U.S. government officials via a back channel, seeking to trade insights that might help us advance client interests and bring Pakistan into closer accord with Washington objectives. We were eager to keep pressure on Pakistan to reform, even as we conveyed to the ambassador our analysis of what, for the U.S. government, constituted red lines not to be crossed.

The ambassador was a courtly man with elegant manners. Yet he was a former senior intelligence official, not given to volunteering the truth. When I discussed his situation with Senator Lugar's chief of staff, Ken Myers reminded me that "Pakistani officials retain a remarkable capacity to deliver a bald-faced lie with a straight face," a point borne out later when Osama Bin Laden was "discovered" living only a mile from the Pakistani equivalent of West Point.

Early in the life of Cassidy's contract with the embassy, the wild tiger we were riding—trying to help Pakistan's moderate ambassador while not undercutting U.S. policy—bucked us. At the end of October 2007, Musharraf suddenly placed Benazir Bhutto under house arrest. His promise of free elections appeared to crumble. I spent a restless night trying to figure out what to do. I sat on our back deck in Arlington, staring up at the stars and trying to work the problem.

It wasn't really that complicated. I had come to Washington

to advance public policy, to work on education, nuclear nonproliferation, and other issues. I had not come to Washington to defend dictators. We could justify helping Pakistan in Washington if Musharraf was welcoming Bhutto, helping the U.S. in the fight against al Qaeda, and moving towards a pluralist democracy. With free elections now shelved, our assignment, it seemed, had become inconsistent with American interests. I worried that I had been over-rationalizing my welcome paychecks, justifying work that strayed too far from first principles.

The next morning, I resigned from the project team, probably coming off as a righteous prig. My partners were trying to protect our staff from pending layoffs. We were playing tackle football here, not croquet: The Marquess of Queensbury rules did not always apply.

What the firm did next, though, was quite remarkable. The Pakistani ambassador was notified that under the changed circumstances on the ground in Islamabad, the firm could no longer provide honest and effective counsel. We would be messengering a check returning the embassy's retainer.

The ambassador's response was: "It is a very decent thing you have done." Hours later, the Pakistani embassy leaked word to *The Washington Post* that they had found it necessary to terminate their contract with the firm. Cassidy lobbyists left this false report uncorrected.

Some days later, in Pakistan, Bhutto was assassinated in a hail of bullets. In the ensuing turbulence, her estranged husband came to power. A new Pakistani ambassador, Hussain Haqqani, was sent to Washington. One of his first visits was to the firm, where he hailed the previous resignation on principle, and asked to engage Cassidy with a new contract. It was one of the few times in Washington that I saw a good deed, originally punished, subsequently get rewarded. This time, however, rather than leave my partners in the lurch in a crisis, I stayed off the reconstituted team. Soon, I turned down a long-term contract extension with the firm. A new reality was inescapable; it was time for me to plan an exit.

Many on the outside would be skeptical, but the ethical red

lines were rather clear. There were not that many gray areas. We were providing professional services. So in the end, my biggest challenge as a lobbyist was a familiar one. I had a deep-seated fear of boredom. No matter how novel the case, and no matter how difficult the environment, there was a sameness creeping into every assignment I took on. I wanted a new challenge. After many years, Congress flipped from one party's control to another. The nation was attacked, and promptly launched multiple wars. The firm was bought and sold. Partners battled, died, or quit to form rival firms. Still, Cassidy & Associates marched on.

The firm indulged me infinitely in my outside pursuits. I kept some eclectic pro bono clients, such as the Save Darfur campaign and the remarkable little arms control lobby, John Isaacs' Council for a Livable World. One year, I took off for weeks to teach a course on presidential campaigns at the University of Pennsylvania. I wrote a spy novel. I continued writing academic articles about Washington policymaking and best practices for NGO advocates.[34] I returned to teach a graduate course on foreign policymaking at Georgetown. After working to get earmarks for Hampshire College, I helped run a Hampshire Board of Trustees development campaign, spending weeks at a time in Amherst.

Even if I was away from the capital, however, the tether of the damn BlackBerry tugged. There was no escape from the Washington grind. The responsibility of helping meet marketing targets and funding the payroll was ever-present.

My brothers understood my persistence. Andy and Pete had held the same job for years; only our younger brother Jason had taken extraordinary risks to pursue multiple careers. Our childhoods, marked as they were by consistently downward economic mobility, had produced in us an absolute determination to build financial security for our families.

Late at night, talking on the back porch with my kids, I'd dream of escape. Once again, good fortune came my way with the remarkable University of Virginia opportunity. It afforded me the chance to be part of an innovative start-up, to help design an educational program, to be an entrepreneur helping build something enduring. It seemed to promise the calm of a collegial campus, a respite from the petty politics of Congress.

One day after weighing the UVa offer, I finally worked up the courage to jump. It was a soft landing. I could imagine the Cassidy train, with longtime colleagues aboard, barreling ahead and disappearing into the horizon. I could look up at the stars and smile. I wasn't at all certain what adventures lay ahead, but I sensed once more the invigorating flow of adrenaline.

CHAPTER FIFTEEN

Cold War Days: Inside the Kremlin

Moscow, Union of Soviet Socialist Republics
August 1981 and August 1987

The Cold War waxed and waned for decades. For those of us who came of age in its midst, it was a conflict marked by fits and starts. Some days, an episodic spike in tensions would erupt. American and Soviet leaders would scare the hell out of citizens in both nations, putting nuclear forces on alert and unleashing volleys of bellicose rhetoric. Then the crisis would pass. We would conveniently forget for months at a time that some of the sixty thousand nuclear warheads in the world targeted our home communities.

Then another eruption would occur—trouble in Cuba, or a proxy invasion some place in Asia or the Middle East that few in the U.S. could locate on a map. Routines in our hometowns once again became tense. The burden of living in the nuclear crosshairs crept back into our consciousness, despite our many efforts over the years to suppress it.

My earliest memory of thinking about our nation's capital stemmed from one such episode. Our family sat in our living room on Peninsula Road—the one with the amazing view across the lagoon of Mt. Tamalpais—watching our old RCA black-and-white TV. It was an Oval Office address President Kennedy was giving at the height of the Cuban Missile Crisis. Kennedy was unspeakably grim. I had no real clue what was happening, just that I saw Mom afraid for the first time. She is a ferociously strong woman, yet she rarely hid us from worldly concerns. Family dinner-table conversation was adult from a very young age. That warm October evening in Marin County, we were watching the same TV that brought us Walt Disney shows every Sunday night at 7:30 p.m., 6:30 Central.

For us kids, months of forgetting would intervene. Then another U.S.-Soviet confrontation would erupt. Sometimes we'd be startled by something as simple as the "duck-and-cover drill" we practiced at Ross Elementary School. I wanted to ask my third grade teacher, the beautiful Polish refugee, Miss Iwanicki, how kneeling under a desk would protect us from a nuclear bomb.

Then another foreign crisis would unfold. The Soviet invasion of Czechoslovakia in 1968. The superpower standoff during the 1973 Arab-Israeli war, when Richard Nixon put U.S. nuclear forces on high alert. The grain embargo and Olympic boycotts. A Soviet brigade "discovered" just south of Miami. Thousands of Cuban refugees floating toward Florida.

Diplomats maneuvered, armies marched, air forces patrolled with nuclear bombs. *Time* magazine, the authoritative source of news in my youth, warned us of a "ring of crisis" from Somalia to the Indian subcontinent. Even as a child, my *Dr. Strangelove* fears of madman bombers haunted my dreams. I had a recurring nightmare about walking down Shady Lane toward our home in Ross. Trees turned to nuclear ash. Neighbors' skin melted like ice cream in a radioactive sun. Viet Cong laughter echoed in the gray smoke.

With the ascension in the early 1980s of Ronald Reagan and his tough-talking Cabinet officers, Al Haig and Caspar Weinberger, the time of dark thoughts was upon us once more. The difference now was that I was an adult, and I had a security clearance—high enough to see classified intelligence on troubling events behind the headlines—and a job staffing the majority whip of the U.S. Senate.

President Reagan gleefully led the name-calling, pinning on the Soviets, who'd lost more than twenty-five million citizens helping us defeat Hitler, the epithet "Evil Empire." Reagan's cheerfulness belied his determination. The Soviets were the villains of his narratives, and the Reagan White House was driven to put Moscow on the defensive. As the war of words escalated and direct contacts between the two capitals ceased, Alan Cranston was alarmed.

Cranston was optimistic, to the point of some naïveté, about Soviet intentions. He was an idealist, a rare Scotsman who saw only the best in his adversaries. He was determined to show that the Soviets were much like us, afraid for their own future. He believed that they often were acting defensively out of fear of U.S. power and NATO encirclement.

Cranston knew Ronald Reagan quite well from California politics. Reagan scared him. Cranston considered the president lazy, shallow, and ill-read, a tool of Orange County John Birch Society ideologues. Cranston feared how easily hard-liners could manipulate a man so ignorant of history.

The senator was determined to help end the deep freeze in U.S.-Soviet relations, to try to resume bilateral discussions on nuclear arms control, even if he had to jumpstart the dialogue himself. After he was reelected to his third Senate term in 1980, Cranston permitted himself the luxury of joining the Foreign Relations Committee, a panel notorious for not helping senators with reelection back home. In this regard, Robert Caro's observation that "power reveals" is instructive; Cranston came to politics determined to advance world peace. When he had accumulated significant power, he tried to use it to advance the cause of his choosing: improving U.S.-Soviet relations. It was similar to the surprising and admirable route taken by Lyndon Johnson when he reached the apex of power. The favorite of Texas oilmen and Southern segregationists, LBJ, as President, declared war on poverty and racism.

Secure in his leadership post, Cranston expanded a bipartisan group of senators he had originally convened in 1978 to prepare for Senate passage of SALT II, the second strategic arms limitation treaty with the Soviets. His group of thirty senators would meet monthly in his spectacular whip office in the Capitol. His friend Senator Charles Mathias, Republican of Maryland, gave him bipartisan cover for the invites to the "SALT Study Group."

Even some of the most conservative senators—Stevens, Lugar, and Domenici—would show up and query his guests. Cranston would host the head of the CIA, the NSC advisor, or the secretary of state. They would speak with blistering candor about what the U.S. government needed to do to avert a nuclear exchange. No transcripts were made of these extraordinary sessions. Only two staffers were let in the room—Cas Yost and I—and we were admitted only so we could brief other senators' staff on what their bosses had said and heard.

When U.S.-Soviet relations reached a low point in mid-1981, Cranston abruptly announced he'd lead a bipartisan Senate delegation to Moscow with Mathias. Their goal was to reason with Soviet Foreign Minister Andrei Gromyko. Secretary of State Haig was not pleased; he doubtless thought Cranston, a San Francisco Bay Area liberal, was soft on Communism. Haig, against whose confirmation Cranston had voted, grudgingly granted the senators and their legislative aides an audience in a last-ditch effort to cancel the trip.

It was a blistering hot July day when we entered Haig's office on the seventh floor at the State Department. Haig had seated himself in front of an enormous plate glass window, through which a blinding glare off the white marble in one hundred-degree summer heat offered only an imperious silhouette. We were forced to squint in his direction. One suspects this was exactly the wizard-like pose Secretary Haig sought. His disdain was palpable. He sneered, his unnaturally ruddy complexion suggesting too much sun, too much drink, or both.

The Reagan administration wasn't talking to the Soviets that year. That was the whole point. Nothing positive, Haig made clear, could come from a couple of do-gooder senators trying to make nice in Moscow. His strategy was to make the Soviets squirm. Neither Secretary Haig nor the White House could stop the Senate trip. Haig made clear to us, nevertheless, that he believed we were on a fool's errand. No, we could not carry any Reagan administration message. No, he wasn't interested in resuming SALT talks. Yes, according to Haig, the frightening deterioration in relations was all the Soviets' fault. Reagan likened Americans clamoring for a freeze in the U.S.-Soviet nuclear stockpiles to "foreign agents" who would "weaken America."[35]

I was put in charge of advance work for the trip. I had Yost as my wingman, and he proved my savior. A senior Republican staffer whose father had been Nixon's UN ambassador, Cas was a veteran of interbranch squabbles. He harbored no illusions about the Soviets, or the Reagan White House. (Cas, ever the bipartisan public servant, later served as a top official on the National Intelligence Council under President Obama.) During a layover in Paris, Yost sat me down with a bottle of good red wine and proceeded to instruct me on how the game was to be played.

"Assume every person you meet works for the KGB," Cas explained. "Say nothing you do not want overheard. Expect every conversation to be taped, even in the U.S. ambassador's residence, even inside the U.S. embassy. Don't drink with the Russians; they'll put you under the table. Don't sleep with them; they'll have you on camera. Don't leave any documents lying about; their intelligence services will copy them in a heartbeat. Smile politely, but assume the worst of intentions in all exchanges."

The next day, Cas and I left Paris for Moscow, ahead of the senators, to negotiate the long-delayed schedule of meetings. His tutorial was quickly put to the test.

Soviet Foreign Minister Andrei Gromyko was our great white whale, the key interlocutor Cranston and Mathias wanted to meet. The cynical veteran of Stalin's WWII inner circle, Gromyko was clearly calling the shots among the aging Soviet leadership, but no U.S.S.R. diplomat in Washington would even confirm he would grant us an audience.

We arrived late on a warm summer evening and were dispatched to Spaso House, which for nearly a century had been the Moscow residence of the U.S. ambassador. The pastel yellow walls and tinted roof glowed in the northern twilight. The domestic staff members in the house were all Soviet citizens. In the hallway to our bedrooms, we were surprised by a beautiful young Russian named Elena, poised in a soft pink sweater she filled quite bounteously.

"May I offer you a snack?" asked this coquettish Meg Ryan look-alike. "Maybe some roast beef sandwiches and an ice cold beer?"

Cas accepted dryly, before she added, "Just let me know if there is anything else at all I can get for you—anything at all!"

As she traipsed off to the kitchen, her blonde curls bouncing back at us, Cas, with a smirk, said under his breath, "Not real subtle."

The following day consisted of a series of fruitless meetings about meetings. The Soviets were proposing an itinerary for the senators that included tours of schools and factories, a few courtesy calls with low-level functionaries and the head of the State Duma (lower house of the legislature) mixed in. Cas was doing a slow burn. *What to do?* The senators were due to fly into Moscow the next evening.

"This is total bullshit!" Yost exploded in my room after Elena delivered our nightcaps. "This is what we are going to do: We are going to the U.S. embassy in the morning and we are going to call the senators on a secure line. We are going to tell them to cancel their visit. Commie bastards think they're going to shaft some of the only guys in Washington with the balls to stand up to the Reagan administration? The senators are not going to fly six thousand miles to tour a goddamn pencil factory."

He crumpled up the draft schedule and threw it in the trash. "Fuck 'em!" he said without even the hint of a wink.

Early the next morning, an anxious emissary from the Foreign Ministry appeared at Spaso House with a new schedule. *Soviet Marshal Nikolai Ogarkov?* Check. *Foreign Minister Andrei Gromyko?* Confirmed. The walls, indeed, had ears.

After the senators arrived, our work rolled forward. First was the meeting with Ogarkov, the Soviet official in charge of nuclear missile forces. We drove to a military complex not far from Red Square. High-ceilinged hallways with dim lighting yielded to a more formal chamber that felt a bit like the office of an elementary school principal. Our escorts bowed nervously and backed out the door. Standing before us was the man who controlled tens of thousands of nuclear weapons targeted at the United States and our allies. I kept thinking: *If war ever breaks out, this is the guy who will kill my family.*

Ogarkov had a dark olive complexion that seemed to blend with his drab tan fatigues, which were bedecked with dozens of medals. His demeanor was serious, but his face seemed sad. He looked like a grandfather worrying about his progeny.

Cranston led him into a dialogue about a nuclear exchange.

"Could a 'limited' nuclear war ever be contained?" Cranston asked.

"No," Nikolai Ogarkov stated through a translator. "Escalation is inevitable."

"Could missile defense afford protection?" Senator Cranston probed. "Star Wars" plans for U.S. missile defense was the issue of the day.

"No," Ogarkov responded matter-of-factly. "Offense is cheaper than defense—interceptors can always be overwhelmed."

"Could either side ever 'win' once a nuclear launch was initiated?" Cranston pressed.

Ogarkov paused for the translation, before interrupting.

"No. Mutual suicide." He said it in English, more in sorrow than in anger.

These last words were really all Ogarkov needed to say. Cranston took the marshal's blunt observation and repeated it to all who would listen, for years to come. Ogarkov's response even became a bittersweet joke in future Cranston campaigns, including his ill-advised 1984 presidential bid. When Cranston staffers would encounter colleagues from other long-shot candidates during our doomed campaign travels, we'd ask if we actually had a chance. The smart-ass answer was always, "No. Mutual suicide."

The audience with Andrei Gromyko was expected to be the high point of our Moscow visit. We headed to the meeting with great anticipation. I still have on my wall, thirty years later, a snapshot taken just before we entered the ancient Soviet Foreign Ministry building. In the faded photograph, Senator Cranston is grinning optimistically next to me, as if one good conversation could straighten out decades of terrible misunderstandings. I am wincing, gazing anxiously into an uncertain future, aware that we stood in the crosshairs of a dozen U.S. nuclear-armed missiles.

The four of us met with ministry functionaries for a time. More photographs were taken. The conversation, however, proved to be of little interest. These were Communist Party apparatchiks, powerless to

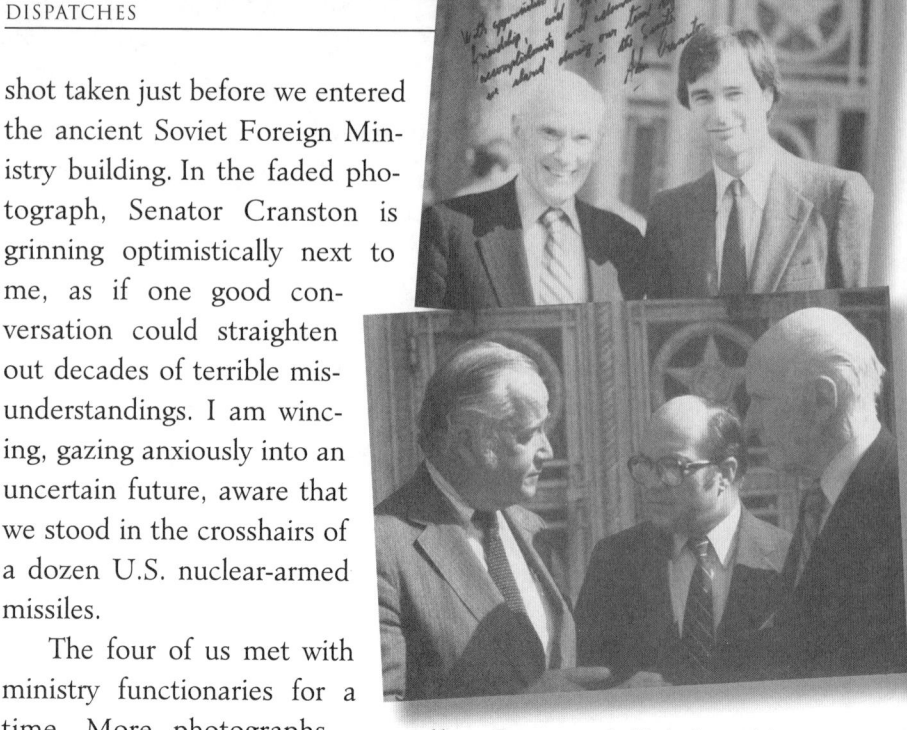

Above: Cranston and aide in front of the Soviet Foreign Ministry, Moscow, August 1981. Below: Acting U.S. Ambassador Jack Matlock with Cranston and Mathias. Soviet Foreign Minister Andrei Gromyko proceeded to give us a tongue-lashing right out of the 1950s.

President of the Soviet State Duma with party apparatchiks inside the Kremlin. Clockwise: Cranston, Mathias, and Mathias aide Cas Yost. Mathias was a favorite senator; his wicked sense of humor helped us recover from this deadly boring meeting full of Communist Party blather.

deviate from the Party line. Then we were escorted into an ornate conference room. Behind a heavy mahogany table was the legendary Soviet Politburo member, veteran of Potsdam and Yalta, Andrei Gromyko. His retinue was fanned out to his right and left. He was muttering under his breath in Russian. He nodded, but did not shake hands.

Senator Mathias opened eloquently: "We are here to learn if there might be a path forward." He explained that the SALT II Treaty was shelved by the Senate while the Soviet military continued its two-year-old occupation of Afghanistan. Confidence-building measures were needed to get a constructive dialogue going once again.

"You Americans bear responsibility for killing arms control," Gromyko interrupted in Russian, not waiting for the interpreter to catch up. "You're playing games with the 'China card.' Your grain embargoes are trying to make our people go hungry. *Your* Star Wars. *Your* Olympic boycotts. *Your* hostile rhetoric about 'Evil Empires.'"

"Sir, with all due respect," Mathias said, "there is no greater American supporter of mutual, verifiable nuclear arms reductions than Alan Cranston. The senator has here in his pocket a tally sheet showing we had the votes to pass SALT II in the Senate right up until the day you invaded Afghan—"

"We only took *defensive* measures," Gromyko interrupted, in Russian, as we waited for the translation. "This was long after your right-wing lawmakers killed SALT!"

Mathias tried to intervene. Cranston also tried to get the floor, reaching into his pocket and producing his trademark roll call tally sheet, but Gromyko was unyielding. For nearly an hour, the crusty Soviet foreign minister railed on and on about alleged American abuses. He paused only a few times for the interpreter to catch up. Then he would interrupt his staff—now in English—to embellish: "I did not say 'lies.' I said '*damn* lies!'"

Just as the translator finally caught up with the last of Gromyko's blasts, the foreign minister pushed away from the table, nodded slightly our way, then strode out the side door from which he had entered. The dialogue we had flown thousands of miles to develop had ended.

Gromyko's rude flourish had left us feeling bleak, and now the day darkened further. There was one more Moscow meeting yet to convene before we flew west to Bonn. In an elaborate ruse that fooled nobody, we took leave of our Soviet handlers and traveled by private car to a grim suburban apartment block. Taking a rickety elevator to an upper floor, we were escorted by a U.S. embassy staffer into the cramped unit of an elderly Jewish couple from Chicago. Soviet citizens now, they had been refused permission to emigrate from the U.S.S.R. Gathered in the room with them were two dozen refuseniks—Soviets who had also been repeatedly refused the right to emigrate. There were teachers who had been laid off, pensioners who were trapped, engineers who had been fired because they applied for the right to leave the U.S.S.R for Israel or the United States. The abstraction of human rights debates in the Senate was made manifest before us.

Visiting them was a debt of honor for Cranston and Mathias, but an act of obligation for me, a descendant of European Jews. For days, I had carried a list in an envelope in my coat pocket, together with a signed plea for compassion the senators had handed to a Gromyko aide. For weeks prior to our travel, Cas and I had met with relatives of the refuseniks, activists, and State Department staffers who added names to the list and subtracted others. It was a chilling process, deciding who would make the cut and who wouldn't—a veritable Sophie's choice. We also knew full well the Soviets might just throw our written appeal in the trash, instead of making a goodwill gesture of releasing dissidents after our departure.

Who would make it onto our list? Who would not? How to decide? I remember their names still: Scharanksy and Slepak, Vitaly Rubin, Ida Nudel, Alexander Lerner—the Chicago Cubs fan.

Soon, their anxious eyes were before us, trying to keep a game face as they poured weak coffee. Their wan smiles did little to hide their despair. We knew our every word was captured by KGB microphones. The gathering was awkward in the extreme. The senators had little hope to offer, though we Americans were awed by their courage and both senators spoke eloquently. Still, most of the Russians seemed heavily resigned to their fate, a slow, dark existence, harassed at the margins of an entrenched Communist dictatorship.[36]

After a desultory conversation, and a quick photo, we left. Their earnest handshakes and sad faces lingered. Survivor's guilt plagued me. I knew I'd be dining west of the Iron Curtain the next night. Each person before us would still be buried alive in a repressive Soviet system.

I felt powerless. Worse yet, now we had to make idle chatter with the Communists one last time. We'd all be drinking that evening with our Soviet escorts. The party loyalists awaited at a posh restaurant, pretending they were unaware of our detour to speak with the refuseniks. The place was all glass and marble, with horrendous acoustics. Our hosts were resplendent in their silk ties and knock-off Cartier watches, purchased from special Moscow stores open only to senior Party members.

Drink we did, though Yost's warning kept coming back to me. We were in a loud "private" club with bad polka music and hefty waitresses serving chewy beef. Toast after toast was offered; all were of straight vodka in shot glasses. I was staggered until I noticed Cas nodding toward me as he quickly refilled his shot glass . . . with water. He was moving preemptively, preparing for the next round. He winked, and I followed the same procedure through several subsequent toasts until, finally, our Soviet staff counterpart, Valery, was reeling.

"I need air!" Valery gasped, laughing, but clearly wounded. I walked with him out the door and stood alongside as he struggled to light a Marlboro. He bent, hands on his knees, in an alleyway, as if to puke, then rallied as a line of official cars passed noisily by.

"So, I guess you'll be glad when we're gone," I offered meekly. I was aware that my furtive shots of water had made for an unfair contest. "You can get back to your regular job."

"Yeah," he snorted, recovering. He stood gasping for a moment, smiling strangely now, sizing me up anew. Then he squared up and looked piercingly at me, despite his drunken state. He glanced behind us, weighing some burden.

It was just us, two inebriated staff guys with lots of good background noise. For this one time, we could speak freely. So Valery let forth his worldly concerns.

"We didn't look forward to your visit, you know." His English was good, and now there was no stopping him. "Your fancy senators with their good intentions. I worried for weeks about all the goddamn details. I was just afraid to screw up. You have no idea what we have had to deal with. My father died in the war—his three brothers, too. Stalingrad, the Ukraine. All dead. We've been through years and years of trying to keep up, trying to win some respect from the Americans. And now, even those who would talk to us want to lecture us.

"There is a problem? It's *always* the Soviets' fault in your stories. Our people just want peace! You call us some 'Evil Empire.' It is the same old bullshit, always the same."

Valery leered at me, then grabbed me hard by my shoulders. He wobbled, even as he strained to steady himself. By now he could say no more, waving off my lame attempt at a response with a knowing smile. We understood each other.

It was the one unscripted moment of the trip, and by far the most genuine. Thirty years later, however, I still feel guilty about watering down my shots.

Our Soviet venture that tense summer had a most unlikely bookend. A sharp contrast from Alexander Haig's harsh audience and Andrei Gromyko's furor, the next time we visited the Soviet Union, we were invited to tea with Andrei Sakharov. Had anyone predicted this in 1981, I would not have believed them.

The Moscow we encountered in August 1987 was like that of another century. The long Narnian winter of the seventy-year Communist Party rule was beginning to thaw. The new Soviet leader, Mikhail Gorbachev, was radically altering the face of his nation. Doors were open for conversations that would have been unthinkable just six years before under the aging Stalinist bureaucrats. Brezhnev, Chernenko, and Andropov were all dead. Gromyko, too, was gone.

Back in Washington, Ronald Reagan was a lame duck, stage-managed by manipulative staff, and beginning to show the foggy loss of recall that would haunt his declining years. His incipient Alzheimer's almost made it believable he did not know his White House staff was illegally trading U.S.-source arms for hostages with Iran to finance the anti-Sandinista contras in Nicaragua. In part due to Reagan's commendably bold offer at the Reykjavik summit with Gorbachev, a gambit which had mortified hawkish U.S. defense planners in the White House traveling party, there was an opening for Americans interested in finally negotiating deep nuclear arms cuts. Changes in the Soviet regime even allowed critics, such as human rights activists Andrei Sakharov and Yelena Bonner, to speak more freely.

Cranston had just been reelected to what would prove to be his final Senate term. His victory margin was microscopic, less than two votes per precinct. Yet he would become the longest-serving California Democrat ever in the U.S. Senate. He was proud of the accomplishment and he was as ready as ever to take risks with the political capital he had preserved.

One of his indulgences was to draft a scholarly book on how the Soviet Politburo worked. He spent months interviewing prominent U.S. Kremlinologists and intelligence sources before departing on another official Senate trip to the Soviet Union. This time, he took family and friends—his son Kim, a few key political supporters, and his top fundraiser, Joy.

We were invited to places previously off-limits to Americans. These included a wild ride through the Georgian countryside. When, at Senator Cranston's request, the entourage stopped in a random peach orchard, we startled a group of farm workers. Then we barreled back down the road, terrified by our grinning Soviet handlers as they raced our limousines around rocky cliffs and down to the heart of Yalta.

At the Black Sea resort, we were summoned by the vacationing Soviet ambassador Anatoly Dobrynin. His "dacha" was a high-rise condo with fancy marble and opulent elevators, built on the shores of some very senior Communist Party summer camp. Senator Cranston queried Dobrynin on *perestroika*, *glasnost*, and the future of arms control, and they posed for informal snapshots.

Soviet ambassador Anatoly Dobrynin with his wife, his niece, Senator Cranston, and Kim Cranston, August 19, 1987.

A jukebox in the distance was playing disco. Dobrynin's young blonde niece strolled in and out from the veranda, sauntering in a cocktail dress as she pulled on a straw inside a bright red can of Coke. We could have been in New Jersey, for all the resemblance it had to the everyday life of a Soviet citizen, or to what we had seen of the old Communist regime before the Gorbachev revolution.

Gorbachev and Reagan had been exchanging ambitious arms-control proposals. Cranston was amazed that his lifelong political nemesis Reagan had kicked open a door to radical new approaches to arms cuts. The senator was unburdened by the need to run for office again, so he was anxious for bold progress, and he didn't let the irony of Reagan's fortunate opening stop him.

Cranston was fascinated by the "soft revolution" just beginning those months in the Soviet leadership. In Moscow, he was intent on trying to figure out how much support Gorbachev had, and what stomach hard-liners in the Kremlin inner circle had for blocking Gorbachev if he agreed to a sweeping arms reduction deal with President Reagan. Our pre-trip briefings made clear that U.S. intelligence officials believed there were several Kremlin factions vying for influence over runaway events. All of Moscow was on edge, not sure what taboos one could now safely break as the iron grip on Soviet civic life since 1917 began to loosen.

To our great surprise, Cranston was allowed to visit Andrei Sakharov and his wife Yelena Bonner, still under house arrest but just freed from years of internal exile. American embassy staff herded us into the only secure room they had—a chilly plexi-glass box with metal chairs in the embassy attic—to explain to us that there were secret feelers out between Gorbachev and Sakharov about the terms of freedom for the legendary Soviet physicist and human rights champion.

We drove to a nondescript high-rise apartment block and walked up several flights of stairs. You could smell soup, plaster, and wallpaper paste. Doors opened a crack as we passed by, then shut quickly. There were empty chairs in the hallway where KGB watchers normally sat.

We entered their shabby apartment; it had been sealed for years, and the wallpaper was curling. Sakharov's wife Yelena gestured immediately to the ceiling. She put a finger to her ear—reminding us we were all miked for sound. Then, astonishingly, Sakharov held forth on the issues of the day. Despite years of harassment and exile, and repeated KGB confiscation of his notebooks, diaries, and academic papers, Sakharov reviewed with us each of the controversies bedeviling Washington-Moscow relations.

Andrei Sakharov and Yelena Bonner with Senator Cranston and his son Kim, August 22, 1987.

Cranston was able to press him on arms control, on the Politburo, even on Star Wars. I took hasty notes. Sakharov, the father of the Soviet hydrogen bomb before he became the Soviet Union's most famous dissident, looked like a cross between Winston Churchill and the Christopher Lloyd character from *Back to the Future*. In his every pronouncement, Sakharov was certain and proud whenever he rejected foolishness, whether emanating from Moscow or Washington. He relished the audience. We could sense he had not been able to speak freely for years, and that he knew there was a chance he might not have such an opportunity again.

He seized the moment. He unburdened himself of a host of opinions. Even if you are not a Kremlinologist, the shorthand memo of the conversation is still of interest.[37] Sakharov's answers, embellished in English by our doting and forceful hostess, were crisp, soundly rooted in the history of the modern Soviet Union.

When it came time to leave, Sakharov suddenly produced a package wrapped in an old brown grocery bag and tied with white string. He handed it to us silently and I carried it back to the U.S. embassy in Moscow, after which it was spirited out of the country in a secure diplomatic pouch. Several days later, it arrived in Washington and then was sent on to New York by special courier. But not before I had peeked.

Inside the package were hundreds of pages of notes, handwritten in Russian. I'd been carrying Sakharov's last edits of what would become an international sensation and bestseller: his autobiography, *My Life*.

In the months that followed our last 1987 visit to the Soviet Union, Washington policymakers were transfixed by the wild maneuverings of the Gorbachev regime. The reform-minded Gorbachev had improbably seized the national car keys after three successive infirm Soviet leaders had died. He shredded the brakes and stepped on the gas as he navigated a road of twists and turns. Ronald Reagan would soon head back to California retirement. George H. W. Bush won the presidency, then quickly completed a sweeping house cleaning of a National Security Council that

Reagan had allowed to descend into criminality under the Ollie North crowd. Fourteen of Reagan's senior White House staff were subject to federal prosecution.

The accumulated weight of a command economy with ridiculous production quotas and falsified data was sinking the Soviet ship. With the arrival of satellite phones and cable television, together with an easing of travel restrictions, the pressure from East European citizens to enjoy what the West took for granted was mounting. Oppressed citizens behind the Iron Curtain knew unmistakably what they were missing.

The U.S., however, remained very much a spectator as Gorbachev played Pied Piper and led the old Soviet Bolsheviks right off a cliff. Once bonds were loosened under *perestroika* and *glasnost*, there was no way to contain the genie of freedom. Washington policymakers from the far left and hard right offered public advice. In the Senate, Alan Cranston and fellow liberals on the Foreign Relations Committee saw great opportunities to cut bloated nuclear arms stockpiles and finally restrain our own weapons budget.

Though they tried with resolutions and legislation, there was little the U.S. could do to hasten the end of the U.S.S.R. or even to ameliorate the fallout. Soon Cranston and his colleagues were proposing targeted packages of aid; these included the Support East European Democracy (SEED) measures we helped shape and the Lugar-Nunn initiatives to secure loose nuclear materials from former Soviet satellites. Promoting such post-Cold War initiatives, Cranston was able to build what became the last major piece of his substantial legislative legacy. It was a legacy tarnished at the end of his last term by his involvement with four Senate colleagues in assisting a contributor, Charles Keating, to expedite a regulatory decision on savings and loan practices.[38]

The truth was, Washington policy was quite irrelevant to the last paroxysms of the Communist regime in Moscow. A villain that had haunted the entire lifetime of my generation, that had repeatedly appeared in nightmares of my youth, was dying. As quickly as Kremlin czars Brezhnev, Andropov, and Chernenko had checked out in rapid succession, the Union of Soviet Socialist Republics was gone. President George H. W. Bush, probably the best prepared foreign policy president ever to occupy the White House, played it just right. Day after day, he counseled U.S. forces to stay out of the way and for American diplomats to cool the rhetoric. His administration refused to play a heavy hand in appealing to the different factions of the dying Moscow regime that were scheming to cling to power in its perilous last months.

When the Berlin Wall fell in November 1989, my intrepid cousin, the *New York Times* reporter Peter Maass, made it there within hours. He calmly took a chisel and small hammer from his rucksack and gouged out pieces of the gray aggregate from the wall near the Brandenburg Gate. One small chunk of concrete he soon delivered to me. This piece of the Wall now sits on my office trophy shelf, alongside my San Francisco Giants 2010 World Champions mug and a faded photo from a signing ceremony at the Carter White House. When I peer absent-mindedly at my Wall remnant today, I think back to the haunting faces of the refuseniks, and smile to know most are now enjoying retirements in Tel Aviv, Pittsburgh, and even, for a few, a very different Moscow.

Watching the Wall fall and listening to Tom Brokaw and Peter Jennings report soon thereafter on the dissolution of the Soviet Union, Americans felt elation. There was little partisan gloating at the time. This was a great and enduring victory for free peoples everywhere. The idea that the death of the Soviet Union was a direct consequence of American conservatives funding Star Wars or declaiming Evil Empires, or of American liberals pressing human rights and arms control legislation, was absurd, and the notion still is, despite efforts of some revisionist historians, who claim the end of the Soviet Union represented a personal victory for Ronald Reagan worthy of his enshrinement on Mount Rushmore. As a less partisan observer, former Kissinger partner David Rothkopf of the Carnegie Endowment, has written, every American president since FDR found ways to counter Soviet contagions without igniting a nuclear conflagration. Rothkopf concludes that saying Reagan "won" the Cold War is like crediting the rooster crowing at dawn with the rising of the sun.[39] Virtually every Congress over those same decades obtained bipartisan majorities to push both carrots and sticks to thwart Moscow designs while avoiding a nuclear war.

In the end, all patriotic Americans could celebrate the fact that the wicked witch of Soviet Communism had finally been vanquished. It was destroyed by the very people it had oppressed, heroes like Andrei Sakharov and Yelena Bonner. Decades in Washington helped me understand that this glorious result was first and foremost *their* victory, not ours.

CHAPTER SIXTEEN

Obama for America

October 2008
Fairfax, Virginia

Lobbyists worked undercover in the Obama-Biden campaign of 2008; it was a fact readily accepted, at least among many insiders. Amongst the idealistic young campaign staff, we grizzled veterans didn't talk much about our day jobs. We'd mutter something about being "in public affairs"; we felt, however, as if we should be wearing a scarlet "L." The work went forward each day that fall, as we joined with several thousand volunteers in the key Virginia exurbs.

As a fiscally conservative, socially progressive Democrat in a center-right country, I was used to losing campaigns. Democrats had lost to Ronald Reagan for years. They had lost to George H. W. Bush on Supreme Court nominees, lost to Newt Gingrich in the House and Howard Baker in the Senate. They had lost to George W. Bush, when an allegedly states-rights majority on the Supreme Court had ended the Florida recount in December of 2000, and elected Bush II on a 5-4 vote.

The 2008 presidential campaign seemed destined to be another repeat. Democrats had a great advantage because of Bush fatigue, but then nominated a poorly qualified first-term senator with an unusual pedigree. Democrats could yet again manage to snatch defeat from the jaws of victory, I concluded, and found myself more than a little reluctant to get involved.

But my former staff colleague from Senate Foreign Relations,

Gerry Connolly, was running hard for the local Republican-held House seat. The ever-loquacious and often profane Foreign Relations Committee chairman I had admired for years, Joe Biden, was running for Vice President. One of the most liberal legislators ever to have a good shot at the White House, Barack Obama, a former community organizer, was trying to deliver the nation from eight years of George W. Bush's divisive leadership. I changed direction, deciding I could not sit out the contest.

The first time I encountered Barack Obama was in an intimate gathering of eighteen thousand at the Boston Garden in the summer of 2004. I was sitting in a skybox talking with Kim Cranston, Alan's son. We both wondered why John Kerry had entrusted his nominating convention's keynote speech to a raw state senator with a strange name. When Obama took the stage, my first thought was that there's hope for tall guys who look gaunt on TV. His anxious grin was bracketed by ears that would have made LBJ's beagle blush.

Then Obama began to speak. All around us, the yammering of narcissistic politicians began to ease, until the din ceased altogether.

Thirty-plus years in politics have made me wary of the power of an individual speech to inspire the masses. The ability of one man to manipulate a large rally often strikes me as a double-edged sword. The image of Hitler stirring Aryan youth at Nuremberg rallies springs to mind; that did not end well. Full-throated allegiance makes me uncomfortable; it is a type of blind rah-rah partisan passion best relegated to sports arenas or high school and college gyms, not public policymaking.

As State Senator Obama got rolling that night, however, I was far from alone in my enchantment. It is very hard to quiet convention hall chatter. Often, eighteen thousand people just keep talking when a politician at the podium speaks. This night was different, though. We sensed it.

"There is not a liberal America and a conservative America—there is the United States of America," he insisted. "There is not a Black America and a White America and a Latino America . . .

there's a *United States* of America." You wanted to believe him.

The crowd watched in anxious silence, as if they were baseball fans witnessing the unfolding of a perfect game. Here was a speaker tapping into a national hunger for unity. Many were eager for a post-partisan patriotism, one we had known in the weeks just after the 9/11 attacks, before Karl Rove and Dick Cheney unleashed a divide and conquer strategy for governing America with 51 percent public support.

Americans were fighting multiple wars in that summer of 2004. Here before us was a young orator appealing to the better angels of our nature. The danger was apparent; this upstart from the Illinois statehouse was upstaging the national party nominee, John Kerry.

Working hard that fall for Kerry, I moved to Philadelphia for the last month of the campaign, helping design and run the Get Out the Vote war room in the swing state of Pennsylvania. My prior campaign experience had been in the brief run Alan Cranston had made for the White House in 1984. I'd also worked on a team headed by Madeleine Albright and Greg Craig, preparing Massachusetts Governor Michael Dukakis on international issues. When it came to Democrats seeking the presidency, my record as a campaign volunteer was a consistently losing one.

Working Pennsylvania for John Kerry in 2004, we were astonished to watch what transpired. Remarkably, the Bush-Cheney-Rumsfeld folks, who had personally ducked on going to Vietnam, tried to demean Kerry's war combat record. Even more remarkable, the strategy actually worked. What stuck with voters was Rove's caricature of Kerry as a French-speaking, wind-surfing millionaire of questionable patriotism.

Heading into Election Day, we still thought Kerry would win. Pennsylvania, Ohio, and Florida were once again key swing states. As we prepared for the balloting, I learned again that my legislative skills were insufficiently hard-nosed for Philadelphia street politics. We'd set up a large headquarters phone bank to communicate with regional offices in every county throughout the Keystone State. Then, a week before Election Day, we'd all moved to a union-controlled warehouse deep in the city's ghetto.

It was a storage facility for some porn or sex products distributor—we kept finding dildos and lewd photos in cartons in the stairwells. Local labor bosses insisted on reissuing staff credentials daily, which was necessary, they maintained, in order to screen out gate-crashers and Republican spies. Entry was through a single metal door; it was guarded twenty-four hours a day by brawny Sylvester Stallone look-alikes wearing leather jackets and dark glasses. One conference room held a bullpen of nervous D.C. lawyers armed with pre-drafted legal challenges, lest any friendly precincts not open on time. Though my staff had lined up food for delivery on Election Day, the local security team intervened.

"No, no, no," the head man said. "*Our* people makes da food, 'n' *our* people delivers it."

"Huh?" I was lost.

"C'mon," he warned. "We can't have our boys and girls spending the day on the toilet, now can we?"

Apparently one of the Donald Segretti-style trash-the-enemy plays common on Election Days in Philadelphia was to lace food headed to opponents' headquarters with powerful laxatives. "Politics here 'onna street," one of the Rocky-style guards explained to me, "is whatcha might call a *contact* sport."

There was press speculation as to whether John Kerry's Philadelphia campaign would submit to local ward bosses' demands for "walkin'-around money"—envelopes of cash handed to union, religious, and ethnic community leaders to turn out the vote. After weeks of deliberation, the Kerry team paid the locals. A whole lot of people who decidedly did not attend college with the good senator were delivered to the polls to vote.

We opened our Election Day headquarters at 5 a.m., as a soft drizzle fell. By noon, the first ecstatic calls came on my cell phone. "We've won!" Breathless friends called from Washington, Boston, and California with the news. "The Wicked Witch is dead!"

By early afternoon, the wave was unmistakable. Every D.C. insider who had ever met a reporter or pollster had gotten the news. The early ballot boxes from the Midwest, from swing precincts in key states, showed irreversible numbers. Kerry was stomping Bush. The TV networks knew it. *Bush* knew it. In Boston, campaign speechwriter Bob Shrum took Kerry aside and said, "Let me be the first to call you 'Mr. President!'"

Exit polls declared Kerry was ahead by 10 percent in Wisconsin, 7 in Ohio, 9 in Florida. It was going to be a landslide. All we had suffered through during the Bush-Gore recount—the hanging chad craziness, the bizarre Supreme Court ruling—followed by the four years of mean-spirited George W. Bush, would soon be over.

Despite my exhaustion, I was elated. I momentarily abandoned my post supervising the war room and stepped out onto the roof to call Mom to tell her Kerry had won. I thought again of the San Francisco Giants and 2002. Seven outs from their first World Series Championship ever, and leading 5-0, they still managed to lose. All those frustrating near misses were finally to be righted. My eyes welled up as I shared the good news we all had from inside the networks and the campaign. Kerry had won.

The rest of the afternoon was spent sleepwalking through routines no longer so urgent. Once the polls began to close, Joy rode in from where she was working in suburban Pennsylvania counties to join the victory celebration. We were both so tired, though, that we just grabbed some pizza and soda, and began the two-and-a-half-hour drive home to Virginia to celebrate with our three children.

It was one of the most sickening drives of my life.

By the time we hit Interstate 95, there was a new caution in the commentators' voices on CBS radio. States that the major news networks had called prematurely for the Democrats were being put back in play. By the time we reached the Maryland state line, things were falling apart. With every mile, the mirage of a Kerry landslide evaporated. It seemed Bush could pull off a Houdini number that would make the 2000 Florida recount look like child's play.

I'd seen this movie before. It was the very same one where Lucy pulls the football just as Charlie Brown is *finally* going to kick it. The one where Al Gore wins the popular vote, but loses the presidential election. The one where my Giants have iced Champagne waiting in their locker room, but never get to taste it. By the time we pulled up in front of our house in Arlington, I felt as if I would throw up. We had lost. Again.

After Kerry's defeat in 2004, I never thought I'd work on another campaign. I vowed to henceforth protect myself from investing too much hope in the outcome of such a fickle business as politics. I never thought I'd care that much again.

A year later, Senator Dianne Feinstein invited me to a small dinner at her Washington, D.C. home. She wanted to introduce one of her newest colleagues to her most loyal supporters. He was the freshman senator from Illinois, the guy who'd quieted the 2004 convention crowd in Boston, and who'd been elected handily to the U.S. Senate on the night of Kerry's November 2004 debacle.

Joy had a business meeting, so I brought our sixteen-year-old daughter, who had been working with student activists on her high school campus to address U.S. policy toward Sudan and Darfur. I was a recovering political addict, having sworn off campaigns. I'd heard the talk that this Senate rookie, with all of twelve months experience as a federal legislator, was considering running in the Democratic presidential primaries. I was skeptical in the extreme.

Senator Feinstein's Washington home is known as Willow Oaks. Cloistered behind high, ivy-covered walls where Foxhall Road reaches tony Spring Valley, its intimate rooms give way to an elegant terrace and pool house. Candles flicker amidst walls covered with family photos and side tables filled with banks of flowers. Guests typically include a cross-section of Californians from Congress, Hollywood, and high tech industries.

Young Senator Obama worked the room slowly and smoothly that evening. Like any good candidate, he lingered as he shook with his outsize hands, the bony elongated fingers of a cellist or an athlete. His grin came naturally. Yet he seemed a bit impatient with small talk. You could sense he figured he was the smartest guy in the room, a dangerous notion in the salon of his brilliant

California hostess.

Then Senator Feinstein offered a brief, but warm, introduction. Obama began to speak to the small circle of potential admirers, all still standing. He seemed modest now, though confident, as he moved effortlessly from domestic to international issues. When queries came from the group, he managed deftly to agree with the premise of almost every questioner, before pirouetting in a classic "yes . . . but" style, expanding on each point to develop a broader answer.

My daughter's question was the last. Jenn was testing him. She wanted to know his assessment of the political hurdles to be overcome in order for NATO partners to agree to impose a no-fly zone over Darfur.

Obama did three things at that moment which further marked him as a political natural. First, he listened intently. He nodded as Jenn spoke, making us feel as if we were the only ones in the room with him. Second, he expressed sympathy for her premise—that NATO must act to prevent the genocide perpetrated by Sudan's dictator Bashir against the people of Darfur. He templed his hands. Then he repeated her name as he detailed a thoughtful and knowledgeable approach for action: "Well, Jenn, Chairman Joe Biden and I pressed the Bush administration on this no-fly-zone proposal yet again this week."

His delivery was flawless, his command of details admirable. I held myself back, though, continuing to honor my 2004 vow.

A coincidence later that week clinched at least one Obama recruit. Several hundred student leaders from across the country rallied on Capitol Hill as part of a "Save Darfur Day." After meeting with junior congressional staffers and conducting door-knocks on the House side, leaders of the student delegation were in the Vice President's Lobby in the Capitol when Barack Obama came off the Senate floor to meet them. He cocked his head, squinted, and then pointed.

"Great to see you here, Jenn!" He grinned.

In 2008, Jenn ended up going door to door in Virginia housing projects, using her Spanish-language skills to help get out the vote for the unlikely candidate. I resisted to the end. I was not for Obama in the early primaries, preferring the hard-nosed experience of Hillary Clinton. I maintained that Obama was too young, too aloof, and too liberal. Besides, there was no way he could win. I *knew* it. Even Jack Kennedy had served fourteen years in Congress before his presumptuous 1960 race against seasoned Vice President Nixon.

Determined to let my head dictate to my heart, I believed that we already knew the consequences of having an ill-prepared ideologue in the White House for eight years. Hillary stood a better chance of winning and governing effectively. We talked of moving to Canada if voters put a Mike Huckabee or a Sarah Palin in the White House, as several friends had discussed after W. entered the Oval Office. As a veteran of Udall for President, Cranston for President, Dukakis for President, and Kerry for President, I stuck to my promise to never drink the Democratic candidate Kool-Aid again.

Senator Clinton was the safe choice. I had never been entirely comfortable with her husband's opportunism and dysfunction, no matter how often I agreed with his policy prescriptions. She was a builder of traditional Democratic coalitions, tough and battle-tested. She frightened mostly southern white males, but they would be voting Republican anyway.

By the time I flew to the 2008 Democratic convention in Denver, I was almost sold on Obama. My role there, however, was as a University of Pennsylvania professor. This facilitated my old ruse: I could maintain a certain distance, posing as an interested observer, an academic analyst. I could be halfway committed, sitting in the stands at Broncos Stadium taking notes amidst a flag-waving throng of Democrats.

My emotional detachment continued into the early fall campaign, even as the economy went into free fall, and Republican candidate John McCain, a senator I admired, began behaving erratically. We worried Obama would bring the racists to the polls, the ugly underside of our American melting pot. Democrats feared an October surprise by the Bush team; they'd finally kill Bin

Laden or they would bomb Gaddafi. We feared that some dark past association of Obama, maybe one with the radical left, would be "discovered" just before Election Day. I am ashamed to admit it, but I also feared that Obama, like my heroes the Kennedys and Dr. King, would be shot.

What I feared most, of course, was believing. I hated the idea of once again believing in someone, in some cause, only to have my hopes smashed again. *I've seen this movie*, I thought to myself once more. *I do not like its ending.*

My children shamed me. Each was working for Obama. Joy, too, was walking precincts, working lists, believing in the future. Even Mom, in faraway Kona, Hawaii, was encouraging friends to vote for Obama.

In late September, during the Wall Street meltdown, the McCain camp bizarrely announced a "suspension" of campaign activities. Obama hit his stride, and I finally relented. I called two friends high up in the Obama campaign, Greg Craig (the campaign counsel, who was playing McCain in Obama's debate prep) and Phil Schiliro (Representative Henry Waxman's chief of staff, who was running congressional relations for the campaign). I would be helping to run Get Out the Vote one last time. They had the crazy notion that an African American could win the capital of the Confederacy. So, off I went to the Virginia battleground in Fairfax County.

In 2008, Fairfax was a classic exurban territory. It was precisely the type of region—new outer suburban housing developments—Obama had to win if he was going to beat McCain. The battlegrounds near Bull Run had become a red state/blue state fault line, where farmers were being displaced by government workers in the vast security bureaucracy spawned after 9/11. The stock market crash had devastated housing values in the area. New voters, who had joined Asian and Hispanic immigrants in bedroom communities like Herndon, were up for grabs.

The Obama campaign calculated it needed to win Fairfax, the state's most populous county, by a margin of 180,000 votes, if it were to make up for inevitable losses in the rural counties of southern Virginia. Fairfax County was the key to capturing the Old Dominion's thirteen electoral votes.

We operated our local campaign headquarters out of a Herndon strip mall. Shuttered office space was donated by sympathetic local citizens. The county campaign was directed by national headquarters to "live off the land." We were to solicit local donations for everything we needed, from food to phones to precinct maps. The national campaign provided one paid staffer, and it provided "The Plan."

Our mission was simple. The Obama and Mark Warner for Senate campaigns had spent months registering new Democratic voters in targeted communities. Now we had the addresses of every one of these first-time voters. We merged this information with lists of thousands of "occasional" Democratic voters—folks we knew had made it to the polls in 2004, but who never showed up in 2006. We were to focus all of our resources exclusively on these two groups. We were to beat their brains out. Push them, hassle them, phone them, knock on their doors, flush them out, and even drive them to the polls if necessary. Volunteers were directed to try for five face-to-face contacts with each of these potential voters in the seventy-two hours before the polls closed. We were only to cross potential Obama supporters off our list once we had confirmed at polling stations that they had voted.

My boss in this enterprise was a bespectacled twenty-three year old from Reston named Vijay Das. It was his first campaign. It was, I swore, my last. Vijay was an intelligent, highly excitable Asian-American kid, recently graduated from Vassar College, and on his way to graduate school. He had worked his way up in the Obama organization all year, helping run the registration drive in the area during spring and summer. My instructions were to get volunteers, train them, and dispatch them to the dozens of Fairfax County precincts for which we were responsible.

We followed "The Plan" religiously. The strip mall which housed us was only 50 percent occupied. Business owners who had gone under in the economic crash handed us keys, and the landlords opened warehouse space. A massage school full of skeletons and folding tables was lent to us free; we used it to pack supplies and run training sessions for precinct walkers. We prepared for weeks, doing computer runs, copying scripts, purging and updating voter lists, calling phone banks to secure potential volunteers for the last big seventy-two hour push. Then we waited.

The Saturday before the election, I was at the staging area at 7 a.m. with 10 dozen Dunkin' Donuts and several gallons of coffee. Vijay and I were both nervous. We had route maps and precinct walker kits for 250 volunteers who were to saturate fifty locations. All we needed were foot soldiers.

Finally, as if a light far down the road had turned from red to green, the cars began to roll in. The Rutgers New Jersey Democratic Club in two large vans. VWs covered in left-wing bumper stickers from Brooklyn. Smiling gray-haired ladies from a bridge club north of Baltimore. A dozen office workers from the Council for a Livable World. They came in waves—people I hadn't seen since Philly '04, friends from Cassidy & Associates, my California high school prom date, computer experts, old white guys passing up golf for politics. Within the hour, there were nearly three hundred volunteers in front of us in the parking lot.

What these citizens had in common wasn't so much that they all were passionately *for* Obama. A lot of Clinton supporters were present, but all were united *against* Bush. By the end of his campaign, poor John McCain had embraced so much of the conservative GOP agenda, and changed so many of his basic positions on issues, that we were united primarily against the Bush-Rove-Cheney strategy of governance by division.

McCain had been an admirable senator. He had been a champion for several issues I cared about, from ending the Vietnam trade embargo to advancing campaign finance reform with Democrat Russ Feingold. By late 2008, however, McCain had developed trust issues with voters. His peculiar feigned campaign halt at the height of the stock market crash rankled independent voters, as did his flip-flops on taxes, war spending, and gay rights.

I still didn't believe Obama would win. I would not allow myself to. Even on Election Day, energized by one last rush of adrenaline as I steered hundreds of earnest volunteers to walk precincts from our headquarters location, I held back.

It was preposterous, this idea that Obama would win the White House, with the capital of the Confederacy giving him the last electoral votes he needed to get to 270. There was, however, a perfect storm of issues breaking for him. Years of laissez-faire deregulation had allowed a housing bubble to burst. Retirement savings and home values were plummeting. The United States was bogged down in multiple foreign wars, with many soldiers in their third and fourth overseas deployments. Osama bin Laden, the murderer of nearly four thousand Americans, was still at large, taunting our citizens. Years of Homeland Security alerts had failed to make Americans feel more secure. Independents were going to be voting heavily for the Democrats, or so the pollsters told us.

Our little campaign outpost had one rule for this Election Day: Ignore the exit polls. That was one lesson learned from 2004. We planned to execute "The Plan," and run at a full sprint through the tape at the finish line. We would even deliver water bottles and umbrellas to voters still waiting in the rain outside polling sites when the 7 p.m. closing hour arrived.

After dispatching my last team to lines of voters outside polling sites at the western edge of Fairfax County, I quietly slipped into my car. I couldn't face another attempt at having an office victory party. I drove east, instead, along Route 66, against the commuter traffic. I kept the radio off, listening to an old Crosby, Stills & Nash CD. Then I parked in front of my house and sat in the darkened car for several minutes.

I was bracing myself, breathing deeply. Then I walked in the front door and poured myself a stiff Ketel One and tonic before I sat down with family—both present and on the Internet—to watch the results.

Within minutes, Brian Williams and the NBC team were calling swing state after swing state. Each went for Obama-Biden. It felt as if we were watching a newsreel on the History Channel, with some dated, antiquated report about events from another time. I sat motionless, watching the screen, even as the tumult built around me.

Before the evening grew late, family members were calling and shouting out the news. Out in the streets, car horns were honking, noise-makers were being plied, pots and pans were being banged, and firecrackers were exploding in a few neighborhoods of the Old Dominion.

To my utter amazement, Obama and Biden won. Finally, it felt like the good guys had won.

I had absolutely no idea what to do next.

CHAPTER SEVENTEEN

Renewal

Charlottesville, Virginia
September 2012

"*Inevitably, life did not proceed exactly according to plan.*"
—Martha Nussbaum

Our lives move in arcs. With the energy of youth, we reach up toward delightful heights. We acquire some knowledge. We engage the world. We try to lead purpose-filled lives. Soon enough, though, gravity takes hold. Only the most fortunate of us manage to experience some grace during the descent phase.

The life of societies, like that of our national politics, moves in discernible patterns. As Arthur Schlesinger so aptly described them, their cyclical ebb and flow is made manifest in American public life. The intellectual cycles are predictable, if not inevitable.[40]

Excess begets reform. An aggressive schemer like President Nixon begets a righteous scold like Jimmy Carter. A crusading Woodrow Wilson and a futile "war to end all wars" produces a "return to normalcy" under a somnolent Calvin Coolidge and like-minded champions of laissez-faire, Harding and Hoover. An era of FDR-driven public purpose invariably makes way for an Eisenhower decade of cautious private agendas. From interventionists like John F. Kennedy and George W. Bush are born "Come

Home America" isolationists, from Barry Goldwater and George McGovern, to Ron Paul and Dennis Kucinich. The hyper-government created by the nascent Obama administration's audacious stimulus and health insurance reform, harvested in just two years a bevy of Tea Party activists from the Ross Perot strain of American politics, anti-Big Government politicians who triumphed in the 2010 midterm elections.

The further our society gets from its original agrarian roots, the more urbanized and information-based our service industry foundation becomes, the harder it is to see these natural cycles in our national politics. Adding to the challege is the fact that these cycles are accelerating. This is true in politics, no less than in information technology.

Consider the fact that the Democrats held the House for forty years, then the Republicans, via Newt Gingrich and his Republican Revolution of 1994, maintained a majority for just twelve, and Speaker Gingrich was forced out by his own Republican colleagues after just four. Resurgent Democrats under Nancy Pelosi lasted only four years as the House majority. The great Democratic wave in support of Obama in 2008 ushered in not a generation of liberal rule in the House, but instead just two years, before coming to disaster in the 2010 midterm elections. Speaker Pelosi's Republican successor, John Boehner, had only months to savor his victory before the knives began to come out within his own caucus; some Tea Party stalwarts waited little time before scheming over how to seize his Speaker's gavel.

Faster, faster, faster we go, like a spinning wheel at the funhouse. American consumers moved so rapidly from radio to black-and-white TV, to color. Then from three TV channels to twelve, and then twelve hundred. From LPs to cassettes to CDs to iPods. From cell phones to BlackBerries to Skype. The pace threatens to overwhelm our capacity to absorb and process all the stimuli. When my grandmother Caroline Harris Stoddard saw a man walk on the moon in July 1969, she took ill, bedridden simply from the shock of unimaginable change. Many of us Baby Boomers feel the same way when we try to juggle three remote controls to program our TiVo. We are overwhelmed by the profusion of data.

This is a serious problem for those who rely on the rush of adrenaline. From the very first day I set foot in Washington, my hunger was to find a way to join the action. From a young age, there was a need to figure out what motivated all the players. My goal was simply to participate; the reflective part could come later. An appreciation of academic analysis as a tool of informed public policymaking would be, for me, a slowly acquired taste.

As a young man, I was far too impatient to settle for a life only analyzing what others were doing. This eagerness to participate bred a skepticism about the detachment of the Academy. It fueled suspicion that some political scientists, trained by and for research universities, knew altogether too much science and too little politics. In the obsessive footnoting of every thought, the endless pressure to secure publication in obscure academic journals, there threatened to develop an unproductive closed loop. It suspected novelty. It was slow to reward original thought. Thus, I came to most admire those scholars who were able to engage. The very best could inform public policymaking in the national arena and offer commentary on alternative prescriptions for national progress.

To get something done in American politics, you enter a Darwinian contest. Politics is a contact sport in North America; it always has been, akin to playing tackle football without helmets. Only the strongest thrive. Political combat tempts candidates to act first and consider the long-term consequences much later. Such survival skills don't always serve the national interest.

In my novel about a group of Stanford University scholars, the graduates head "Back East" to engage in government policymaking. These were driven men and women; most went into public life with a clear purpose. It is a notion mainstreamed in my own DNA, some combination of the Protestant ethic and Jewish guilt. From early childhood, my brothers and I were made to understand that one was expected to do something productive with one's abilities. The notion was equal parts Yankee responsibility and the idealism suffusing the California Wonder Years.

So when have you fulfilled your duty? I worried over the question when, unexpectedly, lobbying proved lucrative. The strategies we developed at the firm and applied on Capitol Hill were special-interest policymaking. Even strategies for home state schools and hospitals advanced *parochial* causes, not necessarily those of the entire community. This was not the impulse that had brought me east to Washington.

From hunter-gatherer roots, many men (and, increasingly, women) take validation from their role as breadwinners. It is a simple concept: Even if you fail at everything else, at least you are a reliable provider. Your salary puts food on the table and thus fulfills some basic caveman psychological need. *Was this not sufficient satisfaction? Or was more required of us?*

Struggling with such questions, I tried to figure out when to try something new. Some of the voluntary retirees from the 111th Congress tried to answer a similar question. Democrat Dave Obey had a great line. The pugnacious liberal was notoriously cranky; he had been in Washington for more than thirty-five years when he announced his retirement in 2010. He reminded voters of his usual election year promise: "I won't quit until we pass national health care reform. We did. So I'm going home."

The protagonists in my novel ultimately returned to their campus roots. They staggered back at mid-life, after extended Washington careers, via a half dozen different routes. Many of the characters in this imaginary universe succeeded. They returned to a sylvan campus and found a place for renewal awaiting them. The fiction offered a determinedly happy ending, unlike the unremittingly bleak novels turned out by most Anglo-Saxons at the beginning of the twenty-first century.

Once again, life seemed to parallel a fiction that, in its telling, remains determined to mimic reality. The cycle is complete. I have entered a twelve-step program for recovering political junkies. Both caffeine and campaigns are off-limits; so is any viewing of shouting talk "news" shows. Urgent *Congress Daily* updates go unread. Weeks of *Roll Call* newspapers pile up. My expired subscription to *Hotline* has gone unrenewed. I have stopped commuting each day east across the Roosevelt Bridge. I have stopped obsessing over state-by-state polls. Never again will I attend a political fundraiser. Early mornings are more reflective, less anxious.

It was easier for me, as Obey had put it, to walk away from the work of politics after sharing the experience of one ever-so-rare win. The Barack Obama-Joe Biden team had grown on me and I admired their agenda. They were smart politicians who were committed to public purpose. They appealed most times to our better instincts. They promised change and experimentation, a commitment to wield all the tools of government to clean up a series of leftover national messes. Their soaring rhetoric offered hope and possibility. That there were daunting challenges ahead made their optimism and can-do spirit all the more appealing.

In the aftermath of the election, many friends flocked to the administration, though I had no such interest. Taking top jobs, they began flying as high as Icarus. Soon, of course, came the first casualties, the shattering falls from the sky. The promised closure of the black hole military prison at Guantanamo Bay did not happen. Attempts to pass an energy development and climate change bill got derailed. The wars in Afghanistan and Pakistan dragged on. Secret drone strikes directed by CIA officials in Langley multiplied. Unemployment and underemployment stayed high. The national debt soared.

The inherited policy challenges of 2009 dampened voter enthusiasm in the midterm elections. The idealism of Obama supporters was tested as the cycle of national politics accelerated once again. Scorn for the excessive deregulation that helped produce the Great Recession and made necessary the bailouts of 2008 gave way, within months, to renewed fears of Big Government solutions.

Friends of mine struggled in the midst of the whirlpool. Greg Craig quit the Obama administration in a painfully public dispute over the slow-walking of Guantanamo's closure. Phil Schiliro took grief daily as he labored to manage congressional relations for the Obama administration, catching spears as he hunted down votes for stalled health care reform. Relations with Capitol Hill became ever more difficult with the Tea Party candidates elected to the House in 2010 and the obstructionist faction led by Senator Mitch McConnell tying the Senate up in knots. Before the Obama 2012 reelection campaign was over, Phil had moved his family to New Mexico for a respite from Washington toxins.

While no longer moving along with the parade, I rooted for old friends and allies. Yet, as the spectacle passed by, I found it much easier to ignore the infotainment elements, the silly stories about such "news" commentators as Sarah Palin and Newt Gingrich, or stories about idiot congressmen who e-mailed lewd photos of themselves and couldn't keep their hands off their Twitter accounts. These no longer seemed important developments in our national life.

Blessed with an interesting landing spot at the new Batten School, launched by one of the country's most venerable universities, I am once again part of an educational experiment. There is a garden cottage in which to read and write, a pavilion apartment opening onto the serpentine walls radiating from Mr. Jefferson's Lawn at the center of his beloved Academical Village.

At dusk, the light plays gently off the pillars. You can sit on the steps of the Rotunda and see the first rise of the Blue Ridge Mountains peeking over Old Cabell Hall, an expectant moon appearing slowly on the horizon. There is time for fresh thinking about old problems, and about new challenges. The new public policy school is growing each month, professors engaging students in robust debates over how to refine the curriculum for the century of policy challenges ahead.

Delighted to arrive at the University of Virginia at the same time as new leadership, I was recruited to work with senior administrators on several initiatives. I had left behind, I was sure, the petty infighting of Washington politics. The University was led by a new team under President Terry Sullivan.

A tested administrator and scholar from the large state universities of Michigan and Texas, Sullivan worked in her first months at Virginia to build a consensus for methodical change at one of the world's best public universities. Here was a wonderful opportunity for me to team with scholars, educators, and institution builders in a collegial environment. Here the palace intrigues and backstabbing of the Senate cloakroom and K Street corridor would be replaced by high-minded discussions and a 190-year-old honor code. Mindfulness, courtesy, and forward thinking reigned at this beautiful, reflective oasis, the University of Virginia.

Then all hell broke loose.

In early June 2012, an attempt to summarily dismiss President Sullivan was made by a faction on the UVa Board of Visitors (BoV). They consulted only with selected members, one on one, in off-the-record discussions. Misrepresenting the board's views and intentions, board leaders forced the resignation of the popular new president. In so doing, the board thrust into stark relief many of the issues facing public institutions of higher education in America.

Like Cal, Michigan, Texas, and other state universities, UVa struggled with crushing unfunded mandates. A hard-right agenda pushed by the state government in Richmond insisted on UVa's admitting more students, despite evaporating state support and a tuition freeze. State politicians felt the six percent of funding provided to the University obliged UVa administrators to pay one hundred percent obedience to their dictates.

Experienced academic managers were not in charge of the BoV in Charlottesville. When the board faction moved against Sullivan, the BoV had sixteen members. Together they had donated more than two million dollars to Republicans and Democrats. There was not one professional on the board with any academic leadership experience. The BoV lacked any voting representative of the UVa administration, faculty, or staff. The board's rector (chairwoman), a Virginia Beach real estate developer, was convinced by a handful of colleagues that President Sullivan was moving too slowly to address the serious budget issues confronting all public universities.

The rector and vice rector left a trail of e-mails revealing weeks of covert planning—even retaining D.C. crisis communications firms. A timely Freedom of Information Act request by the enterprising student newspaper, *The Cavalier Daily*, led to the publication of some of the missives sent internally at the height of the crisis. These communications seemed to many to reveal the shallowness of board leaders' thinking about the future of higher education. They also confirmed that leaders had plotted to fire President Sullivan even as they sat through days of routine meetings with her whilst exchanging compliments and pleasantries.

There were legitimate reasons for concern about the pace of the university's response to challenges. But the manner in which the BoV proceeded sparked a revolt amongst the academic community. The coup had been sprung corporate-style, at 5:45 p.m. on a lazy Friday in early June. It was evidently planned for that hour because students and faculty would be away, and most college town reporters would have called it a week. Violating board rules, and any sense of decency, the BoV leaders misled President Sullivan and the public, maintaining that the board had acted unanimously.

The fact was, the Board had not yet acted. And it later emerged later that the board was far from unanimous. BoV bylaws state that a two-thirds vote of the full sixteen-member board was required to remove a president. Yet there was never any board discussion about putting the president on warning or terminating her. An executive subcommittee quorum of only three members did not even convene to consider the matter or vote to accept the forced resignation until *after* it had been announced. For a revered institution that treasured "the community of trust" to which UVa enlisted faculty and student alike, the forcing out of President Sullivan sparked a determined reaction far in excess of what coup plotters had anticipated.

Two weeks of turmoil ensued. Faculty and donors objected to both the process and the result. More than fifty-five hundred alums joined in an online protest, and thousands of UVa staffers and students marched up the Lawn to stand outside a series of ham-handed board meetings. The faculty senate voted 68-2 for reinstatement of the president and removal of the board leadership. Hundred-million-dollar UVa donors fought over the university's direction in comments published by national papers.

Most everybody who loved UVa winced. Our little island of academic tranquility in Charlottesville was shattered. Despite myself, I felt drawn into the battle once more. The Sullivan administration wasn't perfect, and maybe things were moving a bit slowly, but the team had honor, decency, and forward thinking on their side. Soon, I was back on familiar ground, one of dozens of strategists plotting with fellow faculty members and administrators about how best to rally pro-Sullivan forces.

All the UVa deans joined in a public letter of support for Sullivan's reinstatement. Key Batten School donors supported President Sullivan in stories run on the front pages of *The Washington Post*, and throughout Virginia local papers. Provost John Simon—and even Carl Zeithamel, the interim president the BoV had named—publicly opposed the decision to oust President Sullivan.

Professors and donors worked phones. Coalitions of alums unleashed waves of e-mails and petitions. Social media, including Facebook and Twitter, produced an explosion of grassroots supporters. They convinced think tanks and university associations to weigh in. Editorial boards around the country were encouraged to speak up. In framing the issue for media contacts, Sullivan supporters stressed the deceit in the board's dealing, which violated any definition of best practices for board governance. Some on the board were revealed to be pushing online education as a replacement for the university's signature commitment to an "Academical Village." The BoV seemed at times to be pursuing a University of Phoenix vision that would alter the unique undergraduate experience at Virginia, where a community of scholars is intended to live and learn. This classic liberal arts education remains, by any definition, the university's comparative advantage and its true market niche.

As a peripheral figure in the campaign, I was nevertheless conscious of bookends in my working life. It felt a couple of times almost as if we were back in Jack Bingham's office. In our campaign, we seemed to be applying lessons picked straight up from

Politics 101.

In the end, the result in Charlottesville was as surprising as it was gratifying. The Republican governor, Bob McDonnell, belatedly intervened, announcing that he would fire all board members unless they acted with unanimity and finality. Within forty-eight hours, President Sullivan was reinstated by a 15-0 vote of the full board.[41] As part of a package deal, the BoV stood by its forlorn rector and the governor reappointed her, lest she take the fall for an ill-conceived move many colleagues had encouraged.

The university has been left with enormous challenges. It must change, and change rapidly, to continue to deliver first-class learning under the new, uncertain, twenty-first century education delivery model. Terry Sullivan emerged as a leading national voice for education reform. The future of UVa became the subject of a lengthy *New York Times Magazine* cover story.

The irony is sweet: The Board's failure actually empowered pragmatists to bring sweeping change to a bloodied institution, with the entire higher education community watching closely. How President Sullivan resolves a challenge that faces all fifty states will offer key lessons for the future of public higher education in America.

Just before midnight on June 26, following the unanimous board vote that day to reinstate Terry Sullivan, I was walking back to my apartment on the Lawn. I ran into a campus policeman walking his beat.

"I bet you were nervous today," I said. There had been a crowd of some three thousand demonstrators outside the Rotunda, clamoring for the widely-vilified board of Visitors to reverse itself and reappoint President Sullivan. "What would have happened if the Board had rejected her reinstatement?"

The officer had a stocky farmer's build, trim haircut, and a thick neck. He squared up, looked me in the eye, and smiled gently as he asked: "Guess how many cops we had on the Lawn today?"

I thought about demonstrations I had seen at Berkeley and San Francisco State University in the 1960s, ones that involved

Molotov cocktails, riot police, and scores of arrests.

"One," he answered before I could reply. "It was me."

"What if things had gotten ugly?" I asked. "Any other university in the country would have had tear gas and riot police on standby."

"That's just not the way we do things at UVa." It was all he said. That was the whole point. It was the one point too many on the Board, used to the bare-knuckle world of business, had somehow missed.

There were important lessons learned in the UVa confrontation. As Chicago mayor and former White House chief of staff Rahm Emanuel had famously remarked, one should never waste the opportunity presented by a good crisis. The university has moved forward to address the very real challenges identified by the UVa board. Today, the board is improved and reformed, and President Sullivan is hard at work on a future-oriented agenda. I try to do the same in my lectures, as we look at old case studies and try to distill lessons learned.

What I relished most about a role in public policymaking was, ironically, what I liked best about private enterprise. You get tested. It is very much the same as in baseball; the pitcher plots strategy, putting together a game plan and getting physically ready. Then all he can do, alone on the mound at the center of the stadium, is throw his best pitch. There is a clear result. Each and every contest yields a winner and a loser. Home run or strikeout, the consequences are unmistakable.

The same I found to be true whether whipping votes on the Senate floor or helping to meet a payroll in a small business. Score is kept. You can hate the social Darwinists, but they sure as hell let you know who is the winner.

Teddy Roosevelt had it right when he championed the man in the arena. A life lived too cautiously is a waste. Roosevelt's posturing could be over-the-top macho, to be sure. He was right, however, to chastise the critic who carps from the sidelines, always afraid to care too much, afraid to fail.

The joy of life is in the trying, Roosevelt concluded. Beware the pontificating pundit who is never called upon to offer leadership, the Monday morning quarterback who never tries to make a play. Respect the gamblers in public life, the takers of risk who fight to win a majority for a reason. They hunger for the power to shape public policy. Respect the men and women who stand passionately for ideas; who seek power to promote policy, not just to gratify their egos; who believe in something bigger than themselves.

Such men and women became my heroes. They peopled my stories and gave my work greater meaning and fulfillment.

My attempts at fiction were haunted by a search for closure. There persists in this storytelling a conscious echo of T. S. Eliot's themes about return and renewal as life at times appears to come full circle. Many are on this common journey; we strive to see the world beyond the horizon, to travel across the years, to know some of the most interesting characters of our times. We look for transformative insights. We seek lasting friendships. Then we hope to arrive back where we started and to know the place, and ourselves, for the first time.

It is an old story, of course, one as old as Homer. It is the universal story of the search for wisdom, fueled by a hunger for experience. It is the story I first tried to chronicle as a twenty-one year old idealist, happily marooned for a time along the banks of the Potomac, sending home rambling dispatches from the Eastern Front, so many years ago.

Notes

This is a Washington memoir, not a political science textbook. Many of the accounts herein are drawn essentially from contemporaneous notes and lightly edited letters. I have sought in their subsequent compilation to leave in first impressions, to retain some of the considerable enthusiasm of the moment. Their retelling also offers glimpses from the wings of several events since the end of the Nixon presidency, events many have witnessed from different perspectives on our national stage.

To further examine several of the subjects this work touches upon about Congress and the White House, readers may wish to consult some of the supplementary sources cited in the section after this. Where indicated by an asterisk, some of the original documents, contemporary press accounts, and additional photos will be posted at www.dispatchesmemoir.com.

The introductory Hemingway quote is from "An African Betrayal," *Sports Illustrated*, May 5, 1986.

1   The attempt to build Marincello just north of the Golden Gate was funded by Gulf Oil. Carved from the Sausalito headlands, the new city was to consist of scores of high-rise apartment blocks, a shopping mall, and a luxury hotel. Designed in the mid-1960s, Marincello was blocked in a battle chronicled in a permanent exhibit at Fort Cronkhite in the Golden Gate National Recreation Area. See "Saved by Grit and Grace: Wild Legacy of the Marin Headlands," by John Hart, *Bay Nature*, Summer 1973. Also, see "Doing Good for Decades: Felix Warburg," *The Urbanist*, San Francisco Planning and Urban Research Association, June 2012, p. 23. Note that Congressman Clement Miller joined with President Jack Kennedy to help ensure that Marin County's western coastline became part of the national park at Point Reyes. Miller died in a plane crash just months before Kennedy was assassinated.

2   For more on the three-year Nixon Library lobbying effort, see, for example, "Congress Frees Nixon Papers," by Ben Pershing, *Roll Call*, January 26, 2004 or "Nixon Library Joins the Club: Operation by Archives Marks Transition from Private Sector," Christopher Lee, *Washington Post*, March 20, 2006.*

3   See more mid-1970s Hampshire photos at www.dispatchesmemoir.com. For more on the founding of Hampshire by Amherst College, Smith College, Mt. Holyoke College, and the University of Massachusetts, see inaugural address of President Jonathan Lash in *Non Satis Scire*, Summer 2012. Former Hampshire President Charles R. Longsworth notes, "Hampshire College was planned and opened in the years after World War II when the world was in a period of immense change. Hampshire was created as an agent of change." Lash quotes Lois Bailey, the student speaker at Hampshire's opening convocation in 1970, as noting that when she first arrived at Hampshire, she felt as if she had been "reunited with an old dream . . . that education could and should be a joyful experience—indeed a very condition of life, a never-ending series of discoveries that should thrive in every community."

4   *Conflict and Consensus: The Struggle between Congress and the President over Foreign Policymaking*, Harper & Row, 1989.*

5   "Tunney vs. Nuclear Policy," by Tom Braden, *Los Angeles Times* Syndicate, and other selected Braden columns, 1975-76.*

6   "Nuclear Proliferation Threatens U.S. National Security Interests," *Congressional Record*, March 17, 1981, Vol. 127, No. 43. See also Judith Miller and Ellen Hume's page one stories, in the *New York Times* and *The Wall Street Journal* respectively, from March 18, 1981.* This leak was not an exclusive; we were trying to play the two reporters off each other, a risky gambit.

7   See text of "Cranston's Alter Ego"/"Warburg: Cranston's Guru on Foreign Policy," Keith Love, *Los Angeles Times*, March 13, 1986, and "The Young Political Veteran: Foreign Policy Replaced Baseball," Sam Whiting, *San Francisco Chronicle*, August 11, 1989.*

8   Competitive law firms such as Patton Boggs and Verner, Liipfert, Bernhard, McPherson & Hand would inflate their lobbying revenues with fees from legal work to try to stay on par with Cassidy. See "The Million Dollar Club," *Legal Times*, May 25, 1998.*

9   See Chapter 17 of *So Damn Much Money* by Robert G. Kaiser, Knopf, 2009.

10 See Prime Minister Begin's response, partial text in *New York Times*, October 2, 1982, p. 9.*

11 "Notes on New Hampshire," by Tom Braden, *Los Angeles Times* Syndicate, March 2, 1976.*

12 Bingham press release, "Bronx Bombers Bring Fame to 22nd Congressional District," September 21, 1977.*

13 Representative Bingham's 1976 memos on nuclear nonproliferation policy sent to Governor (later President-elect) Jimmy Carter are included on the dispatchesmemoir.com website.

14 Bingham used the domestic regulatory powers transferred to Udall's subcommittee to move a bill enforcing strict but uniform standards for licensing U.S. light water production reactors. Some of us subsequently changed our views on reactor safety after the Three Mile Island accident on the Susquehanna River in Pennsylvania in 1979. See "A Nuclear Expert's Change of Mind," *Los Angeles Times*, July 8, 1979.*

15 Bingham press release, "Bingham Hails House Vote Stripping Nuclear Committee's Powers," December 8, 1976.*

16 See Ed Cowan's *New York Times* story, "Joint Atomic Panel Stripped of Power," January 5, 1977.*

17 Transcript of the House hearings and markup are printed in "The Nuclear Anti-Proliferation [sic] Act of 1977," Government Printing Office, August 3, 1977; see pp. 267-8 for the Representative Solarz quote.

18 See this book's cover, White House photo.

19 See www.dispatchesmemoir.com for photos.

20 "Why I Live in Washington D.C.," *Washington Star*, May 21, 1976.*

21 *The Mandarin Club*, Bancroft Press, 2006.*

22 This presentation is found at www.batten.virginia.edu. It subsequently ran, in edited form, in *The Nonproliferation Review*, November 2012, Vol. 19, No. 3, and in *Contemporary Cases in U.S. Foreign Policy: From Terror to Trade*, Ralph G. Carter, ed., Congressional Quarterly Press, 2014.

23 *The Last Great Senate: Courage and Statesmanship in Times of Crisis*, by Ira

Shapiro, Perseus, 2012.

24 *The Philippine Daily Inquirer* ran a page one photo of the meeting, including his "eight-foot-tall aide," the next day.*

25 The Cranston for President campaign in 1984 lasted only weeks, but lifelong friendships began then and endured. Kam Kuwata was the much-beloved aide who started out as Cranston's driver and rose to become the most respected Democratic campaign manager in California politics, until his untimely death in 2011. For more on the Cranston presidential campaign, see, for example, "Cranston Offers Job Plan and Alters Strategy," by Frank Lynn, *New York Times*, February 16, 1984, and additional archival material on *Dispatches* website.*

26 Kennedy and Cranston escorting an African leader off the Senate floor, tailed by ubiquitous staff aides, June 1986.

27 *The New York Times* photographer Paul Hosefros snapped a cover photo at the very moment, late on the evening of July 31, 1986, when Democrats pitched a compromise to GOP Chairman Richard Lugar of Indiana.* In

the photo, that's Jeff Bergner, Lugar's chief of staff, watching carefully. Bergner and I cooperated for years in a well-exercised bipartisan backchannel, and subsequently co-authored several academic articles, including "Fast Forward: Planning for Alternative Foreign Policy Futures," *Virginia Policy Review*, Vol. V, Issue 2, Spring 2012.*

28 Cranston led the 1987 campaign against Supreme Court nominee Robert Bork, who was defeated by a vote of 58-42. This was one of the first of a series of vicious post-Watergate confirmation battles that gave rise to the term "the politics of personal destruction," as became manifest in the Clarence Thomas Supreme Court nomination and the Newt Gingrich-led impeachment of President Bill Clinton.

29 On the Bork fight and consequences, including the derivation of the term "Borking" a nominee, see, for example, *Governing America: The Revival of Political History*, by Julian E. Zelizer, Princeton, 2012, pp. 245-6.

30 On the Gregg nomination battle, see "Senate Panel Approves Nominee for Korea Envoy," *New York Times*, Robert Pear, June 21, 1989.

31 See Jim Mann, "How Taipei Outwitted U.S. Policy," *Los Angeles Times*, June 8, 1995, and related editorials generated by the Cassidy publicity campaign on behalf of Taiwan.*

32 Julie Eisenhower, one of the most impressive women I ever met, on my left, in 2005. We're visiting Congressman Gary Miller (R-CA) with my Cassidy associate Christine O'Connor, lobbying for a congressional earmark to build a facility to securely house the most sensitive Nixon presidential papers and tapes in California.

33 See "Lobbyists keep counties 'in ball game': Grassroots effort fights for funding," by Keith Chu, *Bend Bulletin*, January 20, 2008.*

34 See *The National Security Enterprise: Navigating the Labyrinth*, Roger George and Harvey Rishikoff eds., Warburg chapters on Congress and on Lobbying, Georgetown University Press, 2011. See also "Best Practices for NGO Advocates," *Virginia Policy Review*, Spring 2012, Vol. IV, Issue 2.

35 See Seth Rosenfeld's *Subversives: The FBI's War on Student Radicals, and the Reagan Rise to Power*. Farrar, Straus and Giroux, 2012, p. 494.

36 On the Soviet refusenik community, see Anne Applebaum's review of *When They Come for Us, We'll Be Gone: The Epic Struggle to Save Soviet Jewry* (by Gal Beckerman) in *The Washington Post*, November 21, 2010. When we were in Moscow years later, we saw many of the same faces from the startling 1976 photo in the *Post* article.* Remarkably, after years of efforts by refuseniks, Ida Nudel was allowed to emigrate to Israel in October 1987, where she became a neighbor of the Ungers in Carme Yoseff.

37 Memorandum of conversation between Senator Alan Cranston and Dr. Andrei Sakharov, August 22, 1987.*

38 Colleagues memorialized Cranston as one of the most effective legislators of the era. Majority Leader George Mitchell stated that, "Thanks to Alan Cranston, the world is safer, cleaner, and more just than it would have been without his efforts." Joe Biden told the story of the first fundraiser Cranston organized for Biden's 1988 presidential bid, in Chicago: "I have only one question," Alan demanded beforehand. "How devoted are you to controlling nuclear weapons and to changing the dynamics of the relationship between the United States and Russia?" Ted Kennedy noted that "his [Cranston's] leadership is legendary . . . [What] we will miss most is his friendship and idealism, which have been an example of excellence in public service to us all." See Government Printing Office, "Tributes to Alan Cranston," October 8, 1992, S. Pub. 102-26 and "Alan Cranston's Legacy," by the author, in *The San Francisco Examiner*, January 5, 1993.* (Bias alert: Many contemporaries believed that the "Keating Five Scandal" was of historic significance, revealing the alleged corruption of such leading Senate figures as John Glenn, John McCain, and Alan Cranston. I was too close for objective analysis, but I saw no evidence that Keating's contributions to urban voter registration campaigns around the country colored the inquiries Cranston made to regulators. Yes, as with all donations from private interests, there was an appearance of impropriety, and a disproportionately large one at that, given the size of Keating's donations to the senators. No, it was not unusual for Cranston to press regulators to make a timely decision on rules impacting major employers, S&Ls, and homebuilders. Unlike some of his col-

leagues, Cranston reaped no personal benefit whatsoever from any of Keating's contributions—no trips on the corporate jet, no overnights at Keating-owned resorts, no contributions to his campaign or to organizations that benefitted his final 1986 reelection efforts. It was only the savings and loan crash of 1987 that made investigators determined to find a scapegoat. Senators on the Ethics Committee agreed to close the case against Glenn, McCain, Riegle, and DeConcini; then they came down harshly on the retiring Cranston.

39 See *Running the World: The Inside Story of the National Security Council and the Architects of American Power*, David Rothkopf, PublicAffairs, 2005, which is deeply skeptical of Reagan fans' claims. As Rothkopf notes, fourteen different members of Reagan's White House staff were prosecuted by the federal government, and a number of convictions stood until pardons were issued. On the disastrous stewardship of American diplomacy under the Reagan team, see also *Men of Zeal: A Candid Inside Story of the Iran-Contra Hearings* by Senators William S. Cohen and George J. Mitchell, Penguin, 1989, and "Blind to the past, leaders blundered into Iran scandal," by the author, *San Jose Mercury News*, March 10, 1987.*

40 See Schlesinger, Arthur, Jr., *The Cycles of American History*, Houghton Mifflin, 1986. Note that Schlesinger credits his father, a longtime Harvard historian, with having developed the theory of the American electorate vacillating regularly between cycles of isolationism and intervention, between public purpose and private gain.

41 See, for example, "Virginia University President Reinstated," *New York Times*, June 27, 2012.

Supplementary Sources

The literature on Congress is voluminous. Yet, from wherever it originates, it often has essential flaws. The Academy has produced hundreds of doctoral dissertations deep in quantitative minutiae, purporting to shed light on voting behavior and legislative maneuvers. Popular books too often are written with an overt political slant designed to rouse citizens to action. Anecdotal memoirs frequently become score-settling exercises, where facts are conveniently ignored *ex post facto*. To better understand Congress, I believe reading works from all three subgenres is required, however flawed each may be.

For graduate seminars taught at the University of Pennsylvania, Georgetown, and the University of Virginia, invariably I've looked to create a blend of several approaches. Forging a synthesis of the best works remains an ongoing project at UVa's Frank Batten School of Leadership and Public Policy.

Dispatches was compiled from notes, legislative files, and contemporary letters, all of which formed the basis of the first draft. These notes were often written in the heat of the moment. So, where possible, fallible memories have been checked for accuracy through subsequent interviews with fellow policymakers. Also helpful in assessing the relative significance of events I witnessed have been texts used in Master of Public Policy degree programs. Following is a highly subjective list of some of the best works on the modern Congress and its relations with the White House.

Selected Political Science Texts and Biographies

Julian E. Zelizer's *On Capitol Hill* (2004), Cambridge is the single best work on the struggle to reshape Congress and to place the post-Watergate reforms in historical context. Zelizer's *Governing America: The Revival of Political History*, Princeton (2012), is also helpful in this regard.

Walter J. Oleszek, Roger H. Davidson, and Frances Lee's *Congress and Its Members* (13th edition, 2013), published by CQ Press, remains the single indispensable text for how Congress works.

Robert Caro's LBJ biographies, including *Master of the Senate* (2002) and *The Passage of Power* (2012), Knopf, give great detail on Congress as it neared the sweeping reforms of the 1960s and 1970s, but see also Elizabeth Drew's slim biography of Nixon and Alan Brinkley's John F. Kennedy biography from the same series.

Hedrick Smith's *The Power Game: How Washington Works* (1998), Ballantine, chronicles the dicey game played by reporter and source, and is especially revealing of the challenges Howard Baker faced as Senate majority leader during the Reagan presidency and, later, as a very successful White House chief of staff during the second Reagan term.

Norm Ornstein and Thomas Mann's *It's Even Worse Than It Looks* (2012), Perseus, offers a startling and bleak analysis suggested by its subtitle *How the American Constitutional System Collided with the New Politics of Extremism*. Particular focus here is on the decline of the Senate and the rise of the Tea Party since the 2010 midterm elections.

Congress Reconsidered (tenth edition, CQ/Sage, 2012), edited by Lawrence C. Dodd and Bruce I. Oppenheimer, is an excellent text. The collected essays in this volume are particularly strong on current procedure and legislative strategy.

Congress: The Electoral Connection (second edition, Yale, 2004), by David R. Mayhew, updates the definitive academic study on the role electioneering and preparation for reelection play in the day-to-day work of the legislative branch.

Legislative Leviathan: Party Government in the House (University of California, 1993), by Gary W. Cox and Mathew D. McCubbins, is insightful though a bit dated. Stat-heavy profiles and good numbers on party loyalty are helpful to readers seeking to understand the role of parties in the House.

The U.S. Senate: From Deliberation to Dysfunction (CQ, 2011), edited by

Burdett A. Loomis, contains a number of strong contributions. Barbara Sinclair's look at party leadership, which ably chronicles the ebb and flow of party power and the precipitous rise of action-choking, partisan-based Senate filibusters, is recommended, as are Bruce Oppenheimer's excellent review of recent energy policy failures and James Lindsay's review of recent Senate foreign policy actions.

Rivals for Power: Presidential-Congressional Relations, edited by James Thurber (Rowman & Littlefield, 2009), captures the evolution of inter-branch tensions from a number of angles. The legislative strategy chapter by veteran professionals Gary Andres and Patrick Griffin is of particular value.

The Most Exclusive Club: A Modern History of the United States Senate (Basic, 2005), by Lewis L. Gould, is recommended for solid chapters on the Senate between 1975 and 2000.

The Speaker of the House: A Study of Leadership (Yale, 2010), by Matthew N. Green, does an excellent job of explaining how modern Speakers wield power in the House chamber.

The American Congress: The Building of Democracy (Houghton, 2004), edited by Julian E. Zelizer, offers a comprehensive political history of modern reform efforts, especially in its "Part IV: The Contemporary Era, 1970s - Today."

The Last Great Senate: Courage and Statesmanship in Times of Crisis (PublicAffairs, 2012), by Ira Shapiro, is a rich and wistful look back at the achievements, characters, and culture of the Senate in the late 1970s.

Revolving Gridlock: Politics and Policy from Jimmy Carter to George W. Bush (Westview, 2005), by Craig Volden and David W. Brady, is an authoritative analysis of the intersection of party politics and legislative action from 1980 through 2005.

Leading Representatives: The Agency of Leaders in the Politics of the U.S. House (Johns Hopkins, 2007) is Randall Strahan's examination of the careers of three Speakers—Henry Clay, Thomas Reed, and Newt Gingrich—to examine the impact possible for motivated, ambitious, and creative leaders.

Parties and Leaders in the Post-reform House (University of Chicago, 1991), by David Rohde, makes a compelling argument that the reforms of the 1970s strengthened parties, enhanced the power of the majority, and are directly related to the rise in partisanship that occurred in the following decades.

Eric Shickler's *Disjointed Pluralism: Institutional Innovation and the Development of the U.S. Congress* (Princeton, 2001) examines the coalitions that produced major changes to congressional leadership, committees, and procedures during four key periods of the twentieth century: 1890-1910, 1919-1932, 1937-1952, and 1970-1989. Another good work on the subject is Nelson

Polsby's *How Congress Evolves: Social Bases of Individual Change* (Oxford, 2003), which looks at the role of air-conditioning (!) among other causes in altering Southern politics and the changes that have taken place in the post-World War II Congress.

For a well-chosen and well-written series of case studies of congressional leadership in the Senate and House, see *First Among Equals: Outstanding Senate Leaders of the Twentieth Century* (CQ, 1991), edited by Richard Baker and Roger Davidson, and *Masters of the House: Congressional Leaders over Two Centuries* (Westview, 1998), edited by Roger Davidson, Susan Webb Hammond, and Raymond Smock.

Sarah Binder begins with the framers in *Stalemate: Causes and Consequences of Legislative Gridlock* (Brookings, 2003), and moves through the present, offering a blend of history and empirical analysis. Ultimately, this work is concerned with the impact of gridlock on Congress' performance, and closes with a call for reforms that could alleviate some of its most detrimental impacts on policymaking.

Though dated, John Kingdon's *Agendas, Alternatives, and Public Policies* (Little, Brown, 1984) remains an important work on agenda-setting and its role in the policy process, including a look at political actors beyond Congress. For an updated analysis of the same issue, and one more narrowly focused on the legislative branch, see Gary Cox and Mathew McCubbins' *Setting the Agenda: Responsible Party Government in the U.S. House of Representatives* (Cambridge, 2005).

With "unorthodox" legislation now more the rule than the exception, Barbara Sinclair's *Unorthodox Lawmaking: New Legislative Processes in the U.S. Congress* (third edition, CQ, 2007) is more relevant than ever.

Selected Memoirs

The Waxman Report: How Congress Really Works (2009), Hachette. Congressman Henry Waxman's memoir is full of insights on the role of money in politics, as well as how to use Capitol Hill hearings to frame issues and to garner maximum political advantage.

Cranston: The Senator from California (1980), Presidio, by Eleanor Fowle is a fawning biography re-released for the 1984 presidential campaign. It effectively captures Cranston's rise from grassroots politician as well as his early career as a journalist and anti-Hitler activist.

The Changing Dream (1975), Doubleday, a campaign product by John Tunney, hints at the platform and vibe promoted for his seemingly inevitable, but never-to-be, presidential campaign.

The single best memoir ever written about a career working with Congress is *A Political Education* (1994), University of Texas, by Harry McPherson. McPherson captures with searing candor and lyrical prose the remarkable transformations he experienced during his career. Beginning as an LBJ Senate aide in the 1950s, he participated in the vast increase in staff, the drive for civil rights and legislative reform, and the move toward the virtual extinction of southern Democrats in the Senate. He had a noteworthy role once LBJ became President.

Index

*Page references in italics indicate illustrations.
GW refers to Gerald Warburg.*

Aaron, Henry ("Hank"), 176–77
Abrams, Elliott, 166
Adelman, Kenneth, 67, 166
Afghanistan, Soviet occupation of, 155–56, 199
Agendas, Alternatives, and Public Policies (Kingdon), 247
AIPAC (American Israel Public Affairs Committee), 71–72, 84, 113
Al-Aqsa (Jerusalem), 127
Albright, Madeleine, 93, 213
Alpert, Richard, 78–79
al-Qaeda, 186, 188
Alvarez, Bob, 48, 87, 89
The American Congress: The Building of Democracy (Zelizer), 246
American Israel Public Affairs Committee (AIPAC), 71–72, 84, 113
American Nuclear Energy Council (ANEC), 91, 102
American Revolution, 161
Amherst College (Amherst, Mass.), 22
Anderson, Kai, 180, 182

Andres, Gary, 246
Andropov, Yuri, 202, 207–8
ANEC (American Nuclear Energy Council), 91, 102
anti-Semitism, 115
Antonelli, Johnny, 144
apartheid (South Africa), 160–63, 241n27
Appropriations Committee, 42
Aquino, Corazon, 158, *158*
Arab-Israeli dispute over Palestine, 114–18, 121, 124
Arab-Israeli war (1973), 192
Argentina's nuclear program, 85–86
Armed Services Committee, 90–91
Arms Control and Foreign Policy Caucus, 84–85
Arms Control Program (Stanford University), 139
arms control/reduction, 155–57, 203–4, 207. *See also* Nuclear Non-Proliferation Act
arms race, 45, 49, 155, 157. *See also* nuclear weapons
Army Corps of Engineers,

95–96
Ashworth, Bill, 72
atom bomb, 45–46
Atomic Energy Act, 46
Atoms for Peace, 46, 49, 85, 132

Bailey, Lois, 239n3
Baker, Howard, 46, *66*, 67, 69, 211
Baker, Richard: *First Among Equals: Outstanding Senate Leaders of the Twentieth Century*, 247
Batten School (University of Virginia), 34, 39, 230, 233
Bechtel, 54, 56–57, 91
Begin, Menachem, 65–66, 70–71, 126
Beit Sha'an (Israel), 118–19, *119*, 125
Bendixen, Sergio, 154, 159
Bergner, Jeff, 162, 167, 241n27
Berk, Chuck, 165
Berlin Wall, fall of (1989), 208
Berman, Howard, 94–95
Bernstein, Bart, 138–39
Bernstein, Carl, 59
Bettauer, Ronald, 103
Bhutto, Benazir, 186–88

Biden, Joe, 157;
     campaign of,
     211; on Cranston,
     243n38; election
     of, 223, 229;
     on nuclear non-
     proliferation,
     143–44; vs.
     Packwood,
     168–69;
     presidential bid
     of, 169; Reagan
     appointees
     attacked by, 166;
     on the Saudi
     arms sale, 169;
     on the Senate
     Foreign Relations
     Committee,
     66, 66–67; on
     the seniority
     system, 47; vice
     presidential bid
     of, 212
bill-signing rituals,
     129–30
Binder, Sarah: *Stalemate:
     Causes and
     Consequences
     of Legislative
     Gridlock*, 247
Bingham, Hiram, 81–82
Bingham, Jonathan B.
     ("Jack"), *90*, 136;
     campaigning
     by/reelection
     of, 85; district/
     home of, 82;
     guidance of junior
     staff by, 82–84;
     as Harriman's
     aide, 82; "How
     Our Laws Are
     Made" booklet

distributed by,
     99; H.R. 4409
     sponsored by,
     106–11, 132 (*see
     also* Nuclear Non-
     Proliferation Act);
     International
     Trade and
     Economic Policy
     Subcommittee
     chaired by, 91,
     101, 107–8;
     vs. the JCAE,
     88–89, 91–92,
     101; lobbying
     of, 102–3, 104;
     at Nuclear Non-
     Proliferation Act
     signing, 131, *131*;
     on nuclear policy,
     86, 90–91, 102,
     105–7, 240n14;
     personality/
     demeanor of, 81;
     politics of, 82;
     pro-Israel stance
     of, 113; softball
     team of, 81; staff/
     office of, 81
Bin Laden, Osama, 187,
     222
Blacker, Chip, 139, 143
Board of Visitors (BoV;
     University of
     Virginia), 231–35
Boehner, John, 185, 226
Boggs, Tommy, 186
Bolling, Richard, 87
Bond, Jim, 72
Bonner, Yelena, 203, 205,
     205, 209
Bork, Robert, 163,
     242n28
Boschwitz, Rudy, *66*, 67

Boxer, Barbara, 17,
     94–96
Braden, Joan (Tom's
     wife), 53–54
Braden, Joannie (Tom's
     daughter), 53, 79
Braden, Tom, 53–54,
     55–56, 57, 80;
     Eight is Enough,
     79
Bradford, Peter, 129–32,
     131
Brady, David W.:
     *Revolving
     Gridlock: Politics
     and Policy from
     Jimmy Carter to
     George W. Bush*,
     246–47
Brady, Jack, 110
Braun, Werner von, 123
Brazil's nuclear program,
     85–86, 132
Brezhnev, Leonid, 202,
     207–8
Brinkley, David, 53
Brinton, Demaris, 154
Brokaw, Tom, 208
Brown, Chip, 25
Brown, Dan, 45
Brown, Jerry, 52, 80
Brown, Pat, 14, 24
Buchanan, Pat, 79
Buckley, Charlie, 82
Burns, Ken, 25, 31
Burrell, Pat, 147–48
Burton, Priscilla, 154
Bush, George H. W., 97,
     158–59, 166,
     206–7, 208, 211
Bush, George W., 18,
     61–62, 97, 143,
     211–12, 215–16,
     225–26

Byrd, Robert C. ("Bobby"), 38, 166, 167–68

Caesarea (ancient Mediterranean port), 117
California's public schools, 22, 114–15
campaign fundraising, 184–86, 243–44n38
Canaanites, 119
CapCure Foundation, 181
Carter, Jimmy, 225; battles with Congress, 105–6; Cabinet appointments by, 89; nomination/election of, 52, 90, 100–101; Nuclear Non-Proliferation Act signed by, 111, *131*, 131–32 (*see also* Nuclear Non-Proliferation Act); on nuclear policy, 86, 102, 106; popularity of, 115; staff of, 60
Cassidy, Gerry, 64–65, 142, 173–75, 182
Cassidy & Associates, 60; clients of, 176–79, 181–82; daily routine of, 175–76; Darfur project of, 189; expertise of, 178; federal funding for schools/hospitals secured by, 174, 181–82; growth of, 174, 180; Nixon Library project of, 181, *242*, 242n32; Obama supported by, 221; Pakistan project of, 187–88; policymaking strategy by, 182–83; stature/success of, 63–64, 173–74, 178–80, 186, 239n8; *Washington Post* series on, 64–65, 173–74

The Cavalier Daily, 232
Chamberlain, Neville, 97
The Changing Dream (Tunney), 248
Cheney, Dick, 96, 213
Chernenko, Konstantin, 202, 207–8
Chevron, 54, 56–57
Chicago Seven, 47
China, 179–80
China Program (Stanford University), 139
Christianson, Gerry, 165
Christopher, Warren, 179
Church, Frank, 69, 108, 175
Church of the Holy Sepulchre (Jerusalem), 127
CIA interventions in Central America, 158–59
civil rights movement, 161
Clark, William, 166
Cleland, Max, 156
climate change legislation, 95–96
Clinton, Bill, 143–44, 169, 180, 218, 242n28
Clinton, Hillary, 218
Cochran, Thad, 16
Cochran, Tom, 48, 89
Cold War, 45, 156, 191–93, 208–9
committee assignments, 87–91
Communism, 97, 164, 179
Comprehensive Anti-Apartheid Act, 162–63
Con Ed, 102–3
Conflict and Consensus: The Struggle between Congress and the President Over Foreign Policymaking (GW), 175
Congress: accessibility of, 41–42, 171; as partisan, 41, 175; as populist, 41; power dispersed in, 178; "President's Birthday Week" recess for, 110–11; pro-Israel legislators in, 115; receptions hosted by, 52; reformers in (Class of the Ninety-Fourth Congress), 47–48, 88; relevance of, 175; U.C. (Unanimous

253

Consent) votes in,
110–11; and the
war on terror, 161.
See also House of
Representatives;
Senate
*Congress and Its
Members*
(Oleszek,
Davidson, and F.
Lee), 245
Congress Reconsidered
(L. C. Dodd
and B. I.
Oppenheimer),
246
*Congress: The Electoral
Connection*
(Mayhew), 246
CongressWatch, 86
Connolly, Gerry, 165,
169, 211–12
Connor, Chris, 176
Coolidge, Calvin, 225
Co-Op City (South
Bronx), 82
Council for a Livable
World, 189, 221
counterterrorism
measures, 33
Cowan, Ed, 92
Cox, Gary W.: *Legislative
Leviathan*,
246; *Setting the
Agenda*, 247
Cox, Tricia Nixon, 15, 19
Craig, Greg, 161–62,
213, 219, 229
Cranston, Alan, *43*, 70;
appearance of,
153; on arms
control/reduction,
155–57, 207;
biography of,
248; vs. Bork,
163, 242n28; on
CIA interventions
in Central
America, 158–59;
effectiveness/
reputation of,
243–44n38;
fundraising by,
153–55; idealism
of, 136; on the
Intelligence
Committee, 93;
and the Keating
Five Scandal,
243–44n38; leaks
to the press by,
61–62; letter
to Begin on
Israeli invasion
of Lebanon,
70–71; nuclear
proliferation
opposed by,
61–62, 186; offers
GW a position,
136–38; political
enemies of, 153;
presidential bid
by, 159–60,
197, 241n25;
press secretary's
work for, 60; vs.
Reagan, 153,
159, 193; Reagan
appointees
opposed by, 165–
66; reelection of,
203; roll call tally
sheets of, 138,
156, 163, *164*,
199; on SALT
II, 193–94; on
savings and loan
practices, 207;
on the Senate
Foreign Relations
Committee, 66,
66, 68–69; on
South African
policy, 161–62,
241n26; in the
Soviet Union,
194–200, *198*,
203–6, *204–5*;
on the Soviet
Union, 193; staff
of, 94–95, 154,
154; Stanford
connections
of, 139; trips
overseas, 158,
158
Cranston, Kim, 203,
204–5, 212
"Cranston Sees
A-Weapons
Danger in
Iraq, Pakistan"
(Hume), 62
*Cranston: The Senator
from California*
(Fowle), 248
Critical Mass Energy
Project, 48, 86
Crossfire, 79
Cuban Missile Crisis,
191–92
Cubie, Jim, 48, 86–87, 89
cultural revolution, 26
Czechoslovakia, Soviet
invasion of, 192

Darfur, 217
Das, Vijay, 220–21
Daschle, Tom, 68
Davenport, Jim, 144
Davidson, Roger H.:

*Congress and
Its Members*,
245; *First
Among Equals:
Outstanding
Senate Leaders
of the Twentieth
Century*, 247;
*Masters of
the House:
Congressional
Leaders over Two
Centuries*, 247
Davis, Tom, 16–17
Dead Indian Ranch
(Wyoming), *4*,
4–5
Dead Sea, 126
Dead Sea scrolls, 125–26
DeConcini, Dennis,
244n38
DeLay, Tom, 51
Democratic Study Group,
84–85
Democrats: on Asian
civil wars, 164;
conservative,
southern, 88; on
defense, 156;
losses by, 211; vs.
Republicans, 156,
226
Dewar, Helen, 62
Dine, Tom, 169
Dingell, John, 91
*Disjointed Pluralism:
Institutional
Innovation
and the
Development of
the U.S. Congress*
(Shickler), 247
Dobrynin, Anatoly,
203–4, *204*

Dodd, Chris, 47, 157, 166
Dodd, Lawrence C.:
*Congress
Reconsidered*, 246
Dole, Bob, 167, 173
Domenici, Pete, 194
Donaldson, Sam, 80
Dreier, David, 16
Drell, Sid, 138–39
duck-and-cover drills,
192
Dukakis, Michael, 213

Eagleburger, Larry, 166
Edmund Walsh School of
Foreign Service
(Georgetown
University),
93–94
Eight is Enough (T.
Braden), 79
Eisenhower, David, 13,
16–17
Eisenhower, Dwight D.,
13, 225
Eisenhower, Julie Nixon:
effects of her
father's downfall
on, 18–19;
graduation from
Smith College,
28; Nixon Library
role of, 15–18,
19–20, 181,
242, 242n32;
relationship with
her father, 17
Eliot, T. S., 113, 236
Emanuel, Rahm, 235
Environmental Action, 48
environmental groups,
101
Environmental Protection
Agency, 19

Environmental Study
Conference,
84–85
Evans, Connie, 48

Fabiani, Jim, 180
failure, response to,
97–98
Fairfax County
(Virginia), 219–22
Fawcett, Sharon, 19
Federal Election
Commission,
37–38
Federalist 10 (Madison),
103
Feingold, Russ, 221
Feinstein, Dianne, 17,
94–96, 143–44,
216–17
FEMA, 181
filibusters, 41, 152, 167,
175
Findley, Paul, 85, 105,
110
Fingar, Tom, 139, 143
*First Among Equals:
Outstanding
Senate Leaders
of the Twentieth
Century* (R. Baker
and Davidson),
247
Flander, Murray, 60
Ford, Gerald, 51–52, 80,
86, 109
Ford House Office
Building, 73
Foreign Relations
Committee. *See*
Senate Foreign
Relations
Committee
Fortier, Don, 107,

109–11, *131*
Founding Fathers, 81
Fowle, Eleanor:
    *Cranston: The
    Senator from
    California*, 248
Frank, Jane (Harman), 50
Fulbright, J. William, 175

Galbraith, Peter, 72, 165, 186
Gaza, 116, 124
Genton, Gina, 154
George, Alexander, 138–39
George, Roger, 139
Georgetown University: Edmund Walsh School of Foreign Service, 93–94; Inter-Cultural Center, 93; students at, 98, 100
Gephardt, Dick, 185–86
Giants (San Francisco), 144–49, 215
Gingrich, Newt, 51, 95, 185–86, 211, 226, 242n28
Gingrich Revolution, 180
glasnost, 207
Glenn, John: on India's nuclear program, 49, 85; on the Israeli invasion of Lebanon, 70; and the Keating Five Scandal, 243–44n38; at Nuclear Non-Proliferation Act signing, 131, *131*; on nuclear policy,

85, 105, 108–10; on the Senate Foreign Relations Committee, 66, 66–67
Goering, Herman, 123
Golan Heights, 125
Golden Gate National Recreation Area, 3
Goldwater, Barry, 135, 165, 175, 225–26
Gorbachev, Mikhail, 157, 202–4, 206
Gore, Al, Jr., 86, 216
Gore, Al, Sr., 46
Gould, Lewis L.: *The Most Exclusive Club: A Modern History of the United States Senate*, 246
Graham, Katharine, 80
Grateful Dead, 2
Great Recession, 229
Greeks, 119
Green, Matthew N.: *The Speaker of the House: A Study of Leadership*, 246
Gregg, Donald, 166
Griffin, Patrick, 246
Gromyko, Andrei, 194, 195, 196, 197–200, *198*, 202–3
Gruson, Lyndsey, 26, 31–32, 44–45
Guantanamo Bay, 229

Haganah, 120
Hagel, Chuck, 94
Haig, Alexander, 67, 192, 194–95, 202

Haight-Ashbury, 2
Hamilton, Alexander, 103
Hammond, Susan Webb: *Masters of the House: Congressional Leaders over Two Centuries*, 247
Hampshire College (Amherst, Mass.), 78–79, 104; activism at, 26–29, *28*; admissions rate at, 22; alcohol/drug use at, 25; Board of Trustees development campaign, 189; and endowments from companies doing business in South Africa, 161; environment of, 26; experimentalism/intellectual fervor at, 21–22, 25, 30–31, 90, 239n3; founding of, 239n3; *non satis scire* motto of, 21
Haqqani, Hussain, 188
Harding, Harry, 34, 38, 139
Harding, Warren G., 225
Harman, Jane Frank, 50
Har Megiddo (Armageddon, Israel), 117
Harriman, Averell, 82
Harris, Fred, 52
Hart, Gary, 159, 160
Hartley, Gregg, 19, 180

Hashemites, 118
Hastert, Dennis, 96
Hawke, Frank, 178
Hawk 'n' Dove (Washington, D.C.), 87
Hayakawa, S. I., 47, 57
Hayden, Carl, 135
Hayden, Tom, 47, 57
health care reform, 98
Hebrew University (Israel), 123, 124
Helms, Jesse: Cranston on, 153; filibusters by, 175; on the Senate Foreign Relations Committee, 66, 66, 68; staff of, 167
Hiroshima, 46
Hiss, Alger, 18
history and myth, 115, 116
Hitler, Adolf, 192, 212; *Mein Kampf*, 68. *See also* Holocaust
Hodges, Russ, 145
Holocaust, 115, 122, 123–24
Holyoke (Massachusetts), 26–27, *27*
Homeland Security, 222
Hoover, Herbert, 225
House Democratic Caucus, 88–89, 91
House Democratic Steering and Policy Committee, 88
House Energy and Commerce Committee, 91
House of Representatives: lobbyists' campaign donations to members of, 184–86; vs. Senate, 37, 83, 110
House-Senate conference committees, 83–84
House Speaker, 87–88, 94
housing bubble, 222
How Congress Evolves (Polsby), 247
"How Our Laws Are Made," 99
H.R. 4409 bill, 106–11, 132. *See also* Nuclear Non-Proliferation Act
Hruska, Roman, 171
Huckabee, Mike, 218
Hume, Ellen, 60–62, 239n6; "Cranston Sees A-Weapons Danger in Iraq, Pakistan," 62
Humphrey, Hubert, 153
Hussein, Saddam, 61
hydrogen bomb, 45

Indian Point nuclear power station (New York), *90*
India's nuclear weapons program, 49, 85, 132, 143
intellectual cycles, 225
Intelligence Committee, 93
Inter-Cultural Center (Georgetown University), 93
Interior Committee, 90
International Relations Committee, 85, 91
International Trade and Economic Policy Subcommittee, 91, 101, 107–8
Iran-Contra scandal, 153, 158–59, 166, 203
Iraq's nuclear program, 114
Iraq War, 86, 97
Isaacs, John, 189
isolationism and intervention, cycles of, 225–26, 244n40
Israel, 113–28; Americans vs. Israelis, 126; ancient history of the lands, 118–19, *119*, 122, 127; Arab-Israeli dispute over Palestine, 114–18, 121, 124; Arab lands within, 117, 121; democracy in, 124; diversity in, 126; Holocaust survivors in, 123; Kibbutz Dafna, 120; Lebanon invaded by, 65–66, 69–71, 74; plate tectonics in the area, 125; Route 90, 119–20
Israel Defense Forces, 116, 125
It's Even Worse Than It Looks (Ornstein

and Mann), 245

Jackson, Henry ("Scoop"), 46, 87, 166, 175
Jackson, Jesse, Jr., 185
Jackson, Jesse, Sr., 159
Javits, Jacob, 48, 49, 175
JCAE. *See* Joint Committee on Atomic Energy
Jefferson, Thomas, 41, 103, 135
Jennings, Peter, 208
Jericho (West Bank), 125–26
Jerusalem, 116, 125, 127
Jews, persecution of, 115
Jezreel Valley (Israel), 117, 125, 127–28
Jobs, Steve, 2
Johnson, Lyndon, 69, 100; on a free society, 103; on the JCAE, 46; military escalation in Southeast Asia by, 97–98; presidential powers of, 47, 80; war on poverty/racism declared by, 193
Johnson, Vic, 135
Joint Committee on Atomic Energy (JCAE), 104; abolition of, 87–92, 101, 106, *131*, 132; abuses by, 46, 55, 89; Atoms for Peace program, 46, 49; H. Baker's role on, 67; and India's nuclear program, 85–86; and the Nuclear Fuel Assurance Act, 54–55, 56–57, 86; power of, 45, 87, 104–5; public hearings held by, 89; reformers attend meetings of, 48–49; secrecy/closed-door meetings of, 45, 47

Joplin, Janis, 2
Jordan, Barbara, 76
Jordan River (Israel), 120
Joseph, Gloria, 78–79
journalists: bias by, 29, 60, 63; hacks, 63; leaking stories to, 61–63, 239n6; legislators' need for the press, 60, 62–63; relationship with sources, 60–61; as role models, 59; unbiased reporting by, 59, 81
Juster, Norton, 25

Kaiser, Robert, 64
Kassebaum, Nancy Landon, *66*, 68
Kaufman, Ted, 67
Keaney, Dave, 165
Keating (Charles) Five Scandal, 207, 243n38
Kefauver, Estes, 69
Kelley, P. X., 178
Kennedy, Edward ("Ted"), 42, 53; vs. Byrd, 38; on Cranston, 243n38; on nuclear reduction, 155; on South African apartheid, 161–63, 241n26; and Tunney, 50
Kennedy, Joe, 103
Kennedy, John F. ("Jack"), 4, 238n1; anti-Communism of, 97; assassination of, 26; battles with Congress, 100; during Cuban Missile Crisis, 191–92; on the Foreign Relations Committee, 69; interventionism of, 225–26; on nuclear weapons, 49, 143; popularity of, 13, 24, 115; presidential bid of, 218
Kennedy family, 14, 164–65
Kennedy School of Government (Harvard University), 136, 137
Keohane, Bob, 138–39
Kerr, David, 25
Kerr, Gordon, 76–78, 81, 107, 110–11,

132–33
Kerry, John, 69, 151, 157, 166, 169–70, 212–16
Kerry-Lugar-Berman bill, 186
KGB, 195, 200, 205
King, Martin Luther, Jr., 4, 26, 135
King, Martin Luther, Jr., bust of (U.S. Capitol), 135
Kingdon, John: *Agendas, Alternatives, and Public Policies*, 247
Kirkland, Willie, 144
Kiryat Shemona (Israel), 126
Kissinger, Henry, 53, 86
Kizzia, Tom, 25
Knesset (Israel), 126
Krakauer, Jon, 25, 31
Kristallnacht, 122
Krukow, Mike, 146, 149
Kucinich, Dennis, 225–26
Kuhn, Tom, 102
Kuiper, Duane, 146, 149
Kuwata, Kam, 154, 159, 241n25

Lake, Tony, 94
The Last Great Senate: Courage and Statesmanship in Times of Crisis (Shapiro), 246
Leading Representatives: The Agency of Leaders in the Politics of the U.S. House (Strahan), 247

Lebanon, Israeli invasion of, 65–66, 69–71, 74
Lee, Frances: *Congress and Its Members*, 245
Lee Teng-Hui, 65, 177, 179
Lefever, Ernest, 67, 166
Legislative Leviathan: (G. W. Cox and McCubbins), 246
Lehn, Al, 167
Lerner, Alexander, 200
Leventhal, Paul, 48
Levine, Mel, 50, 94–95, 157
Lewis, Jerry, 15
Lewis, John, 138–39
Libby, Scooter, 61
Lien-Fu Huang, 177
Lincecum, Tim, 149
Lincoln, Abraham, 135
Lindsay, James, 246
lobbyists, 173–90; campaign donations by, 184–86; hazards for, 183–84; on K Street, 173; legitimacy of, 174–75; nuclear industry, 104–5; Obama-Biden campaign work by, 211; Obama on, 183; service performed by, 102. *See also* Cassidy, Gerry; Cassidy & Associates
Loma Prieta earthquake (California), 181

London School of Economics, 136
Longsworth, Charles R., *28*, 239n3
Loomis, Burdett A.: *The U.S. Senate: From Deliberation to Dysfunction*, 246
Los Angeles Times, 62, 63
Lovejoy, Sam, 25, 29–30, 43
Lugar, Richard ("Dick"): on aid to the Marcos regime, 157; at the SALT Study Group, 194; on the Senate Foreign Relations Committee, *66*, 66–67; on South African apartheid, 161, 162–63, 241n27

Maass, Peter, 63, 208
Machu Picchu (Peru), 81–82
Madison, James, 41; *Federalist 10*, 103
Majak, Roger, 84, 135
The Mandarin Club (GW), 72, 139, 142, 144
Mandela, Nelson, 163, 177
Manhattan Project, 45
Mann, Thomas: *It's Even Worse Than It Looks*, 245
Marcos, Ferdinand, 157, 158, 163
Marcos, Imelda, 158
Marcus, Stanley, 84
Mare Island (California),

259

Marincello (proposed city; California), 238n1
Marin County Planning Commission (California), 3
Mason, Arthur, 180
Massachusetts Sixth Regiment, 45
Masters of the House: Congressional Leaders over Two Centuries (Davidson, Hammond, and Smock), 247
Mathews, Jessica Tuchman, 101
Mathias, Charles McC., 135, 157; in Moscow, 193–200, *198*; on the Senate Foreign Relations Committee, 66, 68
Matlock, Jack, *198*
May, Ernest, 100
Mayhew, David R.: *Congress: The Electoral Connection*, 246
Mays, Willie, 145
McCain, John, 170, 176, 218–19, 221, 243–44n38
McCarthy, Joseph, 163, 166
McClure, Jim, 130
McConnell, Mitch, 170, 230
McCormack, Mike, 91
McCovey, Willie, 144,

145
McCubbins, Mathew D.: *Legislative Leviathan*, 246; *Setting the Agenda*, 247
McDonnell, Bob, 234
McGovern, George, 80, 156, 159, 160, 173, 175, 225–26
McMahon, Brien, 46
McNair, Bob, 45, 47, 54
McNamara, Dan, 180
McNamara, Robert, 53–54
McNeely, Mary Lou, 137
McPherson, Harry: *A Political Education*, 248
media. *See* journalists
Mediterranean–Mesopotamia route, 125
memoirs of political life, 7–8
Meyers, Ken, 187
The Middle East Policy Survey, 71
Milken, Mike, 181
Miller, Clement, 238n1
Miller, Ellen, 48
Miller, Gary, *242*, 242n32
Miller, George, 47, 94–95
Miller, Judy, 61–62, 239n6
Miller, Steve, 2
Mitchell, George, 168, 243n38
Model Cities program, 26–27
Mondale, Walter, 131, *131*, 159–60
Moon, Sun Myung, 63
The Most Exclusive Club:

A Modern History of the United States Senate (Gould), 246
Mount Holyoke College (South Hadley, Mass.), 22
Mt. Tamalpais (Marin County, Calif.), 23–24
Musharraf, Pervez, 186–88
MX missiles, 156
Myers, Henry, *90*
My Life (Sakharov), 206
myth and history, 115, 116

Nader, Ralph, 48, 86
National Archives and Records Administration (NARA), 12, 15, 17, 18, 181, *242*, 242n32
National Democratic Institute, 113, 124
National Security Council, 159, 206–7
Natural Resources Defense Council (NRDC), 48
Nazis, 122–23. *See also* Holocaust
NCAA, 182
Negroponte, John, 166
Netanyahu, Benjamin ("Bibi"), 114, 126
Newsweek, 179
New York Times: on Cranston's letter to Begin, 70–71; on the invasion

of Iraq, 61; on the JCAE's demise, 92; on nuclear exports, nonproliferation, and waste disposal, 89; on SFRC briefing on Israeli attack on Lebanon, 71–73; on U.S. South African policy, 162, 241n27
New York Times Magazine, 234
9/11 attacks (2001), 33, 97, 213
Nixon, Edward (Richard's brother), 14
Nixon, Frank (Richard's father), 11–12
Nixon, Pat, 12, 19
Nixon, Richard, 103, 225; accomplishments of, 19; angst of, 12–13; anti-Communism of, 18; during Arab-Israeli war, 192; bust statue of, 18; childhood home (*see* Nixon Museum and Birthplace); Congress's relationship with, 47; vs. Cranston, 153; at Duke Law School, 12; foregos Julie's college graduation, 28; gravesite of, 12; impeachment proceedings against, 67, 165; and the Kennedy family, 164–65; pardon for, 51–52, 80; personal attacks on opponents, 163; popularity of, 115; presidential papers, 14–15, 17, 242n32; resignation/downfall of, 1, 5–6, 19, 165; at Whittier College, 12; xenophobia of, 24
Nixon Foundation, 13–14
Nixon Library, 14–18, 19–20, 181, *242*, 242n32
Nixon Museum and Birthplace (Yorba Linda, Calif.), 11–15
Nixon tapes, 12
North, Oliver, 141–42, 206–7
North Korea's nuclear program, 143
Northridge earthquake (California), 181
Nosenzo, Louis, 103
NRC (Nuclear Regulatory Commission), 91, 129, 130
NRDC (Natural Resources Defense Council), 48
Nuclear Fuel Assurance Act, 54–55, 56–57, 86
nuclear industry lobbyists, 104–5
Nuclear Non-Proliferation Act (1978), 111, *112*, 129–32, *131*, 143–44. *See also* H.R. 4409 bill
nuclear policy jurisdiction, 90–91, 240n14. *See also under* Bingham, Jonathan B.
nuclear power, 25, 29–30, 85–86
nuclear reform, 48, 55–56, 86, 89, 104–5, 240n14
Nuclear Regulatory Commission (NRC), 91, 129, 130
nuclear weapons, 45–46, 49–50, 62–63, 102, 132, 143, 239n6. *See also* arms control/reduction; Nuclear Non-Proliferation Act
Nudel, Ida, 200, 243n36
Nussbaum, Martha, 225
Nye, Joe, 105, 106, 111

Obama, Barack, 2–3, 211–23; campaigns of, 211, 216–22, 230; on Darfur, 217; as driven by causes, 51; election of, 223, 229; and

Feinstein, 96; inauguration of, 101; on lobbyists, 183; on the Nuclear Non-Proliferation Act, 143–44; personality of, 216–17; on the SFRC, 69, 169; speaking skills of, 212–13; stimulus and health insurance reform by, 226
Obamacare, 98
Oberdorfer, Don, 62
Obey, Dave, 228
O'Connor, Christine, *242*, 242n32
Ogarkov, Nikolai, 196–97
Oil, Charcoal, and Atomic Workers union, 91
Oleszek, Walter J.: *Congress and Its Members*, 245
On Capitol Hill (Zelizer), 245
O'Neal, Tip, 88, 106, 107
Oppenheimer, Bruce I.: *Congress Reconsidered*, 246
Oppenheimer, J. Robert, 45
Ornstein, Norm: *It's Even Worse Than It Looks*, 245

pace of change, 226–27
Packwood, Bob, 168–69
Pakistan: Bin Laden found in, 187; under Musharraf, 186–88; nuclear program of, 85–86, 114, 132, 143, 186; U.S. policy toward, 186–87
Palestine, Arab-Israeli dispute over, 114–18, 121, 124
Palestinian Liberation Organization (PLO), 65–66
Palestinians, 115–16
Palin, Sarah, 218
Palmach, 122
Palo Alto (California), 143
Panetta, Leon, 177–78
Panofsky, Wolfgang, 138–39
Parties and Leaders in the Post-reform House (Rohde), 247
Patterson, Franklin, *28*
Patton Boggs, 239n8
Paul, Ron, 225–26
Paul, Terry, 180
Peace Now, 121
Pell, Claiborne, 66, *66*, 68, 166
Pelosi, Nancy, 17, 94–96, 226
People's Daily (Beijing), 139
Percy, Charles ("Chuck"), 69, 157; and the Bradens, 53; flip-flopping by, 170; on India's nuclear program, 49, 85; on nuclear nonproliferation, 85, 105; on the Senate Foreign Relations Committee, 66, *66*, 68, 71–73
perestroika, 207
Perot, Ross, 226
Perry, Dan, 154, 159
personalities, 38, 151, 168, 170–71
Philistines, 119
Pioneer Valley activists (Massachusetts), 27–28
Plame, Valerie, 61
Planned Parenthood, 182
PLO (Palestinian Liberation Organization), 65–66
Point Reyes National Seashore (California), 3, 238n1
political combat, 227
political cycles, 27, 225–26, 229
A Political Education (McPherson), 248
political scientists, 227
politicians as issue activists vs. issue exploiters, 51
politics of personal destruction, 163–67, 242n28
Polsby, Nelson: *How Congress Evolves*, 247
Potomac fever, 7
Powell, Jody, 60, 64–65, 178
power distribution, 103–4, 171
The Power Game: How

Washington Works (H. Smith), 245
power seekers, 7
precedents, 37, 38
the press. *See* journalists
Pressler, Larry, *66*, 68, 170
Privett, Steve, 147, 176
public interest groups, 59, 86. *See also* lobbyists
public policy career: for causes, 51; for power, 6–7, 31–32; for public purpose vs. private gain, 244n40

Qumran (West Bank), 125–26

Ramses II, 119
Reagan, Ronald, 14, 52, 141–42; Alzheimer's of, 203; appointees of, 165–66; and arms reduction, 62, 157; and the Cold War's end, 208–9; vs. Cranston, 153, 159, 193; Democrats' losses to, 211; election of, 160, 165; and Gorbachev, 203–4; and the Iran-Contra scandal, 153, 158–59, 166, 203; popularity of, 115; prosecution of staff members of, 244n39; retirement of, 206; South African policy of, 161, 162; on the Soviet Union, 192–93, 195
Realpolitik, 98
Redwood High School (Larkspur, Calif.), 25, 75–76
refuseniks, 200–201, 208, 243n36
religious fanaticism, 127
reporters. *See* journalists
Republicans vs. Democrats, 156, 226
Revolving Gridlock: Politics and Policy from Jimmy Carter to George W. Bush (Volden and D. W. Brady), 246–47
Ribicoff, Abraham, 48, 49, 85, 102, 105
Rice, Condoleezza ("Condi"), 139, 143
Richardson, Bobby, 145
Riegle, Donald W., 244n38
Rivals for Power (Thurber), 246
Riverdale (New York), 82
Roff, Hadley, 54, 56, 57
Rogers, David, 62
Rohde, David: *Parties and Leaders in the Post-reform House*, 247
Romans, 119

Room of Secrets (U.S. Capitol), 45
Roosevelt, Franklin Delano, 225
Roosevelt, Teddy, 104, 235
Rosen, David, 48, 76, 77
Rosenberg, M. J., 84
Ross, Cody, 148
Ross Creek (Marin County, Calif.), 95–96
Rothkopf, David, 208–9, 244n39
Rove, Karl, 18, 61, 213
Rowand, Aaron, 148
Rubin, Vitaly, 200
Russell, Richard, 46
Russo, Marty, 180
Russonello, John, 159
Rutgers New Jersey Democratic Club, 221

Sakharov, Andrei, 202, 203, 205, *205*, 209; *My Life*, 206
SALT II, 193–99
SALT Study Group, 194
Sandoval, Pablo ("Panda"), 147
San Francisco Bay Area, 2
San Francisco Chronicle, 63
San Francisco State University, 234–35
Santana, Carlos, 2
Santorum, Rick, 175
Sarbanes, Paul, *66*, 67, 166
Saudi Arabia, 182
Saul, King, 119

savings and loan practices, 207, 243–44n38
Scaggs, Boz, 2
Scharansky, Anatoly, 200
Scherr, Jacob, 48, 89
Schiliro, Phil, 219, 229–30
Schirmer, Kitty, 101
Schlesinger, Arthur, Jr., 97, 225, 244n40
Schlesinger, James, *131*
Schreiber, Liev, 31
Sderot (Israel), 126
Sea Ranch (Sonoma County, Calif.), 4
Sechrest, Colleen, 154
Selig, Bud, 176
Senate: committee jurisdiction in, 102; confirmation battles in, 163, 165–67; vs. House of Representatives, 37, 83, 110; lobbyists' campaign donations to members of, 184–86; majority vote in, 152; personalities in, 151, 168, 170–71
Senate Dining Room (U.S. Capitol), 17
Senate Energy Committee, 109
Senate Foreign Relations Committee (SFRC), *66*, 66–74, 134, 156, 161, 166, 169, 207

Senate Hart Building, 94
September 11 attacks (2001), 33, 97, 213
Setting the Agenda (G. W. Cox and McCubbins), 247
sexual revolution, 26
SFRC. *See* Senate Foreign Relations Committee
Shapiro, Ira, 152; *The Last Great Senate: Courage and Statesmanship in Times of Crisis,* 246
Sharon, Ariel, 69, 70
Shavuot, 121
Shickler, Eric: *Disjointed Pluralism: Institutional Innovation and the Development of the U.S. Congress,* 247
Shields, Mary, 180
Shrum, Bob, 215
Shultz, George, 169
Silicon Valley, 2
Simon, John, 233
Simon, Paul, 68, 71–72
Sinclair, Barbara, 246
Slepak, Vladimir, 200
Smith, Gerard, 105, 106
Smith, Hedrick: *The Power Game: How Washington Works,* 245
Smith College (Northampton, Mass.), 22
Smock, Raymond:

Masters of the House: Congressional Leaders over Two Centuries, 247
Solarz, Steve, 108, 162
Sons of Champlin, 2
South African apartheid regime, 160–63, 241n27
South Bronx, 82, 85
South Korea's nuclear program, 85–86, 132
Soviet Union: Afghanistan occupied by, 155–56, 199; collapse of, 157, 206–9; Czechoslovakia invaded by, 192; emigration from, 200–201, 243n36; as "Evil Empire," 192–93, 202; under Gorbachev, 202, 206; nuclear arsenal of, 155–57, 191; and SALT II, 193–99; U.S. relations with, 193–98, *198*, 202 (*see also* Cold War)
Sparkman, John, 131, *131*
Spaso House (Moscow), 195–96
The Speaker of the House: A Study of Leadership (Green), 246
Specter, Arlen, 16, 51
Speth, Gus, 89, 101
Sports Coalition, 182

Stalemate: Causes and Consequences of Legislative Gridlock (Binder), 247
Stalin, Joseph, 45–46, 195
Stamm, Dianne, 135
Stanford Business School, 96–97
Stanford Linear Accelerator, 139
Stanford University, 136, 138–39, 143, 174
Star Wars missile defense plan, 197
State Department, 103, 106–7, 108, 111, 167, 179
Steny Hoyer Research Center (Silver Spring, Md.), 12
Stevens, Ted, 194
St. John's Hospital (Los Angeles), 181
Strahan, Randall: *Leading Representatives: The Agency of Leaders in the Politics of the U.S. House*, 247
Sullivan, Terry, 39, 230–34
Sunlight Basin (Wyoming), 5
Support East European Democracy (SEED), 207
Supreme Court's *Citizens United* decision, 103
Sutton, Barbara, 180
Symington, Stuart, 49

Taiwan: vs. China, 179–80; nuclear program of, 85–86; U.S. relations with, 179
Taliban, 186
Taylor, John, 11–12
Tea Party activists/candidates, 226, 230
Tel Aviv, 114
Temple Mount (Jerusalem), 127
Tenet, George, 93
Thomas, Clarence, 165, 242n28
Thomson, Jeri, 43–44
Three Mile Island accident (1979), 240n14
Thurber, James: *Rivals for Power*, 246
Time magazine, 192
Torres, Andres, 148
Tower, John, 165
Tower of Power, 2
Truman, Harry, 45–46
Tsongas, Niki, 67
Tsongas, Paul, *66*, 67
Tunney, John, *43*, 46–47, 48, 49–52, 54–57, 57; *The Changing Dream*, 248

U.C. (Unanimous Consent), 110–11
Udall, Mo, 52, 90–91, 240n14
United States: foreign aid policy of, 157; intervention in El Salvador, 157; and the Iran-Contra scandal, 153, 158–59, 166, 203; nuclear arsenal of, 155–57, 191; on nuclear proliferation, 62–63; Pakistan policy of, 186–87; South African policy of, 160–62, 241n27; Soviet relations with, 193–98, *198*, 202 (*see also* Cold War); Taiwan policy of, 179
University of California–Berkeley, 2, 234–35
University of Massachusetts, 22
University of Pennsylvania, 189
University of San Francisco, 174, 178
University of Virginia, 34–35, 36–39, 189–90, 230–35
Uris, Leon: *Exodus*, 120
U.S. Olympic Committee, 182
The U.S. Senate: From Deliberation to Dysfunction (Loomis), 246

Vallejo (California), 181
Van Hollen, Chris, 169
Verner, Liipfert, Bernhard, McPherson & Hand, 239n8
Versage, Vince, 180

265

Vietnam War, 24, 27–28, 97–98, 178
Volden, Craig: *Revolving Gridlock: Politics and Policy from Jimmy Carter to George W. Bush*, 246–47

Warner, Mark, 220
Warnke, Paul, 165, 166
war on terror, 161
Washington, George, 35, 135
Washington Post, 64–65, 173–74, 233
Washington Times, 63
Washington wallpaper, 129
Watergate, 47, 59, 165, 178
Watergate Babies, 14
Watergate reformers, 88–89
Watsonville Community Hospital (near Monterey, Calif.), 181
Waxman, Henry, 17, 94–95, 219; *The Waxman Report: How Congress Really Works*, 248
Wegman, Dick, 48
Weinberger, Caspar, 192
Weinstein, Allen, 18
Weiss, Len, 109, *131*
Weizmann, Chaim, 123
West Bank, 116–17, 121, 124, 126
Westinghouse, 91
Wiener, Anthony, 175
Wikipedia, 104
Williams, Brian, 222

Willow Oaks (Washington, D.C.), 216
Wilson, Brian, 149
Wilson, Woodrow, 104, 225
wisdom, 113, 236
WMDs (weapons of mass destruction), 61
Wohlstetter, Albert, 109
Wollack, Ken, 71, 72–73, 76, 113
women's rise in politics, 94
Woodward, Bob, 59
Wozniak, Steve, 2
Wright, Frank Lloyd, 24

Yost, Casimir ("Cas"), 93–94, 167, 194–96, *198*, 201

Zablocki, Clem, 85, 105, 131, *131*
Zeithamel, Carl, 233
Zelizer, Julian E.:
    The American Congress: The Building of Democracy, 246;
    On Capitol Hill, 245
Zionism, 123. *See also* Israel
Zorinsky, Ed: on the Senate Foreign Relations Committee, *66*, 68
Zorthian, Greg, 78, 101

Acknowledgements

Jennifer, Zack, and Dylan Warburg were in my mind most every day that I worked on this book. In some respects, it is written fundamentally for them. Many of my errors recounted in this memoir have subsequently been inflicted on my adult children as infamous "lessons learned." I thank each of them for their sage counsel, as well as for their inspiring examples of lives well-lived. Special thanks to my IT chairman Zack, copy editor extraordinaire, who rescued and improved innumerable drafts and provided invaluable editorial counsel.

Bruce Bortz and his team at Bancroft, including Harrison Demchick and Tracy Copes, have been wise and persistent, as always, in presenting the story. Thanks, Bruce, for your friendship, your encouragement and support, and your editing skills. Thanks also to the late Dr. Abe Bortz for his faith in and enthusiasm for the project.

Special thanks to Ali Abbas for his cover design.

Friends of the book have also been invaluable commentators and editors. Thanks especially to Joy Jacobson, Colleen Sechrest, Gordon Kerr, Joe Tanner, Steve McGee, Ben Converse, Max West, Kim Armstrong Strumwasser, Stephen Fennell, Tom Guerin, Jason Warburg, Sandol Stoddard, Mike Walsh, Andy Warburg, Pete Warburg, Michele deNevers, Jeff Bergner, Peter Galbraith, Tom Kizzia, and Gary Hart. Veteran authors John Casey and Peter Maass were exceptionally generous with their insights, for which I am deeply grateful.

My appreciation for labors shared goes to so many people at the House and Senate, Georgetown University, Cassidy & Associates, and the University of Virginia. Special thanks for their wisdom to Kathleen McCloskey, Gerry Cassidy, and Harry Harding, as well as to the late Jack Bingham and Alan Cranston.

About the Author

Gerry Warburg is Professor of Public Policy and Assistant Dean at the Frank Batten School of Leadership and Public Policy at the University of Virginia. He teaches courses in national security policymaking, congressional strategy, and "The Public Policy Challenges of the 21st Century." He served for many years as a legislative assistant to members of the U.S. House and Senate leadership, where he played a lead staff role in advancing such measures as the Nuclear Non-Proliferation Act; abolition of the Joint Committee on Atomic Energy; the Comprehensive Anti-Apartheid Sanctions Act; the Support East European Democracy Act; and legislation advancing a mutual, verifiable U.S.-Soviet nuclear weapons production freeze. He staffed congressional leadership trips to more than a dozen countries, and has served as a consultant to the Nuclear Regulatory Commission and several U.S. presidential campaigns.

Formerly Executive Vice President of Cassidy & Associates, a Washington public affairs firm, he taught previously at the University of Pennsylvania's Annenberg School of Communication, Georgetown University's Walsh School of Foreign Service, and the Stanford in Washington program.

His publications include *Conflict and Consensus: The Struggle Between Congress and the President Over Foreign Policymaking* (Harper & Row); *The Mandarin Club*, a novel (Bancroft Press); two chapters in *The National Security Enterprise: Navigating The Labyrinth* (Georgetown Press); "Nonproliferation Policy Crossroads: Lessons Learned from the U.S.-India Nuclear Agreement" in *Contemporary Issues in U.S. Foreign Policy* (CQ Press). He is the author of numerous opinion pieces, and the subject of profiles, published in *The San Francisco Chronicle*, *The Los Angeles Times*, *The Washington Post*, *San Jose Mercury-News*, *The Philadelphia Inquirer*, *The Washington Times*, *Foreign Policy*, *The Nonproliferation Review*, *The Virginian-Pilot*, and *The Virginia Policy Review*.

A graduate of Hampshire College, with a graduate degree from Stanford University, Warburg was born and raised in the San Francisco Bay Area. He now lives in Virginia.